GIFTS AND COMMODITIES

T0385609

HAU
BOOKS

Executive Editor
Giovanni da Col

Managing Editor
Sean M. Dowdy

Editorial Board
Anne-Christine Taylor
Carlos Fausto
Danilyn Rutherford
Ilana Gershon
Jason Throop
Joel Robbins
Jonathan Parry
Michael Lempert
Stephan Palmié

www.haubooks.com

GIFTS AND COMMODITIES
(SECOND EDITION)

C. A. Gregory

Foreword by
Marilyn Strathern

New Preface by the Author

Hau Books
Chicago

© 2015 by C. A. Gregory and Hau Books.
First Edition © 1982 Academic Press, London.
All rights reserved.

Cover and layout design: Sheehan Moore
Typesetting: Prepress Plus (www.prepressplus.in)

ISBN: 978-0-9905050-1-3
LCCN: 2014953483

Hau Books
Chicago Distribution Center
11030 S. Langley
Chicago, IL 60628
www.haubooks.com

Hau Books is marketed and distributed by The University of Chicago Press.
www.press.uchicago.edu

Printed and bound by CPI Group (UK) Ltd, Croydon, CR0 4YY

For Judy, Polly, and Melanie.

Contents

PART TWO: THEORY

Foreword

I had forgotten that there was still a postcard inside my copy of *Gifts and commodities*, sent from central India in early 1983 when Chris Gregory was doing fieldwork in Bastar. I must have given him some comments, though I cannot have known at the time quite what an influence his model of exchange relations was going to have on my own work. Writing comments once more, for this second edition, leads me to declare my interest in the book and the gratitude I owe its author. But then, again, the astonishment with which I rediscover much that I had forgotten perhaps puts me sufficiently outside that frame to offer some general reflections on what it so creatively accomplishes.

While *Gifts and commodities* has had far-reaching consequences in anthropology, that is not where Gregory began. He was an economist who was drawn, as Eatwell's preface as original series editor made clear, to what was then a fresh concern with the analytical principles of classical political economy (as opposed to neoclassical economics). If—in the theorizing of relations between production and consumption—these principles allowed a historical specificity to the description of economic systems, Gregory saw that this also entailed a cultural specificity that permitted fine discriminations between (in words of the time) societies on the ground. With this came the illumination that the counterpart Marx had proposed to production and productive consumption, namely consumption and consumptive production, demanded that one think about how people replace themselves. And that is where Gregory made his anthropological turn: What had anthropologists been doing for so long but analyzing kinship systems, and what were kin terminologies but a classification of people with respect to their replacement of one another? However, the cultural shock of a colonial, and decolonizing, Papua New Guinea had come first.

The point is that Gregory had let himself be shocked. He was observing what everyone else was observing about apparently rational and irrational behavior—these were serious topics then. Indeed it is sobering to think back on how many (neoclassical) economists, and in their own way anthropologists, were struggling with the apparent perplexities of development, motivation, and the way people invested their energies. Gregory's questions were different. It went over my head at the time, but *Gifts and commodities* in effect offered a brilliant way out of a conceptual impasse widespread among colleagues (myself included). His model, accounting, as good models should, for interaction between sets of relations as they impinge upon one another, might have been demonstrated in Papua New Guinea but it tackled a conceptualization generally the bane of much midcentury thinking on the matter. This was the endless adjudication of "social change" as though it were a matter of balancing "change and continuity" or identifying signs of "tradition and modernity." It is not irrelevant that the only other challenger was a burgeoning Marxist anthropology.

What Gregory did is encapsulated in Chapters VI and VII, on the transformation of gifts into commodities, and of commodities into gifts. These transformations did not just hinge on a very particular moment in history, they defined it. In fact Gregory gives a wonderful account of the ripple effect of such a moment as it was recreated across different regions over time, as similar conditions came repeatedly into being. The moment was a point at which produce and labor could be (not all were) treated by Papua New Guineans as commodities while the land crucial to clan survival was not. If the clan-based system, in Gregory's words, subsidized commodity production through replacing (reproducing) produce and labor, money and other commodities in turn helped replace the basis of the clan as identified through the exploits of its "members." These were especially, although not exclusively, male members, and in many areas of Melanesia the exploits were those which had long been described as "gift exchange."

A political economy perspective dealt with the covarying elements of what (in the vocabulary of social science) were called systems. Given that commodity transactions were also known as exchanges, gift exchange seemed a self-evident counterpart. Much of the early part of the book is concerned with spelling out the implications of bringing "gifts'" and "commodities" into systematic relation. But a hallmark of Gregory's approach is that what springs from ethnography also returns to ethnography. Concepts and their theoretical framing are here a means to description, a clearing ground, not themselves an end. While the systematization (and attendant generalization) is exactly that, what endures of Gregory's work are its extraordinary insights, both into the specificities of social life in preindependence Papua New Guinea, and of its history since colonization, and into the ethnographic preoccupations of anthropologists within and beyond that country. Exchange mechanisms involving (group) alliance, marriage prescriptions and preferences, givers and receivers, forms of reciprocity, indigenous models, and the like, were all in the air. The present-day reader will find that this book gives an unexpected route into such preoccupations. That one might add to them other preoccupations, and in the language of Melanesianists of the day this would have included sexual antagonism, and even perhaps "persons" and "things," would be in the spirit of Gregory's sense of the way in which theoretical frameworks occupy certain niches and then exceed or extend them.

The Preface to this second edition is exhilarating in this respect. It takes us forward. The recent adventures of gifts and commodities offer a history of anthropology in microcosm, and I say anthropology, rather than economic anthropology, for the latter never completely encompassed the scope of Gregory's address. In a nutshell, what he lays out are conditions for the selfreplacement of anthropological inquiry, as the continuing and radical empirical endeavor he envisages, insofar as such replacement must always be at once a matter of changeful modeling and of changing circumstances of study. Hau Books is to be congratulated for seeing the future that this book will surely have for its new readers, including readers anew.

MARILYN STRATHERN
Cambridge, August 2014

Preface to the first edition

While all the systematic research for this book was carried out in Cambridge over the period 1976 to 1981, the initial stimulus for the research derives from the casual empirical observations I made during a period of residence in Papua New Guinea (PNG) from 1973 to 1975. Although I was based in Port Moresby I traveled widely throughout the country and was able to observe the workings of the indigenous economy at first hand. I was completely bewildered by what I saw; what little faith I had in the explanatory powers of orthodox economic theory—which I was employed to teach at the University of PNG—was lost completely. In an attempt to comprehend what was happening to the country I was led inevitably to the rich ethnographic literature on PNG and eventually to the theories of such anthropologists as Morgan, Mauss, Lévi-Strauss, and so on. It struck me that the basic approach of these theorists was similar to that employed by the old classical political economists, Quesnay, Smith, Ricardo, and Marx, whose theories of European capitalism are no longer fashionable today. As the analysis of the colonial PNG economy presupposes some theory of capitalism, I have attempted an analysis that involves a synthesis of the ideas of the classical political economists with those of Morgan et al. in the light of empirical evidence from PNG. The aim of the book is to develop a constructive alternative to neoclassical economic development theory, the dominant orthodoxy in universities and other institutions around the world today. Neoclassical economic analysis deserves critical attention not because of any intrinsic intellectual interest in its theoretical propositions (of which there is little), but because of its pervasive political importance: it is often used to provide theoretical justification for development policies of a highly dubious nature. Orthodox development economics is more concerned with prescription than description. As Lipton (1977: 28) has put it:

> Marx wrote, "The philosophers have only interpreted the world in various ways; the point, however, is to change it." The economists, turned philosophers of international development, have sought too often to change the world without understanding it.

The synthesis of the ideas of the political economists with anthropologists presented here is not, it should be noted, a simple welding together of different theories. It is a critique in the old-fashioned sense of the word in that it involves criticism, modification, and transcendence of their theories. Furthermore, the method adopted differs from these theorists' in one significant respect. Almost every theorist from Adam Smith, through Marx and Morgan, and down to Lévi-Strauss analyzed anthropological data within an evolutionary framework: the colonial context in which anthropologists collected data is abstracted from and the data are analyzed as if they described a precapitalist society. This is a highly questionable procedure: the societies anthropologists study have been subordinated to European capitalist societies and must be analyzed as such. Furthermore it should be noted that anthropological studies describe colonial rather than precolonial situations: of the 138 intensive ethnographic studies made in PNG between 1871 and 1969, for example, 62 of them (i.e. 45%) were made during the period 1960–69. However, to make this point is not to question the political economists' method of using abstract conceptual models. The colonial PNG economy presents the analyst with a very complex mixture of indigenous and imposed economic forms which changes over time and varies from place to place. It is only by pulling the complex whole apart, examining the workings of its parts as if in a vacuum, and reassembling the parts in the concrete historical situation that we can have any hope of understanding colonial PNG. The two-part division of this book into "Concepts" and "Theory" reflects this methodological approach. It should not be deduced from this that this book does not deal with "facts." Facts do not stand opposed to concepts and theories, as the neoclassical approach would have it, but are an integral part of both. In this book anthropological data from different parts of the world are used to illustrate the concepts and distinctions developed in the first part of the book, while in the second part these concepts form the basis of the propositions developed to explain the empirical data on colonial PNG.

While this book is designed as a critique of neoclassical economic development theory in general, and its practice in PNG in particular, it also addresses issues of interest to anthropologists. It puts the "formalist/ substantivist" debate in economic anthropology in a different perspective and attempts to tackle the problem of the relationship between "kinship" and the "economy" head on. The latter problem is handled by introducing into the discussion a modified version of the concept "reproduction" used by Marx. This approach enables "classificatory" kinship terms to be analyzed as exchange relations analogous to "prices." It also enables the development of a system for classifying Melanesian societies, as well as an explanation for the fact that the "big-man" phenomenon is not found everywhere in PNG. Finally, by examining the anthropological data in the context of the economic history of PNG, it suggests some reasons for the efflorescence of gift exchange that has occurred with colonization.

CHRIS GREGORY
Cambridge, July 1982

Preface to the second edition

ON THE TERMS OF A DEBATE: GIFTS, COMMODITIES, AND GOODS

I am grateful to Hau Books for bringing out this second edition of *Gifts and commodities*. The original 1982 text was scanned and reformatted; I took the liberty of correcting a few typographical errors but have made no attempt to produce a revised edition. That would be neither possible nor desirable because so much has changed over the past four decades: my thinking has moved on; anthropological and economic thought has moved on; and the political economy of Papua New Guinea (PNG) has moved on. All books are a product of their time, and no one is more conscious of this fact than the author. Books become part of a historical archive the moment they are published; a second edition cannot, and should not, try to rewrite history.

It is a sobering experience for an author to observe the thirty-year history of the reception of his book. A book acquires a life of its own after it is published. The author loses all control over how it should be interpreted. The worst that can happen is that the book is ignored; the best is that it is critiqued, and I have been most fortunate in this respect. My critics fall into three broad classes. First are those who have made a constructive critique by modifying and developing my general conceptual framework and using this to address new theoretical questions that locate the debate about gifts and commodities in different historical, geographical, and theoretical contexts. Second are those who have made a "negative" critique in the sense that they reject my conceptual framework on the grounds that it is historically obsolete or fundamentally flawed. Third are those who have simply misunderstood what I was trying to say. This third group, perhaps a majority, accuse me of making an argument that is precisely the opposite of what I said. As I have responded to these critics in *Savage money* (1997: 41–53), I will not consider them again here, suffice to repeat that my problem in *Gifts and commodities* was to understand efflorescence of gift exchange in the "ambiguous" colonial economy of PNG where things are now gifts, now commodities, depending on the social context. The empirical reality we study is a complex muddle, but our theories don't have to be. Clarity of thought is a supreme academic value yet it does pose the risk of being simply misunderstood.

No theory can escape the curse of history, but the task of modifying and developing theoretical concepts and arguments in the light of changing historical circumstances is a difficult one about which reasonable people will disagree. Good theory does not fall from the sky; academic debate must be grounded in comparative ethnography, political and economic history, and historical geography. I make no claims to fully understand the extraordinary political and economic changes that have occurred in the world over the past three decades and their implications for theory, but I try (Gregory 1997: Chap. VII). My theoretical perspective has also been colored by interactions with colleagues at universities in Australia, PNG, and the UK, where I have spent most of my academic life, and in shorter academic sojourns to Germany, the USA, and Japan (a country that has much to teach us about the efflorescence of gift exchange in an advanced capitalist economy). My empirical understanding has also been influenced by the people I have met while doing fieldwork in India (where I spent a year studying the rural marketing system in 1982–83 and have made some fourteen shorter return trips over the past thirty years) and Fiji, where I lived from 2008 to 2012. It is from this perspective that I offer my reflections on developments in the theory of gifts and commodities over the past thirty years. My aim is neither to rebut my critics nor to argue the merits of my perspective, but rather to clarify some of the key issues in post-1970s debates about the gift/commodity paradigm as I see them so that young scholars and nonanthropologists can make up their own minds about the explanatory adequacy of the competing theories and move the debate along.

But what precisely is *the* problem of gifts and commodities? How did I pose it in *Gifts and commodities*? How have others posed it over the past thirty years? How should it be reformulated for today and tomorrow? Should the very words "gift" and "commodity" define the terms of the debate? If not, what alternative conceptual language should be used? Constructive critique can only proceed when there is agreement on the terms of the debate; "negative" critique implies disagreement, the negation of the basic assumptions of an opponent, and raises the problem of incommensurability.

Establishing the appropriate terms of debate was the problem I confronted in my Ph.D. *Gifts and commodities* is a revised version of my Ph.D. thesis (Gregory 1979) which has the somewhat longer title: "Gifts and commodities: A critique of the theory of 'traditional' and 'modern' goods with particular reference to Papua New Guinea." As this longer title suggests, I sought to change the terms of debate of mainstream economics by using the theoretical language of classical political economy and economic anthropology. My problem was to understand the economic history of colonial PNG. I was trained in mainstream economics but found the terms of debate—*traditional* and *modern goods*—unsatisfactory. Economic anthropologists refer to mainstream economists as the "formalists." This is correct in the methodological sense that mainstream economists are primarily concerned to develop mathematical models of the economy based on assumptions about the world, be they about perfect knowledge of rational consumers or about perfect competition between firms. From the perspective of the theory of value, mainstream economics is more accurately called a theory of *goods*. This theory assumes a subjective marginalist utility theory of value, and the word "goods" is the linguistic expression of this assumption. Marginalists reject the labor theory of value of the classical political economists and the language of *commodities* in which it is expressed. Economic anthropologists in the pre-1970s era were concerned with noncommercial exchange using the language of *gifts*. Their problem was that of understanding the moral obligations to give, receive, and repay gifts. This was based on a radically new theory of value that had the notion of reciprocity at its core.

The historical problem I was concerned with in *Gifts and commodities*, to repeat yet again, was the paradoxical one of understanding the efflorescence of gift exchange during the colonial period. The colonial state's imposition of a commodity economy from above did not destroy the indigenous gift economy but created the unintended conditions for it to flourish from below. My problem was to understand this *ambiguous* relationship between gifts and commodities in the colonial period. I did this by modifying the terms of debate used by political economy and economic anthropology. The first part of this book is an attempt to develop a conceptual framework that synthesizes the two approaches; the second part uses this conceptual framework to provide an interpretation of the economic history of colonial PNG. The conceptual framework in the first part has received the most critical attention, and most misunderstanding, so I take the opportunity here to briefly clarify what I was trying to do.

Pre-1970s economic anthropology privileged the concept of *exchange*, but political economy focused on the more inclusive concept of *reproduction*, a notion that includes exchange as one of its moments in the dynamic circular process of production, consumption, redistribution, exchange, and reproduction of things and people. The annual cycle of grain production provides the central organizing image of this conception of reproduction: to grow wheat one needs wheat as seed, tools, land, and labor as inputs; some of the output at the end of the year has to be set aside as seed for next year's production and the rest distributed and exchanged to buy new tools, pay wages, and dividends. This notion of reproduction focuses on material reproduction but not human reproduction. Marx ([1857] 1973: Introduction) called the former "the conditions of production and productive consumption" (PPC) and the latter "the conditions of consumption and consumptive production" (CCP), but neither he nor his twentieth-century followers, such as Sraffa (1960), developed the idea. It struck me that the kinship systems of the type found in Melanesia and Aboriginal Australia were the CCP analogs of Sraffa's PPC. If, following Lévi-Strauss ([1949] 1969: 65), the bride was the "supreme gift," then this gift had to be "consumed," exchanged, and reproduced every generation. My conceptual framework, then, expands and develops the Marxian/Sraffian notion of reproduction by conceiving of kinship as a form of human reproduction rather than as mere exchange, as Lévi-Strauss had it. My conceptual framework is a synthesis of these two traditions. I distinguish some six types of gift exchange and five types of commodity exchange (see Figure 3.14) as moments of a generalized concept of reproduction that itself takes many forms. Part One is demanding and reveals that my conceptual opposition of gifts to commodities is anything but simple; but I confess that my analytical method of successive approximations, which proceeds from the simple to the complex, and from the abstract conceptual to the concrete historical, has provided lots of ammunition for hostile critics who want to dismiss my argument as simplistic by tearing one-sentence quotes out of their conceptual and historical context.

The terms *gifts*, *commodities*, and *goods* are ancient words that are not going to fade away any time soon. This is because the three terms are the linguistic signs of quite different paradigms of value. What has changed, and will change, is the substantive context of these theories of value, the list of specialist terms of the theoretical lexicon in which it is expressed, the semantic contrasts embedded in the conceptual frameworks, and the pragmatic way the concepts are used as tools for understanding historically and geographically specific problems. In Chapter I, I give a potted intellectual history of the three paradigms as I understood it in the late 1970s.

I draw the reader's attention to the fact that I never used the word "reciprocity" as a term of debate in *Gifts and commodities*. A digital search will show that it is occurs twice, both times in quotations from other authors. This was a conscious decision on my part, and I now see that it involved a departure from the orthodox interpretation of Mauss that ruled at the time. Mauss famously posed three questions about the obligation to give, to receive, and to repay. The "principle of reciprocity" is one possible answer to the last question, and Lévi-Strauss, Polanyi, and Sahlins all developed this concept in their own ways. This interpretation of the concept of the gift elevates "reciprocity" to the status of an explanatory variable. In Sahlins' work (1972: 191ff.), for example, the commodity becomes redefined as "negative" reciprocity and the gift as "positive" reciprocity; the latter has many subordinate forms, such as "balanced reciprocity," "generalized reciprocity," and so on. In other words, the terms "gift" and "commodity" become species of the genus "reciprocity." The implication of this is that two theories of value merge into one: the "norm of reciprocity," as Gouldner (1960) called it. For Lévi-Strauss ([1949] 1969: 24) this "principle" has its origins in the incest taboo, "that composite mixture of elements from both nature and culture"; for Polanyi (1944: 48), reciprocity "is enormously facilitated by the institutional pattern of symmetry."

The problem with this theory of value is that it depicts exchange as a general category independent of production, distribution, and consumption; but I could see that the reciprocity theorists, and Mauss, were dealing with a concept of exchange that called into question Marx's distinction between PPC and CCP discussed above. The framework of analysis I develop in Chapter II was designed to solve that problem. This perspective involves a different reading of Mauss, one that locates him, and his interpreters, in a lineage of thought that includes the historically informed classical tradition of political economy. My constructive critique of reciprocity and its associated conceptual framework has passed by largely unnoticed. A prominent exception is Marilyn Strathern, of whom more below.

A noteworthy development in the intellectual history of the gift since the 1980s has been the extraordinary attention it has received in disciplines outside anthropology, be it literature (Hyde 1984), philosophy (Derrida 1992), sociology (Godbout and Caillé 1998), history (Davis 2000), or law (Hyland 2009). The theory of reciprocity has driven much of this interest, but so too has Mauss' original text as scholars have reinterpreted novels, ancient legal cases, historical archives, and other kinds of empirical data. Anthropology, for its part, has gone off in many new directions since the 1980s. Some anthropologists have completely rejected the gift/commodity paradigm and redefined the terms of debate using a rehabilitated theory of goods. Others have reconceptualized the distinction by calling into question the descriptive adequacy of Mauss' theory of moral obligation and reciprocity; historical and ethnographically informed critics have rediscovered the presence of the gift in the heartland of European commodity production and called into question the adequacy of prevailing theories of the commodity. In sum, the debate between those who propose a theory of value based on the gift/commodity distinction and those who reject it is still with us today but in radically new guises. In what follows I review some of the significant developments in anthropology as I perceive them. I deal firstly with scholars who, for the most part, are concerned to develop a constructive critique of the gifts/commodity paradigm and the economic anthropology/political economy tradition of thought of which it is part;

and I deal secondly with scholars who reject the terms of this debate in favor of an approach that involves a constructive critique of the formalist theories of mainstream economics, the theory of goods paradigm.

CONSTRUCTIVE CRITIQUES OF THE GIFT/ COMMODITY PARADIGM: THE PNG CASE

The principal historical problem I was concerned with in *Gifts and commodities*—the efflorescence of gift exchange in PNG in the colonial era when commodity production was being established—is one that is well documented in the ethnographic archive. The word "efflorescence" itself seems to have been first used by Andrew Strathern (1979), but descriptions of the phenomenon appeared earlier in two pioneering ethnographies on Melanesian gift exchange published in 1971: Andrew Strathern's *The rope of Moka* (1971) and Michael Young's *Fighting with food* (1971). These, as Anthony Forge (1972) notes, were the first full-length ethnographies ever published of gift exchange in "big-man" societies. Malinowski's ([1922] 1961) classic work on the *kula* was based in the Trobriand Islands, a chiefly society. Subsequent ethnographic work established the fact of efflorescence beyond any doubt. The transition from "stone to steel," as Salisbury (1962) characterized the local experience of colonial history, freed up labor time for men that was channeled into ceremonial exchange activities rather than increased commodity production for the market. Of importance, too, to my understanding of this process were Marilyn Strathern's *Women in between: Female roles in a male world, Mount Hagen, New Guinea* (1972) and her pioneering work on Hagen migrants in Port Moresby, *No money on our skins* (1975). While Andrew Strathern's work analyzed the strategies big-men employed as they competed with other big-men in the sphere of *moka* exchange, Marilyn Strathern's work focused on implications of this for women in the sphere of production. *Moka* gifts involve the exchange of pigs and shells. Pigs eat sweet potatoes, and feeding them places huge labor demands on women in the run-up to a *moka* exchange when their big-men husbands have to accumulate large numbers of them to give away. Successful big-men are masters of persuasion and oratory, but those who migrated to Port Moresby faced a different problem: money did not stay on their skins because it had to be used to pay for food, clothing, and shelter and to support kin at home.

These ethnographies, and others, posed for me the question of the conceptual adequacy of existing theories of the gift and the commodity, and the historical question of the reasons for the efflorescence of gift exchange in an era when commodity production was being imposed. My book tried to answer these questions by placing the new ethnography in a broader comparative and historical context, one that focused on economic history and the history of ideas about exchange and reproduction. I confess that I was very nervous about the bold generalizations I was making because the conventional wisdom among experienced Melanesian ethnographers at the time, such as Ann Chowning (1977), for example, was that Melanesian cultures were extremely diverse and that generalizations were well-nigh impossible.

This conventional wisdom was soon to change with the publication of Marilyn Strathern's classic *Gender of the gift* (1988), an exhaustive survey of the ethnographic literature that identified a common set of suppositions about gender relations in Melanesia that sent the debate about gifts and commodities off in fresh directions by posing new questions and adding some new terms and concepts to the theoretical lexicon. It is a "constructive" critique of my book in that she modifies and develops two key aspects of my work: my conceptual argument about the distinction between PPC and CCP, and my historical argument about the efflorescence of gift exchange. Whereas my book addresses 1970s debates in political economy and economic anthropology, her book addresses 1980s cross-disciplinary debates about gender. The historical question of the efflorescence of gift exchange in a world of commodity production was no longer her concern. Her long periods of fieldwork over the period from the mid-1960s to the mid-1970s had documented this fact in extensive detail and her attention shifted to more comparative and general theoretical issues. Her new question, as expressed in the subtitle of her book, was with "problems with women and problems with society in Melanesia." Her analysis is based on my gift/commodity distinction which she modifies and develops in new ways. A long quote is justified.

The contrast sustained in this book between commodity systems and gift systems of exchange is taken directly from Gregory's (1982) work.

Gregory himself insists that the two types of exchange are found together. Certainly this is true for contemporary Melanesian societies for as long as they have been studied by Westerners, and his own account is embedded in a study of change and the coexistence of both forms in colonial and postcolonial Melanesia. Nevertheless, insofar as he grounds the predominance of gift exchange in a "clan-based" as opposed to a "class-based" society, he does suggest that the character of the predominant form of exchange has distinctive social correlates. It is important to the way I proceed that the forms so contrasted are different in social origin, even though the manner in which they are expressed must belong commensurately within a single (Western) discourse. Thus a culture dominated by ideas about property ownership can only imagine the absence of such ideas in specific ways. In addition, it sets up its own internal contrasts. This is especially true for the contrast between commodities and gifts: the terms form a single cultural pair within Western political-economy discourse, though they can be used to typify differences between economies that are not party to the discourse, for example non-Western economies that may behave according to a particular political-economy theory without themselves having a political-economy theory. (M. Strathern 1988: 18, emphasis added)

Strathern calls this contrast a "fiction" (ibid.) and notes that "reciprocity in exchange cannot be taken as an independent social form" (ibid.: 144), and then redefines the "fiction" of the gift by modifying and developing the CCP concept.

"Gift economy," as a shorthand reference to systems of production and consumption where consumptive production predominates, implies, in Gregory's terminology, that things and people assume the social form of persons. They thus circulate as gifts, for the circulation creates relationships of a specific type, namely a qualitative relationship between the parties to the exchange. This makes them reciprocally dependent upon one another. Some dependencies are conceived of as prior to transactions, while others are constructed during the course of the transaction itself. In the latter case, parties may come to the transaction as independent social entities, a condition for the kind of reciprocity that ceremonial exchange partners in Hagen, for instance, sustain between themselves.

> The outsider may establish these points through the examination of so-
> cial arrangements (political and kinship) contingent on the circulation
> of persons and things; but it is the actors, of course, who construe the
> qualitative nature of the relationships in terms of an "exchange" or as
> a matter of parties to the exchange being in a state of "reciprocity." As
> Sahlins (1972: 134) warned, "everywhere in the world the indigenous
> category for exploitation is 'reciprocity'." (M. Strathern 1988: 145–46)

Strathern goes beyond my work by introducing a contrast between the
individual and the dividual. The latter is an "androgyne" who "is rendered
individual in relation to a counterpart individual" (ibid.: 15). She ac-
knowledges her debt to Marriot (1976) for this term, but it is interesting
to note that it was used by nineteenth-century English legal scholars,
who distinguished between dividual and individual obligations, where
the former are divisible among multiple persons, the latter indivisible
(Colebrooke 1818: para. 333). There are subtle differences between the
way Strathern, Marriot, and Colebrooke use the term "dividual," but I
leave that problem for the historians of anthropological thought.

    This intervention liberated the concept of the gift from the hegemo-
ny of the "norm of reciprocity," reformulated its relationship to the gift in
terms of the language of dividuality, and linked it to gender in a way that
differed greatly from that of Lévi-Strauss. Strathern's book stimulated
much debate. The studies that followed it in PNG, Macintyre (2011: 91)
notes, "concentrated on the ways that Western and Melanesian economic forms interacted." This had a number of interpretive consequences
both for Strathern's theory of the gift/commodity distinction and mine.
Critics interpreted her "analytical fiction" as a geographical fact, and I
am critiqued for failing to understand the complex empirical relationship between gifts and commodity. This is a misreading of both her work
and mine.

    The political economy of PNG has been transformed beyond all rec-
ognition since the time Strathern published her ethnographic accounts
and I mulled over its colonial economic history. Our accounts are now
history, part of an archive. The plantation economy of the colonial days
has given way to one based on mining, timber, and other natural resources. This has brought extreme wealth to a few but poverty and envi-
ronmental degradation to many. Democratic political institutions have

managed to survive, but not without allegations of grand corruption. Tribal warfare has revived in certain areas, and violence against women is an issue of major concern.

Patterson and Macintyre's edited collection, *Managing modernity in the Western Pacific* (2011b) brings the ethnographic picture up to date. They note (2011a: 18) that debates in Melanesia have been led by exponents of the "New Melanesian Ethnography," on the one hand, and the "New Melanesian History," on the other. Marilyn Strathern's work, among others, has inspired the work of the former, while that of Nicholas Thomas (1991), among others, has been influential in the latter. They follow Michael Scott's (2007) call for a third way that critically adopts aspects of both positions.

This makes good sense to me because it is what I was trying to do when I divided *Gifts and commodities* into two parts called "concepts" and "theory." One might, following Strathern, call these two parts "fictions" and "facts." In Part Two I struggled to capture the dialectic between the emergence of commodity production in colonial PNG, on the one hand, and the countertendency for commodities to be transformed into gifts, on the other. The driving force here, as I saw it, was the contradiction between the policies and actions of the colonial state and the values and desires of the colonized PNGians. Chapter VI is a straight economic history of the transformation of labor, primary products, and land into commodities; Chapter VII examines the countertendency by means of twelve case studies from different regions in PNG. I argued that the nonemergence of land as a commodity not only created the conditions for gift exchange to flourish in the past but would also lead to conflict in the future as people struggled to gain from the implicit exchange-value that land had acquired. It gives me no pleasure to see that this has happened. Patterson and Macintyre (2011a: 19) note that influential foreign advisors continue to advocate for the privatization and rationalization of land tenure, while for Melanesians in rural areas "land has become a kind of cultural last redoubt in their ambivalent attempts to both profit from and slow the flows of globalization." What I was unable to predict, of course, was the culturally specific way this ambivalence has manifested itself in different places and at different times.

Keir Martin, whose work critically develops that of Strathern, myself, and others, addresses this ambivalence in his recent book, *The death of the big men and the rise of the big shots: Custom and conflict in East New Britain* (2013). He shows how emerging income inequality between the well-educated and relatively wealthy urban kinsman and his relatively poor relatives at home raises the issue of what he calls "the limits of reciprocity." The *tok pisin* term "big shot" has derogatory overtones; the way it is used by the poor relative invites anthropologists to think again about culture as a system of shared values. The term is not current in the highlands but the notion certainly is. Ketan (2004), in his recent ethnography of the local political leaders in the Mount Hagen, calls them "super big men." This refers to people who seek prestige, status, and wealth by standing for parliamentary elections. This new emerging class of "super big men" stand accused, in the eyes of the public and their political rivals, of using public office for private gain.

CONSTRUCTIVE CRITIQUES OF THE GIFT/ COMMODITY PARADIGM: BEYOND THE PNG CASE

I turn now to the work of critics and others who have sought to develop the gift/commodity paradigm in constructive ways using data from places beyond PNG. This literature can, for the purposes of this Preface, be classified under three broad headings: history, value, and morality. By "history" I mean those who have been primarily concerned with understanding the historical relationship between gifts and commodities in a comparative context; by "value" I mean those who have sought critically to address the question of value as defined by the political economy and economic anthropology paradigms; and by "morality" I mean those who raise the question of the morality of exchange.

History

Nicholas Thomas' *Entangled objects: Exchange, material culture and colonialism in the Pacific* (1991), Carrier's *Gifts and commodities: Exchange and Western capitalism since 1700* (1995), and Akin and Robbins' *Money and modernity: State and local currencies in Melanesia* (1999) are among those that fall into the first category. Given that my method is one that calls for theory to be grounded ethnographically, historically, and geographically, my general response is to welcome critiques like these, even though I may have a minor quibble here and there with aspects of the critique. I offer a few general comments on the first two books because the third is a collection of essays and does not admit of easy summary.

Thomas' critique involves two important moves. He generalizes my account by situating PNG in the regional context of the Pacific as a whole and complicates my dialectical analysis using the image of "entanglements." The result is a regional history of objects that calls into question the role of traditional valuables, such as *kula* shells and Fijian whales' teeth, in the colonial and postcolonial period. Comparative regional history of this kind reminds us of the need for concrete analysis of concrete situations and to avoid easy overgeneralization. This was brought home to me during my four years in Fiji. On the face of it, Fijian whales' teeth are like *kula* shells in that they are scarce, highly valued marine artifacts used as instruments of exchange. But the similarities stop there. Whales' teeth are not ranked like *kula* shells and nor do they have a transaction history like *kula* shells. There is an important sense in which whales' teeth are not gifts of the classic Maussian kind because they are not transacted between equals who are obliged to give, to receive, and to repay in an agonistic way. There are many ways to present a whale's tooth, but most involve the giver making a gesture of respect rather than hostility. One classic form of a whale's tooth transaction involves a commoner who kneels in front of a chief and presents a whale's tooth while making a *request*. Request, not obligation, is the dominant moral sentiment; status inequality rather than equality characterizes the social relations between transactors; and extreme deference rather than antagonistic showmanship characterizes the behavior of the giver.

Carrier's book flatters me by borrowing my title. His subtitle, *Exchange and Western capitalism since 1700*, defines the historical and geographical specificity of his analysis. It establishes the fact, known to native English-speakers from their everyday experience but which received theories of the economy blind us to, that gifts flourish in the heartland of capitalist commodity production. One of Carrier's arguments is that Christmas Day differs from market day and that the conceptual distinction between gifts and commodities may be a useful way for thinking about the historical relationship between these two events. He shows (1995: Chap. 8), for example, how gift-giving at Christmas time emerged during the nineteenth century, when capitalism was at its most expansive. It subsequently flourished and accounted for about one-sixth of all retail trade by the end of the twentieth century. This thesis echoes the one I developed in *Gift and commodities*: the efflorescence of gift exchange in Melanesia in the colonial period.

Carrier is concerned to critique the "Maussian model" of gift exchange, but this model, as he suggests, tells us more about the anthropological understanding of Mauss than it does about Mauss himself. This interpretation has been the subject of much criticism of late. For example, Hart's (2014) recent essay on Mauss presents a revision of the standard interpretation by drawing attention to the "Chinese wall" that Mauss himself kept between his academic and political interests. This separation, Hart notes, has made it easier for anthropologists to ignore Mauss' politics and to fail to understand the significance of the coeval relation between gifts and commodities that informs the analysis and conclusions of his essay on *The gift*. Mauss was a political activist and financial journalist, a side of him that most Anglophone anthropologists are unaware of because his writings on this remain untranslated. Hart's analysis of these writings is the basis of an alternative interpretation of *The gift*. The following is a sample of the argument he develops.

> Mauss's chief ethical conclusion is that the attempt to create a free market for private contracts is utopian and just as unrealizable as its antithesis, a collective based solely on altruism. Modern capitalism rests on an unsustainable attachment to one of these poles, and it will take a social revolution to restore a humane balance. If we were not blinded by ideology, we would recognize that the system of prestations survives in our societies—in weddings and at Christmas, in friendly societies and more bureaucratic forms of insurance, even in wage contracts and the welfare state. (Hart 2014: 42)

The implication of the work of Carrier and Hart is not so much that our understanding of gift exchange is wrong but that our theories of capitalism are in need of revision. We have overlooked the "presence of other mechanisms in our societies that have been hidden from view and marginalized by the dominant form," Hart argues (ibid.: 42). It is important to stress that many of the transactions that are hidden have been deliberately concealed, such as those in that grey area between the gift and the bribe. Hart makes this point elsewhere when he revisits his famous distinction between the formal and the informal economy and argues that there has been an informalization of the formal economy (Hart 2012). In other words, corruption is not something exceptional but, rather, has become part of business-as-usual. This raises the question of the morality of exchange, but before getting to that it is necessary to review those constructive critiques of the gift/commodity paradigm that focus on the value question in the narrower socioeconomic sense of the word.

Value

The value question is widely recognized as the central problem in the economics discipline. This is because it defines the political battle-line that that separates two incommensurable paradigms, the theory of goods on one side and the theory of commodities on the other (as I illustrate in Chapter I). For economic anthropologists, on the other hand, the value question has not loomed large. Graeber has sought to change this state of affairs with his *Towards an anthropological theory of value: The false coin of our dreams* (2001). He criticizes me (ibid.: 41) for drawing a distinction between the "value" of commodities and the "rank" of gifts, and for suggesting that the value problem is only relevant for the study of commodities. This was not my intention. I, too, consider the value question to be a matter of central concern, but I can see that my terminology has enabled him to draw his conclusion. Concerned as I was not to develop a "commodity-centric" view of gift exchange, I used the term "value" in its narrowest economic sense. The word "value" covers a broad terrain and has many levels of meaning. In addition to economic values such as use-value and price, we have familial values such as respect and familial love; religious values such as purity and auspiciousness; moral values such as virtue or vice; and a conception of the Good that imagines a possible future where people live well. This is a vast semantic field, and in *Gifts and commodities* I limit myself to a relatively narrow socioeconomic conception. If I were rewriting my book today I would use the expressions "exchange-value" and "rank-value" to signify that I consider them as two species of a genus.

Valuation in this socioeconomic sense is a process whereby valuers assign cardinal or ordinal values to entities, be they things or persons.

When the valuers are buyers and sellers in a market, the value created is an exchange-ratio between objects that renders otherwise heterogenous objects equal, as in $1 = 6 apples = 3 pears. When the valuers are Brahmin priests, they rank themselves higher than the kings; kings for their part rank themselves higher than merchants; and so on down the order. Brahmins also rank food, giving vegetables a higher rank than fish, fish a higher rank than chicken, and so on. The everyday fact of valuation is not in question, although it is not just Brahmins who rank people or only market participants who set prices. The historical reality is that both types of valuation coexist everywhere and are done by everyone, but not always without conflict, as illustrated by the ideological battle for supremacy between kings and priests throughout history.

The academic debate arises when it comes to (a) the descriptive question of what standard of value underlies a valuation and (b) the prescriptive question of what standard should inform the valuation. Answers to the descriptive question include labor time, utility, government regulations, religious purity, familial respect, and familial love. Answers to the prescriptive question include the free market, government regulation, the theology of a Brahmin priest, and the rebellious values of the subaltern.

My attempts to understand modes of valuation in the "ambiguous" Melanesian context were informed by my reading of the ethnographic literature and the history of theory as it related to economy and kinship. I was struck by the similarities between Marx's and Sraffa's reproduction schemes and kinship systems considered as models of human reproduction. Marx and Sraffa argued that prices spring from the methods of PPC, which suggested the general hypothesis that the ranking of people and things—personfication, as I called it—springs from the methods of CCP. This was my reformulation of Sahlins' theory of reciprocity, which, in turn, I saw as a reformulation of Marx's theory of the origin of commodity exchange ("negative" reciprocity). Obligations to give, receive, and repay have their origins in familial relations of consanguinity, affinity, and contiguity.

Graeber's constructive critique of the gift/commodity paradigm goes way beyond my early concerns. He raises the value question as a central problem not only for economic anthropology but also for humanity. Since 2001 he has single-handedly blitzed the field with the publication of eight single-authored monographs (2001, 2004, 2007a, 2007b, 2009,

2011a, 2011b, 2013), all of which are informed by a coherent theory of value whose prescriptions for possibilities in the future are rigorously grounded philosophically, ethnographically, historically, and theoretically. *Towards an anthropological theory of value* (Graeber 2001) is just one part of this grand design. It develops a constructive critique of Marilyn Strathern, Terry Turner, Nancy Munn, and me and a "negative critique" of Bourdieu and Appadurai, whom he identifies as formalists in the theory of goods tradition.

I will return to Graeber's negation of Bourdieu and Appadurai in the final section, where I consider post-2000 developments in the theory of goods. Of interest here is his constructive critique of Mauss' theory of the obligation to repay. Graeber (ibid.: Chap. 6) explores this obligation in great detail in a thoroughgoing analysis of the classic ethnography on Polynesian gifting, where gifts do not always have to be repaid. Mauss' question, he argues, needs to be reformulated: "*When* do they have to be repaid? What sort of gifts? In what circumstances? And what precisely can count as a repayment?" (ibid.: 217 emphasis added). Graeber's use of the simple word "when" transforms Mauss' universal question into a historically contingent one. His conclusion? Reciprocity "can mean almost anything. It is very close to meaningless" (ibid.). This is how it struck me also in the 1970s, but it did not occur to me to question Mauss' question, as Graeber has done so persuasively.

The norm of reciprocity has come under fire from other directions too. Urbanization and poverty among Aboriginal people in Australia has given rise to a new phenomenon that Peterson (1993) has called "demand sharing." He coined this phrase to describe transactions he observed in the context of contemporary Australian Aboriginal culture, but the phenomenon is quite general. The classic form of demand sharing is a polite verbal request of the kind "I want to owe you five dollars" (ibid.: 860); the impolite form is "Give me five dollars." Such requests, Peterson notes, can be refused by hiding, secretive behavior, and lying (ibid.: 864). He argues that "demand sharing reflects the underlying tension between autonomy and relatedness that runs throughout Aboriginal life" (ibid.: 870), an argument that has echoes with Keir Martin's idea of the limits of reciprocity. Martin does not refer to Peterson's work in his (2013) book, but the idea of demand sharing is there. It is the big shots who are the subject of most demands in PNG: their desire for autonomy pushes

them in the direction of refusing by hiding or lying; their desire for relatedness pulls them in the other direction. What is at stake here is the
adequacy of the ruling interpretation of Mauss' notion of the obligation
to return. MacDonald makes this explicit in her development of Peterson's argument.

> One reason demand sharing has both fascinated and eluded anthropo-
> logical analysis can be seen to be the blinkers produced by the Maussian
> legacy: the emphasis in almost all economic anthropology on exchange
> as an obligation to return. The obligation to give in response to demands,
> without expectation of return, sets up a different dynamic in social rela-
> tions, and thus invites a different approach which focuses on the eco-
> nomics of demand sharing as part of a system of sociality. (MacDonald
> 2000: 91)

MacDonald illustrates her argument with material drawn from her study
of the Wiradjuri, an urbanized New South Wales community whose
contemporary culture has been shaped by two hundred years of colonization and commercialization.

PNG and Fiji have a shorter history of colonization and commercialization, but their common commercial history has created common
transactional forms that coexist with culturally specific forms of gift-giving. What is at stake here, once again, is the distinction between an obligation and a request. The latter is called *kerekere* in Fiji and it has been the
subject of much theoretical debate in anthropological circles and much
moral condemnation in government circles. While there is no doubt that
this value has its origin in Fiji's deep past (Sahlins 1993), it is also clear
that recent history has both preserved the classic forms and given rise
to many new forms beyond those at issue in the Sahlins/Thomas debate
(Thomas 1993). What is interesting about requests is that when they
take a verbal form such as "I want to owe you five dollars," they give expression to the hybrid nature of economic reality today. Is this a request
for a gift in the language of the market or vice versa? This is a question
for which the addressee has to find a quick answer as he or she struggles
to deal with the request.

Demand sharing excites strong negative emotions among policy
makers in all places and at all times, as the following quotation illustrates.

Hence as Basil Thompson put it as long ago as 1908, "*Kerekere*, which was formerly the pivot of native society, now wars unceasingly against the mercantile project of the people." The tales of *kerekere* certainly lose nothing in the telling, but it is as certainly true that *kerekere* puts a premium on laziness and is often a serious or even disastrous drain on those Fijians who are endeavouring to accumulate and to invest. (Spate 1959: 24)

Anthropologists, by and large, are neutral or positive in their judgments. Participants, for their part, are ambivalent: demanders like it, demandees do not. This everyday reality of moral judgment raises the question of the morality of exchange, also a subject I did not address in *Gifts and commodities*.

Morality

Parry and Bloch's edited collection *Money and the morality of exchange* (1989) has done much to rehabilitate the study of moral economy within the discipline of anthropology.

Moral economy does not begin with Thompson's (1971) famous article, as many people suppose, but is as old as commercial life itself (Baldwin 1959). Moral economy is the theory of the *just* price, and is to be distinguished from political economy, which is the theory of the price (without an adjective). In other words two quite distinct value questions are at stake here. The first concerns the socioeconomic basis of price determination: what enables two heterogeneous objects to be brought into equation in the market place? What is the common substance that enables us to say, for example, that $1 = 6 apples = 3 pears? (For nineteenth-century political economists the answer was to be found in the labor time of the producer; for modern economic theorists it is to be found in the marginal utility of the consumer.) The second question raises the issue of the moral judgment of the resultant price: Is it a fair price? Is it fair that shopkeepers raise the price of food when there is a drought?

Moral economy brings together moral philosophy and political economy. Adam Smith was both a moral philosopher and a political economist and his legacy was two classic treatises, *The theory of moral sentiments* ([1759] 2009) and *An inquiry into the nature and causes of the wealth of nations* ([1776] 1970). These books have created a problem for modern-day economists because the former has sympathy for others as it central theme while the latter has economic self-interest. This apparent contradiction is referred to as the "Adam Smith problem," but it is the modern-day economists' problem because they see their theories as value-free.

Anthropological studies of the morality of exchange extend the scope of moral economy to include gifts as well as commodities. "Exchange" in Parry and Bloch's sense includes both gift exchange and commodity exchange. If there is a moral economy of the just price, then we must allow for the existence of the moral economy of the "just" gift. Just as cardinal valuation systems like prices pose the question of the just price, ordinal valuation systems pose the question of the just rank of a thing or person. It is one thing to ask why a particular *kula* valuable has such a high rank compared to another, quite another to pass moral judgment on the way that a *kula* valuable was given. Or, to take another example, it is one thing to ask if religious purity is the basis of caste ranking, but quite another to say that a lower-ranking person did not present a gift to a Brahmin in a respectful way. These two sets of questions coexist in a general moral economy of gifts and commodities, as Robbins (2009, 2013) has rightly noted in his critical development of my theory. A consideration of the religious values that inform gift exchanges raises new problems, as Parry's (1986) analysis of the "Indian" gift illustrates. But before I get to that, a brief consideration of the recent literature on the morality of commodity exchange is necessary.

When the World Bank Chairman James D. Wolfensohn gave his famous "corruption as cancer" speech in 1996 the morality of commodity exchange became a hot issue and academic interest in the subject soared (as the reader can confirm by a Google Scholar search). The Enron affair, for its part, was the stimulus for a book on the anthropology of corruption (Haller and Shore 2005), one of the first anthropological studies of the subject. Corruption is a difficult subject to study because, by definition, it involves secret transactions, but the reports of investigating bodies can provide new insights into the values that inform gift-giving. I have recently published an essay (Gregory 2014) that uses material from a case involving Australian politicians. At stake was the status of a gift of $10,000 from one politician to another, a relatively trivial sum compared to other corrupt insider-trading dealings involving millions of dollars.

The case is a classic example of the anthropological commonplace that gift exchange is all about social relationships, not the substantive content of the gift. The case is too complicated to go into here, suffice to say that it involved relationships between fathers and sons, family friends, and neighbors who went to great lengths to conceal the gift through a complex web of transactions involving the buying and selling of cars, the transferral of forged registration papers, and money transfers of various kinds and a commission. The investigation had to decide whether the core transaction was a gift or a bribe. The participants argued that it was a gift. The commissioners, for their part, judged that the giver had acted corruptly, but there was insufficient evidence to find that the receiver had. In other words, the transaction was a classic hybrid: it was a bribe when it left the hands of the giver but metamorphosed into a gift by the time it reached the receiver. Of course, other interpretations of the transaction are possible, but the law of libel prevents one from airing them.

"Commercial gifts" of this kind are hybrids whose interpretive status as gift or commodity, and whose moral valuation as good or bad, are in question. A "bribe" is an outsider's moral valuation of a transaction that an insider participant may interpret as a being either a gift or a commodity. A judge may be unsure and give a muddled judgment, as in the above case, but the participants never are. They may disagree as to whether it is a gift or commodity, with the giver arguing one way and the receiver the other. Alternatively, they may tacitly agree not to disagree by not posing the question. Whatever the case, it is as if the greater the degree of ambiguity of a transaction, the greater the need for someone to make neat distinctions in order to make sense of what is happening. This applies as much to participants, interested outside observers, and judges as it does to anthropological theorists.

I come now to a consideration of Parry's ethnographically informed theory of the Indian gift. India, he argues, is the land of the "alienable gift" (Parry 1986). This paradox is a fundamental challenge not just to my theory of the gift but also to the theoretical tradition as a whole. Before I give my ethnographically informed comments on Parry's theory, some contextualization is necessary.

Gifts and commodities was published in 1982, one year after Trautmann's *Dravidian kinship* (1981). I did not come across this book until the late 1980s, but when I did it struck me as the most significant study of the gift since Mauss. Trautmann is a Sanskrit scholar interested in ancient history and kinship theory. The ancient Sanskrit literature on gift-giving is vast and his book is a critical survey of kinship theory and Indian ethnography in the light of this literature. Whereas my book was a constructive critique of Lévi-Strauss' theory of the "supreme gift" outlined in *The elementary structures of kinship* ([1949] 1969: 65), Trautmann's book was a destructive critique in the sense that he successfully shows that Lévi-Strauss' theory has limited applicability in India. In those areas of Oceania where fathers bestow daughters in marriage to another group, the general rule is that the married woman retains membership of her natal clan (even though her reproductive capacity is severed); in India, by contrast, wedding rituals symbolically sever the formal link between father and daughter (but paradoxically by strengthening the emotional bond between brother and sister). The Brahmanic notion of *kanyadan*, "the one-way gift of a virgin," is the linguistic expression of this ideology (but one that is not generally accepted everywhere in India). Trautmann, an Indologist and kinship theorist, has done anthropology a great service by reviewing the extensive ancient Sanskritic literature on *kanyadan* and by revealing the extraordinary resilience of this ideology. If Lévi-Strauss has given us an account of the elementary structures of Oceanic kinship, then Trautmann has given us an account of the historical geography of Indian kinship; in the process he has shown that Oceanic models should not be applied to India. Trautmann also shows that *dan* is first and foremost a gift that is given to a Brahman. The traditional function of the Brahman is to receive *dan* and the function of the warrior caste is to give it. The idea that brides are *kanyadan* came later and is, for the most part, restricted to the Gangetic plain, where bride-takers are reckoned to be superior to bride-givers.

Mauss, who was also an Indologist, was well aware of this literature on the one-way Brahmanical gift called *dan*, noting, quite rightly, that it "is probable that entirely different relationships obtained among noblemen, the princely families and the numerous castes and races of the common people" (Mauss [1925] 1974: 53). This Brahmanical theory of the gift is a dominant ideology in North India, and the ethnographic research of Parry (1994) and Raheja (1988) has provided new insights into its working today. They show, in their different ways, how religious gifts called *dan* can embody negative religious values such as impurity, sin, and inauspiciousness as well as positive values such as purity and auspiciousness. There is no obligation to return negatively valued gifts because the receiver is a low-status priest whose duty it is to remove these bad values.

While the ethnographic fact of negatively valued exchanges of this type is beyond question, the same cannot be said of the other claims Parry has made. He argues, for example, that even *kanyadan* has these negative religious values. This challenges the generally accepted idea that the Indian bride is Lakshmi, the goddess of good fortune and the epitome of auspiciousness. The idea that the bride, as *kanyadan*, is inauspicious is simply wrong according to many of my Indian interlocutors, who say that *dan* is a gesture of respect to a superior, be it to a wife-taker or to a Brahman whose traditional function it is to receive *dan*. *Dan* is always a one-way and upward transaction because it is only given to high-status people. This theory has the support of Sanskritists like Heim (2004), who criticize Raheja and Parry for overlooking the key role of respect; the classic texts, Heim demonstrates, place great emphasis on respect as a value that informs *dan*.

My own ethnographic research in central India confirms the insights of Trautmann and Heim. The Halbi-speakers of the Bastar plateau with whom I work are adamant that their brides are not gifts of the *kanyadan* type. Wife-takers and wife-givers have equal status in Bastar, and the wedding ritual celebrates this fact with many elaborate displays of mutual respect between the same-sex parents of bride and groom. Opposite-sex parents, by contrast, are deemed to be brother and sister, a fictitious kin relationship which ensures that 100% of all marriages are with "cross-cousins," that is, that cross-cousin marriage is an effect rather than a causal "marriage rule." Halbi-speakers have many words for "gift" but only one that is called *dan*. This gift is given at death rituals. It involves the giving of a tray of uncooked food to the son of the sister of the deceased man by his brothers; when the deceased is a woman, the gift is given to her brother's son by her husband's family. Halbi-speakers say that the cross-nephew is "just like a Brahman," code for saying that he is the most respected kinsman a man or woman can have. This respect is often shown in everyday greeting rituals: for example, the mother's brother touches the feet of his sister's son rather than the other way around. The giving of *dan*, on the other hand, is not part of everyday life. Halbi-speakers make a sharp distinction between the world of gifts of the *dan* variety and the world of commodities, but one that also exploits the ambiguity between the two values. Like mortuary rituals everywhere, the death of a relative involves the immediate suspension of work, the beginning of a period of mourning, and the engagement of ritual experts to manage the ritual cleansing of the deceased's home. What appears to be unique among Halbi-speakers is the use of a symbolic market ritual to bring the period of mourning to a close. Female affines walk around "selling" homemade sweets and roti to members of the deceased's family. This mock market ritual is called *hat nikrani*, the "coming-out market." This is a time for joking and laughing. The "profit" from this activity is used to buy puffed rice and sweets which are distributed the next day. This symbolic market is a classic liminal rite where ambiguities reign supreme: gifts take the ritual form of commodities; sadness is expressed by laughter and joking.

When Parry (1986: 462) says that *dan* is "a transactional theory quite unlike Mauss's Melanesian, Polynesian and American examples," he is only partially correct. The classic Melanesian gift is an agonistic two-way tussle between equals but the classic Polynesian gift is akin to the Indian gift in that it is a one-way, upward, respectful transaction between transactors of unequal status. The Tongan bride is also akin to the North Indian bride in that her social status is higher than her elder brother's status and she should be given to high-status family who are under no obligation to reciprocate. But the social similarity between the Polynesian gift and the Indian gift ends when it comes to the religious values that are believed to inform them: Hinduism has given the Indian gift its culturally specific form, Polynesia is, for the most part, Christian today, but the question of how far these values have permeated those that inform gift-giving is an empirical one.

Expressions like the "Indian gift" and the "Polynesian gift" have their origin in distinct geographical locations, but the migration of Indians and Polynesians to every corner of the globe poses the question of the meaning of these terms today. To the extent that migrants take these gifting traditions with them when they migrate, the adjectives lose their geographical referent and begin to signify the values of a transplanted ethnic community. The fact of migration also raises the question of the strength of ties to the homeland and of how they are renewed. These are empirical questions which only detailed ethnographic research on transnational families can answer, but one economic consequence of great significance is well documented: the emergence of massive global flows of money in the form of remittances which are estimated to exceed the size of global flows of foreign aid. What is less well documented and understood are the microeconomic foundations of these global flows in the domestic moral economies of specific communities.

If my current research on Indo-Fijian transnational families is anything to go on, then it would seem that familial values are extraordinarily resilient. For example, around 25% of the indentured laborers taken to Fiji in the latter part of the nineteenth century came from various Dravidian-speaking areas in the south, the rest from mainly Hindi-speaking areas in the north. Fiji Hindi and English evolved as the lingua franca over the subsequent four to five generations, but distinct "cultural groups," as Mayer (1961) has termed them, emerged based on the two regionally distinct cultural areas that scholars such as Trautmann and others have mapped. Since the time of Mayer's fieldwork in the 1960s, intercultural marriage between "northerners" and "southerners" has become more common, but the distinctive kinship values and ritual practices are preserved by means of a patrilineal principle: children follow the kinship values and ritual practices of the father. Wives, for their part, become bicultural. A southerner women, for example, will follow southerner wedding ritual practices with her parent's kin but will follow northerner practices when marrying off her own children. She uses Hindi kin terms when addressing kin but in different ways when addressing northerners and southerners. For example, marriage with the mother's brother is possible in Southern India. Indo-Fijians do not practice this form of marriage but use Hindi kinship terms as if they do. Familial transfers of money and other exchanges of the *dan* type are informed by these familial values and the religious values of which they are a part.

The "Indian gift," then, flourishes in Fiji, which poses the question of how it interacts with "Polynesian" gifts and commodities of different kinds. This is a very different question to the one I posed in *Gifts and commodities*, but developments in political economy and economic anthropology since the 1980s can provide the conceptual tools and methods for trying to answer it; some of the pre-1980 ideas that I relied upon may be relevant too. Whatever the case, a critical stance informed by comparative ethnography, economic history, and cultural geography is needed. The gift/commodity paradigm is a broad church that has the capacity for unlimited critical development. The other option is to seek inspiration from those who reject the gift/commodity paradigm by changing the fundamental terms of debate. This involves a negation of the fundamental value premises of the paradigm.

NEGATION OF THE GIFT/COMMODITY PARADIGM: RECENT DEVELOPMENTS IN THE THEORY OF GOODS

The debate between the "formalists" and the "substantivists" defined the agenda for discussion in the economic anthropology of the early 1970s. The formalist tradition was epitomized by the work of Frank Knight, a Professor of Economics at the University of Chicago, who wrote a long dismissive review of a book by Herskovits, arguing that the principles of economics are known intuitively and that those ethnographers or historians hoping to discover them by inductive empirical methods were embarked on a "wild goose chase" (Knight 1941: 254). The substantivist tradition was epitomized by the work of Karl Polanyi, whose classic text, *The great transformation* (1944), illustrated the need for a method that combined economic history and comparative anthropology. While the work of these two scholars illustrates the fact of incommensurability that lies at the heart of the debate, I found that the terms of the debate—formalist/substantivist—oversimplified the issue because, among other things, the substantivists were by this time battling the neo-Marxists. This debate needed to be put into its broader context of the history of ideas, and Chapter I, "The competing theories," tries to do that.

My book was designed as a fundamental critique of the theory of goods, and in particular of those mainstream economists who applied their methods to the PNG situation (identified in Chapter V). My critique has been a complete failure in the sense that it has had no impact on thinking in the dominant mainstream paradigm: members of the economics discipline have simply ignored it. Critical attention has come almost entirely from anthropologists. For me this is further evidence, if it were needed, of the fundamental incommensurability of the paradigms. There is no common language, there are no agreed terms of debate. What has surprised me has been the way the goods paradigm has developed over the past thirty years. Just as many developments in the theory of the gift have taken place outside the discipline of anthropology, so, too, many important developments in the theory of goods have taken place outside the discipline of mainstream economics. Included in the latter are many prominent members of the anthropology profession who reject the assumptions of the pre-1970s gift/commodity paradigm.

A turning point in the history of economic thought was President Nixon's decision to go off the gold standard in August 1971. This marked the end of state regulation of exchange rates and the beginning of "market triumphalism," as Sandel (2012) has called it. For members of the economics discipline this marked the victory of the Chicago School free-market Knightian tradition over the state regulators in the British Keynesian tradition. Nixon's decision meant that foreign currencies could be bought and sold on the free market, and the financial sector began its explosive growth as new profit-making possibilities emerged. The era of globalization had begun, and scholars everywhere started trying to make sense of what was going on as market values conquered ever more new domains of life. Anthropologists have rightly turned their attention to the problem of globalization and its moral implications: ethnographers have started doing fieldwork in Wall Street and other financial centers; theorists have grappled with the implications of the changes for theory by posing new questions and developing new concepts. The common problem—globalization—has created common ground with scholars from other disciplines, and a new paradigm, called "cultural economy," has emerged. This is a loose coalition of scholars from many disciplines united more by what they oppose than by what they propose. What they oppose is the conceptual framework and value theories of pre-1970s political economy and anthropology; but what theory of value do they propose?

Cultural economy uses the language of "goods," but it is a constructive critique of the prevailing orthodoxy in the sense that I have used that notion above. The emergence of this new paradigm has been a three-decade-long evolution of thought rather than a sudden revolution. It only became apparent to me when I read Appadurai's latest book, *The future as a cultural fact: Essays on the global condition* (2013), and puzzled over its significance in the light of the now vast interdisciplinary literature on the subject. Graeber (2001: 26–33), armed as he was with his value-theory sensitive radar, detected the signs of change in his critique of the early work of Appadurai and Bourdieu. Developments since 2001 enable us to situate the work of these scholars, and others like them, more precisely. The March 2008 launching of the journal *Cultural Economy* (Bennett, McFall, and Pryke 2008) marked the formal coming of age of the new paradigm.

Any discussion about cultural economy must begin with Appadurai because his much-cited writings have done much to set the agenda. Indeed, his many neologisms can be seen as a struggle to find the terms of the new debate in much the same way that Jevons, Walras, and Menger struggled to do so in the 1870s (see Chapter I). Appadurai's fundamental question concerns the "spirit" of post-1970s financial capitalism. This question has its origins in the 1970s, when deregulation of the foreign exchange market stimulated the explosive growth in the financial sector. The globe defined the geographical limits of this market, but the future provided unlimited scope for the development of new forms of money making; the derivative, a truly fantastic mathematical entity that only exists in the future as an abstract number with a price, was born and with it a new spirit of finance capitalism.

Weber's ([1930] 2001) classic study has inspired Appadurai's question about the spirit of capitalism today, but he turns to Frank Knight to develop his answer. Appadurai is more concerned to develop a constructive critique of Knight's theory in the light of post-1970s developments in the global economy than he is to develop a negative critique of political economy and economic anthropology. This is a perfectly legitimate strategy. As a result, the work of Taussig, myself, and others in the political economy/economic anthropology tradition gets short shrift as Appadurai hurries on to his principal theoretical inspiration, Knight.

What distinguishes Knight from many other mainstream economists is his theory of uncertainty and risk. Knight's theory of goods is premised on the assumption of the brute fact of uncertainty, the unhappy truth that the future is unpredictable. Risk, Knight (1921) argues, is calculable using probability theory, but while this theory may work in the controlled environment of the casino, it does not work in the uncertain world of global markets. This fact has not stopped the majority of mainstream economists, and many financial traders, from adopting the contrary assumption. Knight is a protestant mainstream economist; it is this dissident tendency within mainstream economics that cultural economy rehabilitates. Appadurai's version of cultural economy builds an "ethics of possibility" based on Knight's assumption of the brute fact of uncertainty, and opposes this theory of value to an "ethics of probability" based on the mathematics of probability (Appadurai 2013: Chap. 15). Moral implications follow. An ethics of possibility is a virtue because it is based on sound assumptions; financial traders who base their trades on the assumption of uncertainty contribute to public welfare. An ethics of probability is a vice and must be denounced because it assumes that the future is predictable; financial traders who base their trades on these assumptions, Appadurai (ibid.: 244) argues, are no different from astrologers, tarot card readers, and other practitioners of the mystical arts. Anthropologists cannot stand aside from this; the future of anthropology must be based on an ethics of possibility. "In this regard," Appadurai (ibid.: 300) notes in the last sentence of his book, "we have nothing to lose but our chains." This call to arms has a distinct Marxian ring, but the Knightian theory of value that informs it could not be more different.

Appadurai's theory of value has been extended and developed by scholars from different disciplines, but most importantly, for our purposes, by the anthropologist Michel Callon, Latour's former collaborator in Actor Network Theory, who turned his attention to matters of economics in the 1990s. Callon is a logically rigorous thinker who has tidied up Appadurai's sometimes imprecise language and rehabilitated *homo economicus* in a new guise in his Introduction to *The laws of the markets*.

Whether we choose to enhance the economic theory of the agent or denounce it, in both cases we formulate the same critique: *homo economicus* is pure fiction. This introduction as well as the entire book in fact, maintains the contrary. Yes, *homo economicus* really does exist. Of course, he exists in the form of many species and his lineage is multiple and ramified. . . . He is formatted, framed and equipped with prostheses which help him in his calculations and which are, for the most part, produced by economics. Suddenly new horizons open up to anthropology. It is not a matter of giving a soul back to a dehumanized agent, nor of rejecting the very idea of his existence. The objective may be to explore the diversity of *calculative agencies,* forms and distributions, and hence of organized markets. The market is no longer that cold, implacable and impersonal monster which imposes its laws and procedures while extending them ever further. It is a many-sided, diversified, evolving device which the social sciences as well as actors themselves contribute to reconfigure. (Callon 1998: 51, emphasis added)

Homo economicus is reborn in the plural with a new name, *calculative agencies,* in a new theoretical home, cultural economy, where the future is uncertain and global financial markets rule. "Calculative agencies," we are told elsewhere (Callon and Muniesa 2005: 1236), "are not human individuals but collective hybrids, 'centres of calculation.' . . . These agencies are equipped with instruments; calculation does not take place only in human minds, but is distributed among humans and non-humans. . . . Calculative agencies, along with calculable goods and calculated exchanges, constitute the three elements that define concrete markets as organized collective devices that calculate compromises on the values of goods."

Callon's careful and precise use of the language of "goods" betrays the formalist tradition he is rehabilitating, but three important innovations must be noted: the individual economic agent is replaced by a network of posthuman *calculative agencies*; rational choice theory is replaced by market *calculation* done by agents who are *calculative,* with goods that are *calculable* in exchanges that are *calculated*; certainty of market outcome is replaced by *radical uncertainty.*

The standard utility theory of value gives pride of place to the agency of individuals, but this constructive critique adds nonhuman agents into the mix. This theory can be seen as a reformulation of Adam Smith's invisible hand of the market; but Appadurai takes an extreme animist position within the school when he argues that things have "intentionalities, projects, and motives independent of their human handlers" (2013: 257).

This market-oriented theory of goods with its lexicon of specialist terms stands opposed to, say, Marx's theory of commodities with its lexicon of specialist terms. Terms such as calculative agents, calculable goods, and calculated markets populate Callon's lexicon while terms such as commodities, exchange-value, use-value, and surplus-value populate Marx's list. Economic anthropology has extended Marx's lexicon by adding terms such as gift, rank, reciprocity, and obligation, which raises the question of where the gift fits into Callon's conceptual framework. Callon's answer builds on Bourdieu's (1977) notion of temporality. His analog of the gift/commodity distinction is a continuum defined by the degree of calculative agency. This, in turn, depends on the time frame. "The shorter the interval, the more the gift will be experienced as calculative' (Callon 1998: 15).

This brief sketch is hardly an adequate account of cultural economy, but it does reveal that this new paradigm rehabilitates the formalist tradition by negating the substantivist tradition. It introduces a new theory of value based on human and nonhuman agency in the calculated exchanges of goods. This has nothing in common with Graeber's theory of value, but, so far as I can tell, neither Appadurai nor Callon replies to Graeber's critique. They simply ignore him, in the same way that mainstream economists ignored my 1982 critique of the theory of goods paradigm.

It may be impossible to debate across incommensurable paradigms, but we should nevertheless try to do so. Cultural economy raises at least two important questions that call for discussion. One of these concerns its notion of uncertainty and the related issue of temporality, the other concerns its theory of the workings of the market mechanism. Appadurai (2013) critiques mainstream economics for failing to confront the brute fact of uncertainty and draws implications for the future of anthropology. Callon (1998: 1) also critiques mainstream economics by drawing attention to the paradox that it celebrates the market but has very little to say about how it works. He also critiques political economy for its oversimplified notion of capitalism, which he dubs "kapitalism" (Callon 2005: 13).

The points are well taken, but they raise other issues which are not addressed. Firstly, Knight (1921) was not the only person who raised the question of uncertainty in the 1920s. Malinowski ([1925] 1974) and Keynes (1921) also did so at the same time. For Malinowski ([1925] 1974: 31) it provided an answer to his question about why Trobriand fishermen engaged in magical practices when they fished on the high seas but did not when they fished in the safety of a harbor. For Keynes (1937: 213–14) it informed his theory of interest and employment and his theory of why free markets don't always work efficiently. Cultural economy has rehabilitated Knight's theory of uncertainty but not those of Malinowski and Keynes, which theories are quite different from his. This raises the question of the implications that a rehabilitation of Malinowski's theory and Keynes' theory has for our understanding of the market mechanism today.

Secondly, while Callon's point about the abstract purity of theories of "kapitalism" is well taken, the logical purity of his own account of the efficiency of the market mechanism can be questioned too. The reality of the Enron affair and the revelations concerning the corrupt role Wall Street played in the subprime lending crisis poses the question of whether or not corruption should be seen as the "exception" or as part of business as usual. This is a question for students of both the global and the local. Chabal and Daloz's answer in *Africa works* (1999: Chap. 7) is that we must see corruption as an "instrument of disorder," that is, part of business as usual. This thesis is not novel. For the ancient Indian theorists of political economy it was an obvious fact of life.

> Just as it is not possible not to taste honey or poison placed on the surface of the tongue, so it is not possible for one dealing with the money of the king not to taste the money of the king in however small a quantity. Just as fish moving inside water cannot be known when drinking water, so officers appointed for carrying out works cannot be known when appropriating money. It is possible to know even the path of the birds flying in the sky, but not the ways of officers moving with their intentions concealed. (Kangle 1972: 2.9, 32–34)

How different would political economy, economic anthropology, and cultural economy look if we all made such an assumption?

Keynes ([1936] 1967: viii) famously argued that the greatest hurdle facing any scholar is not the development of new ideas but escaping from the old. I escaped from the old ideas of mainstream economics by finding a home in the economic anthropology and political economy paradigms. It should come as no surprise, I suppose, that some anthropologists have sought to escape from the old ideas of pre-1980s economic anthropology by moving onto the economists' domain and developing a constructive critique of their theory of goods. The challenge for the scholar of the future will be to escape from the old ideas of both traditions, but to do this they will have to study the past: intellectual history, political and economic history, comparative ethnography. To quote the wisdom of another elder from the past, "There is no royal road to science, and only those who do not dread the fatiguing climb of its steep paths have a chance of reaching its luminous summits" (Marx [1867] 1965: 30).

CHRIS GREGORY
Canberra, September 2014

Acknowledgments

In the process of writing this book—which is a revised version of my Ph.D. thesis—I have accumulated many debts, of which one of the largest is to John Eatwell, my thesis supervisor. He has carefully read the many drafts this book has gone through and has been a constant source of encouragement and support. My thesis examiners, Maurice Godelier and Bertram Schefold, provided many useful constructive criticisms. Most of my "anthropological fieldwork" was conducted among anthropologists living in or passing through Cambridge. These people, who have been extremely generous with their time and data, are numerous but special mention must be made of the following: Fred Damon, Marilyn Strathern, Andrew Strathern, Paul Jorion, Gilbert Lewis, Jack Goody, Giancarlo Scoditti, Shirley Campbell, Alfred Gell, Jerry Leach, Milan Stanek, Nigel Oram, and the participants at the 1978 and 1981 *kula* conferences. A Research Fellowship at Clare Hall supported me during the period of rewriting and I am grateful to the Governing Body of Clare Hall for giving me this opportunity and also for providing me with a stimulating academic environment in which to work; special mention must be made of Polly Hill, a fellow of Clare Hall, whose work on economic anthropology has been a source of inspiration for me. I would also like to thank the following people who have provided useful written comments on one or other of the chapters: Peter Fitzpatrick, Jim Fingleton, Melanie Beresford, Geoff Harcourt, Suzy Paine, Adrian Graves, and Roy Green. I owe a special debt to my wife Judy Robinson. She has provided crucial moral support and has, along with Dee Moore, helped me with editing and proofreading. Finally I must thank my many PNG friends—from UPNG, the PNG trade union movement, and elsewhere—who have taught me about the "Melanesian Way." I reserve special thanks for Morea Pipi and my friends at Elevala village.

CHRIS GREGORY
Cambridge, July 1982

I owe a special debt to Giovanni da Col, without whose initiative, energy, and enthusiasm this second edition would never have been published. My warm thanks to Marilyn Strathern for agreeing to write the Foreword and for all the support she has given me over the past four decades. Comments from Giovanni and Marilyn on my Introduction to this second edition, along with those from Keith Hart and Keir Martin, have enabled me to improve it considerably. I thank Sean Dowdy, Justin Dyer, and Sheehan Moore, who have labored hard and efficiently on the production side of things with me. A Manchester-based, ESRC-funded grant on the value question in the Asia-Pacific region has enabled me to update my thinking of the gift/commodity distinction. I am grateful to the ESRC for research funding and to the many participants at workshops and seminars we have held. Particular mention must be made to my UK-based collaborators in this project—Karen Sykes, Fiona Magowan, Rodolfo Maggio and Rachel Smith—and to Canberra-based colleagues Jon Altman and Nicolas Peterson. Special thanks once again to Judy Robinson who has been through it all with me.

CHRIS GREGORY
Canberra, September 2014

Introduction

The subject of this book is colonial Papua New Guinea (PNG) and its objective is to provide a critique of neoclassical economic development theory by presenting a constructive alternative that builds on the theoretical work of Marx, Sraffa, Lévi-Strauss, and others, and on the empirical work of anthropologists who have worked in PNG and elsewhere. The problems to be confronted in this book, and the propositions it seeks to demonstrate, are best introduced by examining, very briefly, the political and economic history of PNG.

The term "Melanesia" is used by anthropologists to describe the geographical region that includes such countries as Irian Jaya, PNG, Solomon Islands, New Caledonia, New Hebrides, and Fiji. PNG is part of western Melanesia, the geography and territorial divisions of which are shown in Map 1. The western half of western Melanesia was claimed by the Dutch in 1828; it became part of Indonesia in 1969 after the notorious "Act of Free Choice," when 1025 specially selected representatives of the people voted unanimously in favor of integration. The eastern part of the island was appropriated by the British and the Germans in 1884, with Germany colonizing the northern part—New Guinea—and Britain the southern part—Papua. Australia assumed administrative control of both territories after the First World War. This situation persisted until 1975 when PNG gained its formal political independence. The *de facto* colonization of the country has been rather different, its pace and direction being governed by the geography of the main island. Lying entirely between 1 and 12 degrees of latitude south, the island, with its huge mountainous central spine and its range upon range of mountains with jagged, serrated peaks, is covered with tropical rain forests and large rivers that meander through coastal swamplands on their way to the sea.[1] These factors rendered the highland plateau areas virtually impenetrable and it was not until after the Second World War that the colonizers discovered, to their surprise, that almost half the population lived there. These areas are shown as numbers 8, 9, 10, and 14 in Map 2, which gives the administrative districts of colonial PNG.

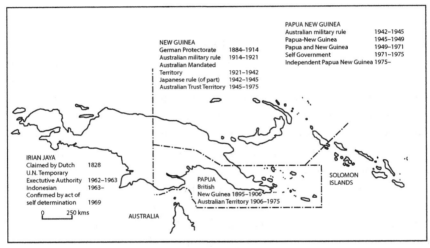

Map 1. West Melanesia.

The economic history of colonial PNG is the history of foreign-owned plantation and mining companies who came in search of cheap labor, gold, and copper. In the period 1884–1920, copra and rubber plantations were established in the coastal and island districts. These plantations survived by exploiting cheap unsophisticated indentured labor from the labor frontier.[2] This frontier moved around the coastal areas in the 1890s

1. See Brookfield and Hart (1971).
2. See Bailey (1957) for a discussion of the concept "economic frontier" in the Indian context.

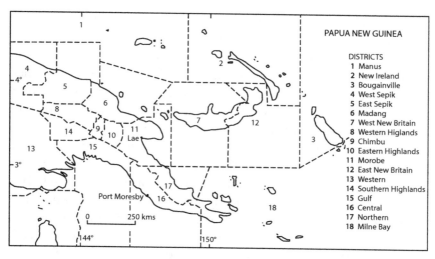

Map 2. Papua New Guinea.

and 1900s, deep into the lowland river areas in the 1920s and 1930s, and into the highland areas in the 1950s and 1960s. Plantation labor contracts were usually of two to three years in duration, and while some recruits signed for a second term, the majority returned to their village to engage in cash cropping as a sideline. This enabled them to earn the money they needed to pay taxes and to buy the imported commodities they desired. The mining companies have had an altogether different impact on the country. A mining company's profit depends not so much on cheap labor as on the rent (super profit) the exploitation of a natural resource provides. Gold was first discovered in the Milne Bay District in the 1880s. These mines had petered out by 1930, when another find was made in the Morobe District. This lasted about ten years. Today a substantial proportion of the country's gross national product is derived from the gold mined as a by-product from the capital-intensive Bougainville Copper Mine, which commenced operations in 1971.

The impact of colonization on the indigenous economy of PNG presents the analyst with something of a paradox. This is because the indigenous economy has not died out with the advent of political and economic development, but has "effloresced" (Andrew Strathern 1979). This runs counter to both the descriptive and prescriptive propositions of neoclassical development theory and it calls into question the descriptive and explanatory adequacy of that theory, to say nothing of the relevance and implications of its policy recommendations.

To understand the efflorescence of the indigenous economy it is of course necessary to have some understanding of the principles that govern the production and exchange of things and labor. It is here that another problem is confronted. While it is generally agreed that the indigenous economy is different from the European capitalist economy, theorists are by no means agreed on how to characterize this difference. Indeed, the problem is so basic that the indigenous economy has not even been satisfactorily named, let alone described or analyzed. The following terms are among the many that have been used to describe the indigenous economy: "primitive communist," "primitive capitalist," "primitive affluence," "stone-age," "peasant," "gift economy," "tribal," and "traditional." This diverse set of terms is evidence of the lack of a generally agreed conceptual and theoretical framework for describing and analyzing the indigenous economy.

The indigenous economy is by no means homogeneous. For example, the country's two and a half million inhabitants (Census 1971) speak over seven hundred different languages, one-seventh of the world's total (Laycock and Wurm 1974). Associated with this is an enormous cultural diversity, a point that anthropologists continually stress (Chowning 1977: 3). The basic unit of social organization in the rural areas was, and still is, the clan. A clan is a land-owning group of people among whom marriage is prohibited.[3] Unlike many African clans (lineages), PNG clans are not, in general, headed by a chief. Prestige and power are usually vested in the hands of a "big-man" who acquires renown in a type of meritocracy system which involves the competitive giving of gifts between clans. For example, if *A* gives 100 pigs to *B*, and the latter replies with a counter-gift of 150 pigs which *A* cannot repay, then *B* is the "big-man" because he gave the last gift. Shells, which are marked[4] according to size, color, and age, are also used as instruments of competitive gift

---

3. This is a simplification, of course. In some areas of PNG the marriage group and the land-owning group are different. See Chapter VII below.

4. Many have confused the ordinal ranking of these shells with the cardinal ranking of money and have erroneously called these shell-gifts "primitive money" or "shell money" (e.g. Einzig 1948; Epstein 1968).

exchange in addition to pigs in some areas. But the big-man system is by no means general.[5] In some areas neither competitive gift-giving nor big-men exist. In these areas political authority tends to be in the hands of elders, who acquire their authority by seniority and command over ritual knowledge.

The analysis of the impact of colonization on a country such as PNG, then, poses a large number of fundamental theoretical problems. The particular problems that this book addresses itself to can be summarized as follows. First, there is a need to develop a general conceptual framework within which a distinction between capitalist and noncapitalist economies can be made. Secondly, a set of concepts for describing the basic features of the indigenous economy of PNG, as well as a system for classifying the different types of indigenous economic systems in PNG, is required. Thirdly, these concepts must be able to generate propositions to account for the historical and anthropological data on the impact of colonization on PNG and, in particular, the efflorescence of the indigenous economy.

A starting point for an analysis of this type is the literature on economic theory. However, as economic theory was developed to explain the particular case of the European capitalist economy, a question immediately arises as to the usefulness of this theory for understanding non-European economies. This issue is highly controversial and a considerable body of literature has been devoted to it. Myrdal (1968: 19), for example, believes that "the use of Western theories, models and concepts in the study of economic problems in South Asian countries is a cause of bias seriously distorting that study." To address oneself to this literature, however, is to miss the point somewhat. The so-called "Western theories" are by no means homogeneous: there are a number of different approaches to the analysis of European capitalism, each with its own methodological approach and theoretical structure. An analysis of the impact of colonization presupposes a certain approach to the analysis of capitalism, and once this problem is resolved the problem of what approach to take to the analysis of noncapitalist economies is, to some extent, resolved as a consequence.

---

5.   Maurice Godelier (personal communication) stressed this point and has developed a "great-man"/"big-man" distinction.

The literature on approaches to the analysis of European capitalism can, without too much oversimplification, be classified under two broad headings: political economy, which was the dominant orthodoxy prior to 1870, and economics, the dominant orthodoxy since 1870. The defining characteristics of these two approaches are developed in great detail in subsequent chapters, but it is necessary to give a brief sketch here as a prelude to outlining the principal argument to be advanced in this book.

Political economy is associated with the work of Quesnay ([1759] 1962), Smith ([1776] 1970), Ricardo ([1817] 1951), Marx ([1867] 1965) and Sraffa (1960), among others. While there are many important differences in the form in which these writers present their theories, they share a common approach to certain basic issues. They were all concerned to lay bare the principles governing the reproduction of the surplus product in different economic systems, and they all gave particular attention to the analysis of surplus reproduction in European capitalist economies. For example, the principal problem of political economy, as Ricardo saw it, was to determine the laws which regulate the distribution of surplus, under the names of rent, profit, and wages, between landlords, capitalists, and workers. This was one of Marx's problems too, but he located it within a broader framework which focused on the "laws of motion" of capitalist production and reproduction. By developing Quesnay's *Tableau économique*, Marx was also able to analyze surplus reproduction in a more rigorous way than Ricardo. Sraffa, in turn, has developed Marx's reproduction model to provide some new answers to Ricardo's question.

Economics, or the "neoclassical" approach, is associated with the work of its founders: Jevons ([1871] 1970), Menger ([1871] 1950), and Walras ([1874] 1954). It is the dominant orthodoxy today, and while its most sophisticated contemporary exponents, such as Samuelson ([1947] 1971) and Debreu ([1959] 1971), have developed the technique of analysis used by Jevons and the others, they have not altered the basic premises upon which the whole approach is based. The economics approach developed in conscious opposition to the political economy approach. It shifted the central concern of economic analysis from the analysis of surplus reproduction in class-based societies to the general analysis of scarcity and individual choice. This involved a shift from a study of the particular "laws of motion" of European capitalism to the universal laws of consumer choice. The principal problem of economics is the analysis of consumer behavior under conditions of unlimited wants and limited resources. This problem is analyzed in terms of a model which assumes that an individual maximizes utility, subject to certain constraints. Associated with this change in approach was a change in the terminology used to describe the object of analysis. The political economists used the term "commodities" to describe objects of exchange, a term whose etymology suggests an objective relation between the things exchanged, that is, prices. Economists, on the other hand, have opted for the term "goods" (see Milgate 1987). This term connotes a subjective relation between an individual and an object of desire. The expression "goods" epitomizes the whole "subjectivist" approach of economics in the same way that the term "commodity" epitomizes the fundamentally "objectivist" approach of political economy (see Bukharin 1919: 36): the project of political economy can be understood as an attempt to relate the surface appearance of things presented by the phenomenon of commodities to class relations in the sphere of production, while economics can be understood as an attempt to examine the consequences of postulated subjective relations between individuals and objects of desire for market behavior.

It is clear from this brief discussion that an approach to the analysis of colonization which uses the economics approach will be very different from an analysis using the political economy approach. One is therefore confronted with the problem of which approach to choose.

One of the central themes of this book is that the political economy approach enables the development of theories which have superior descriptive and explanatory power compared to those of the economics approach. The problem with the economics approach is that its supreme concept, "goods," is subjectivist and universal, which means that the theory of goods, by definition, has no objective empirical basis for distinguishing between different economic systems. The concept "commodity," on the other hand, presupposes—as will be seen in subsequent chapters—certain objective historical and social preconditions. If these conditions are not met, then the political economy approach says some theory other than the theory of commodities applies. It is precisely this situation that one finds in PNG. In PNG-type societies "we see that a part of mankind, wealthy, hardworking and creating large surpluses, exchanges vast amounts in ways and for reasons other than those with which we are familiar from our own societies" (Mauss [1925] 1974: 31). The workings of these economies have been painstakingly described in hundreds of anthropological monographs, and these monographs in turn have been the subject of much interesting theorizing by other anthropologists such as Morgan (1871, 1877), Mauss ([1925] 1974), Lévi-Strauss ([1949] 1969), and others. What is striking about the approach of these anthropologists—and this is another theme of this book—is that their approach is an extension of the project started by Quesnay, Smith, Ricardo, and Marx. Like the early political economists, the central focus of analysis of these anthropologists is the social relations of reproduction of particular social systems. The central concept of their theories is the "gift." This refers to the *personal relations* between people that the exchange of things in certain social contexts creates. It is to be contrasted with the *objective relations* between things that the exchange of commodities creates. The theory of gifts and the theory of commodities are compatible and together they stand opposed to the theory of goods with its focus on the *subjective relationship* between consumers and objects of desire. The gift economy and the commodity economy should be seen as just two of many possible economic systems that the political economy approach is able to differentiate. The concepts "gift" and "commodity" have no meaning within the economics approach, and the phenomena to which they refer are captured by the categories "traditional" goods and "modern" goods. This distinction is a distinction within the category "goods" and, like the concept "goods," has no objective empirical basis. As a consequence, theorists who use the economics approach tend to confuse general economic categories with historically specific categories. For example, they tend to perceive noncapitalist economies in terms of inappropriate categories relevant only to capitalism such as "profit," "interest," "capital," and so on. Such confusions prevent the development of adequate explanatory hypotheses and, to the extent that neoclassical description is used as a basis for prescription, may either mislead policy makers or provide theoretical justification for policies which, from the perspective of political economy, have no objective economic basis.

This book is concerned to elaborate and demonstrate the propositions discussed above at both the conceptual and theoretical level and to illustrate the propositions using data from PNG and elsewhere. Chapter I reviews the literature of commodities, gifts, and goods; it identifies the common basis that links the theory of commodities with the theory of gifts and shows how this common approach (political economy) stands opposed to economics. Chapters II–IV are concerned to modify and develop the political economy approach by producing a synthesis of the theories of Marx and Sraffa with those of Morgan, Mauss, Lévi-Strauss, and others; the analysis presented in these chapters is abstract and conceptual and in the realm of logical rather than historical time. In Chapter V a conceptual critique of the economics approach is presented; the argument here is general but is illustrated by using theories which neoclassical economists working in PNG have developed. In Chapters VI and VII the historical and anthropological evidence from PNG is examined and a number of theoretical propositions are developed and illustrated; these propositions, which attempt to account for the efflorescence of the indigenous economy, and which examine the consequence of this for wages theory and policy, are contrasted with those of the economics approach.

PART ONE

Concepts

CHAPTER I

The competing theories

This chapter reviews the literature on commodities, gifts, and goods; its aim is to identify the competing theories by contrasting the approaches used by different theorists. It outlines the defining characteristics of political economy and economics, and shows how the rise to dominance of economics in 1870 involved a radical departure from the theoretical approach of Quesnay, Smith, Ricardo, and Marx to the analysis of economic systems. It also argues that the political economy approach was taken over and developed, if somewhat unconsciously, by Morgan, Mauss, and Lévi-Strauss, and other anthropological theorists.

The reason why the economics approach rose to dominance in the 1870s is a problem for historians of thought and is beyond the scope of this book. Having identified the different approaches, the concern of the following chapters is to challenge the continued dominance of the economics approach today.

POLITICAL ECONOMY

The theory of commodities

Because wealth assumes the form of an accumulation of commodities in European countries, an examination of the category "commodity" was the starting point for the early political economists. A commodity is defined as a socially desirable thing with a use-value and an exchange-value. The use-value of a commodity is an intrinsic property of a thing desired or discovered by society at different stages in its historical evolution. For example, as Marx ([1867] 1965: 43 fn.) noted, "The property which the magnet possesses of attracting iron, became of use only after by means of that property the polarity of the magnet had been discovered." "Exchange-value," on the other hand, is an extrinsic property, and is the defining characteristic of a commodity. "Exchange-value" refers to the quantitative proportion in which use-values of one sort are exchanged for those of another sort.

These propositions were developed by Smith, Ricardo, and Marx, among others; but Marx's great advance over his predecessors was to see that exchange-value was a historically specific property of the commodity which presupposed certain social conditions for its existence.

Consider Smith, for example. He argued that commodity exchange was the defining characteristic of people. "It is common to all men, and to be found in no other race of animals, which seem to know neither this nor any other species of contracts" ([1776] 1970: 12). Smith's analysis of the commodity form begins with the analysis of commodity exchange in a tribe of hunters and proceeds through what he considered to be the other three stages of mankind—the age of shepherds, the age of agriculture, and the age of commerce (see Meek 1976: 117). Smith's analysis of that "early and rude state of society" was completely fanciful because it was based on the highly unreliable travelers' tales of the social life of the American Indians (see Meek 1976: Chap. 4). Smith ([1776] 1970: 13–14) argued that in a tribe of hunters

> a particular person makes bows and arrows . . . with more readiness and dexterity than any other. He frequently exchanges them for cattle or for venison with his companions; and he finds at last that he can in this manner get more cattle and venison than if he himself went to the field to catch them. From a regard to his own interest, therefore, the making of bows and arrows grows to be his chief business, and he becomes a sort of armourer.

But as anthropologist Franz Steiner has recently pointed out, "Smith was wrong on this point . . . the modern anthropologist cannot fathom a man dextrous in manufacturing bows giving up cattle in a cattle society, one where ritual values and status are connected with cattle, merely in order to make bows" (Steiner 1957: 120).

A similar criticism can be made of Ricardo. Not only did he believe that commodity exchange was universal, he also believed that humanity was divided into three classes: the "proprietor of the land, the owner of the stock or capital necessary for its cultivation, and the laborers by whose industry it is cultivated" ([1817] 1951: 1). What distinguished the different stages of society for him was the proportion allotted to each of these classes "under the names of rent, profit, and wages."

Marx's approach was different. He criticized Ricardo for making

> the primitive hunter and the primitive fisher straightway, as owners of commodities, exchange fish and game in the proportion in which labor-time is incorporated in these exchange-values. On this occasion he commits the anachronism of making these men apply to the calculation, so far as their implements have to be taken into account, the annuity tables in current use on the London Exchange in the year 1817. ([1867] 1965: 81, fn. 1)

The argument that Marx developed in opposition to this was that

> the exchange of commodities evolves originally not within primitive communities, but on their margins, on their borders, the few points where they come into contact with other communities. This is where barter begins and moves thence into the interior of the community, exerting a disintegrating influence upon it. ([1859] 1970: 50)

The proposition that commodity exchange begins on the boundaries of "primitive" communities was, according to Engels, later verified by the anthropological data.[1] In an editorial footnote to Volume III of *Capital* he commented that "after the extensive research ranging from Maurer to

---

1. Marx made a careful study of this anthropological literature in the later years of his life but never wrote it up. See Krader (1972).

Morgan into the nature of primitive communities, it is an accepted fact that is hardly anywhere denied" (see Marx [1894] 1971: 177).[2]

Building on this simple fact, Marx ([1867] 1965: 91) was able to develop a very important proposition: that commodity exchange is an exchange of alienable things between transactors who are in a state of reciprocal independence. "Alienation" is the transference of private property; this, as Marx ([1867] 1965: 91) noted, "has no existence in a primitive society based on property in common." The corollary of this is that noncommodity (gift) exchange is an exchange of inalienable things between transactors who are in a state of reciprocal dependence. This proposition is only implicit in Marx's analysis but it is, as will be seen below, a precise definition of gift exchange. The distinction between a commodity economy and a noncommodity economy, then, is the first defining characteristic of the political economy approach.

The second defining characteristic of the political economy approach is the importance attached to the analysis of the social control exercised over land and other important means of production as the key to understanding economic activity. Jones has stated this precisely. He argued that only an accurate knowledge of the "economical structure of nations" can provide the key to understanding economic activity. By the "economical structure" he meant "those relations between the different classes which are established in the first instance by the institution of property in the soil, and by the distribution of its surplus product" (Jones 1859: 560).

This was the procedure followed by Quesnay, Smith, Ricardo, and Marx, among others; it was this method that gave their theories historic specificity. Quesnay, for example, who wrote in the mid-eighteenth century, distinguished three classes: the productive class, the class of proprietors, and the sterile class. The "productive class" consisted of the farmers who did the work, and incurred the expenses, in bringing agricultural products to the market; the "class of proprietors" included the sovereign, the owners of the land, and the tithe-owners who subsisted on the revenue or net product of cultivation; the "sterile class" was composed of

---

2.   This is not quite true. Whilst the data show that commodity exchange is a
     subordinate and peripheral form of economic activity in clan-based socie-
     ties, it says nothing about the origins of commodity exchange. See Sahlins
     (1972: Chap. 6).

all the citizens engaged in providing other services, or doing work other than that of agriculture. This "economical structure" captured the essence of the eighteenth-century French economy. This is because manufacturing was "sterile" in the sense that it was incapable of yielding any disposable surplus over necessary costs in terms of value (Meek 1962: 381). Furthermore, there was no landless proletariat to speak of. However, by the time Marx came to analyze English capitalism over a hundred years later, this "economical structure" was inadequate for understanding commodity production. Marx captured the changed historical circumstances by removing the class of landed proprietors to a subordinate position, elevating the "sterile" class to the status of "productive," and by dividing the productive "departments"—agriculture and industry—into the opposed classes of wage-laborers and capitalists. All of Marx's categories derive their meaning from these relationships and, like Quesnay's theories, they cease to apply when the historical circumstances render the "economical structure" inappropriate. Thus, theories within political economy have a planned obsolescence.

A third defining characteristic of the political economy approach is the picture of production and consumption as a circular process. Quesnay ([1759] 1962) was the first to develop this with his *Tableau économique*; Marx ([1893] 1971) elaborated the idea in his "reproduction schemes"; and Sraffa (1960) developed the idea even further with his *Production of commodities by means of commodities*. These models all deal with the reproduction of things and they have served two quite distinct purposes: on the one hand they have been used to analyze the conditions of self-replacement; on the other they have been used to analyze growth and change. Sraffa, unlike Quesnay and Marx, used his model only for the purposes of the former, a procedure that will be adopted in this book.

Models of the reproduction of people were not developed by the classical economists. This was because, in the European economies which they studied, the reproduction of things was the predominant sphere. As Marx and Engels ([1846] 1962: 28) noted,

> The family, which to begin with is the only social relation, becomes later, when increased needs create new social relations and the increased population new needs, a subordinate one . . . and must be located and analysed according to the existing empirical data.

Engels was to return to this point forty years later and to verify the converse proposition with respect to non-European societies by an examination of the anthropological data and, in particular, Morgan's *Ancient society* (1877). Engels ([1884] 1970: 449) observed, "the less the development of labour, and the more limited its volume of production and, therefore, the wealth of society, the more preponderatingly does the social order appear to be dominated by ties of sex."

A fourth defining characteristic of the political economy paradigm is the "logical-historical" method of inquiry. Engels (1859: 98) has described this method in the following terms:

> The criticism of economics . . . could . . . be exercised in two ways: historically or logically. Since in history, as in its literary reflection, development as a whole proceeds from the most simple to the most complex relations, the historical development of the literature of political economy provided a natural guiding thread with which criticism could link up and the economic categories as a whole would thereby appear in the same sequence as in the logical development. This form apparently has the advantage of greater clearness, since indeed it is the actual development that is followed, but as a matter of fact it would thereby at most become more popular. History often proceeds by jumps and zigzags and it would in this way have to be followed everywhere, whereby not only would much material of minor importance have to be incorporated but there would be much interruption of the chain of thought; furthermore, the history of economics could not be written without that of bourgeois society and this would make the task endless, since all preliminary work is lacking. The logical method of treatment was, therefore, the only appropriate one. But this, as a matter of fact, is nothing else than the historical method, divested of its historical form and disturbing fortuities. The chain of thought must begin with the same thing that this history begins with and its further course will be nothing but the mirror-image of the historical course in abstract and theoretically consistent form, a corrected mirror-image but corrected according to laws furnished by the real course of history itself, in that each factor can be considered at its ripest point of development, in its classic form.

This method, as Meek (1967) has demonstrated, was used, in one form or another, by Quesnay, Smith, Ricardo, and Marx, among others. These authors also used the "conjectural-historical" method, which must not be confused with the logical-historical method. The former is a highly controversial theory of the evolution of society, while the latter is merely a system of classification. For example, a conjectural historian uses contemporary anthropological evidence to reconstruct the prehistory of Europe. This process necessarily involves the logical-historical method. However, logical history can also be used to classify categories as a prelude to the analysis of the impact of colonization, a procedure which uses anthropological data in an altogether different way.

The theory of gifts

The theory of gifts, as developed by Morgan (1877), Mauss ([1925] 1974), and Lévi-Strauss ([1949] 1969) is a logical extension of the method of political economy to the analysis of anthropological data. Engels was one of the first to realize that Morgan's work was a development of the political economy approach, describing Morgan's *Ancient society* (1877) as "one of the few epoch-making works of our time" ([1884] 1970: 450). *Ancient society* was an attempt to provide a theoretical account for the wealth of anthropological data Morgan collected and published in *Systems of consanguinity and affinity* (1871) and *League of the Iroquois* (1851). Morgan's books introduced European readers to facts of social organization previously unknown or uncomprehended. Morgan was, as Fortes observed (1969: 8), a discoverer, "one not unworthy to be ranked with the discoverer of a new planet." His discoveries provided the empirical basis for the elaboration of the distinction between classes and clans. He did not develop a theory of the gift explicitly; it arose out of the subsequent researches that his work stimulated.

Whereas Smith, Ricardo, and Marx were primarily concerned with the clarification of relations between things and, in particular, the explanation of the phenomenon of prices, Morgan was primarily concerned with the clarification of relations between people and, in particular, the explanation of the phenomenon of kinship terms. While conducting fieldwork among the American Indians, Morgan found, to his amazement, that they used kinship terms in a "classificatory" way. For example, a male called all the male members of his clan one generation above him "father," those below him "son," all the female members one generation above "mother," and so on. He then collected terms from 134 different family groups around the world and discovered that "classificatory" kinship terms were a general feature of non-European societies. He distinguished these from "descriptive" European kinship terms, which tend to be more "individualistic" in their identification of people, especially lineal blood relations. For example, the term "father" is usually only applied to one person, the real father.

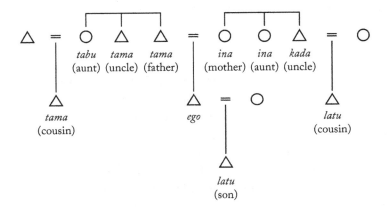

Figure 1.1. Trobriand and English kinship terms compared. *Key:* △ male, ○ female, = marriage, ⌐ siblings, | descent. *Source:* Malinowski (1929: 435).

The distinction between "descriptive" and "classificatory" kinship systems becomes clearer when an actual empirical example, such as the one in Figure 1.1, is considered. This shows the terms used for near relatives by Trobriand Islanders (PNG) and English speakers. It is clear from the way Trobriand Islanders use the terms *tama* and *latu* that there is an indisputable empirical basis to Morgan's distinction. The term *tama*, for example, classifies my father, my father's brother, and my father's sister's son together. However, Morgan's conceptualization of this difference between kinship terms, and his theoretical explanation for it, can be challenged. His argument (Morgan 1877: 404) that classificatory systems result from plural marriages while descriptive kinship systems result from marriages between single pairs is no longer seriously entertained; his argument (Morgan 1871: 490) that the rise of private property in Europe overthrew the classificatory system and led to the emergence of a descriptive system with clearly defined channels for transmission of estates can be neither refuted nor verified because the evidence is simply not available. However, the idea that kinship, property, and systems of land tenure are somehow related was seminal. This point has been taken up and developed by contemporary theorists. Leach (1961: 146), for example, has argued that a kinship system is "a way of thinking about rights and usages with respect to land."

Morgan's theory of "gentile organization" (i.e. clan-based societies) was an empirically based theory of social organization of a society without private property; Gentile organization, Morgan observed (1877: 63), had an organic series:

> first, the gens, a body of consanguinei having a common gentile name; second, the phratry, an assemblage of related gentes united in a higher association for certain common objects; third, the tribe, an assemblage of gentes, usually organized in phratries, all the members of which spoke the same dialect; and fourth, a confederacy of tribes, the members of which respectively spoke dialects of the same stock language. It resulted in a gentile society (*societas*), as distinguished from a political society or state (*civitas*).

In a *societas* all the important means of production, such as land, belong to the confederacy, and the different units of social organization have rights over the land which vary according to the position of the social unit in a hierarchy. For example, members of a clan *x* of tribe *A* have different rights to the land they occupy than do members of clan *y* of tribe *A*. The clan is characterized by rights, privileges, and obligations conferred and imposed upon its members. Morgan gives a long list of these but the following are the most important: the obligation not to marry in the clan; mutual rights of inheritance of the property of deceased members; reciprocal obligations of help, defense, and redress of injuries.

The next significant contribution to the distinction between class-based and clan-based societies was Marcel Mauss' *The gift* ([1925] 1974). Like Morgan's theory, Mauss' theory arose out of a detailed comparative analysis of the extant anthropological data. However, by the 1920s much more reliable data had been collected, especially from the Pacific area. Mauss therefore had data from PNG, the home of the classic gift economy. This country was not even colonized at the time that Morgan wrote.

Like Morgan, Mauss was concerned to contrast the European with the non-European economy; but whereas Morgan concentrated on the contrasts between the social and political structures, Mauss concentrated on the contrasts between the economic structures, in particular, the modes of exchanging things.

One of Mauss' aims was to debunk the prevailing orthodoxy among economists that economies of the PNG type were "natural" economies which produced for subsistence rather than exchange. After surveying a vast amount of historical and anthropological literature, he came to the conclusion that, "It appears that there has never existed, either in the past or in modern primitive societies, anything like a 'natural' economy" (Mauss [1925] 1974: 3). He noted that "we see that a part of mankind, wealthy, hard-working and creating large surpluses, exchanges vast amounts in ways and for reasons other than those with which we are familiar from our own societies." He called this system of production and exchange a "gift economy" and found that it was widely distributed throughout the non-European parts of the world.

But in what sense is production for gift exchange unfamiliar? How does it differ from production for commodity exchange?

"We live in a society where there is a marked distinction between real and personal law, between things and persons," said Mauss (ibid.: 46). "This distinction is fundamental; it is the very condition of part of our system of property, alienation and exchange. Yet it is foreign to the customs [in the non-European societies] we have been studying." In other words, in a class-based economy, where there is private property, a person has alienable rights over the things that he owns. This requires that a sharp distinction be drawn between a thing and its owner. But in a clan-based economy, where there is no private property, people do not have alienable rights over things. As a result "the objects are never completely separated from the men who exchange them" (ibid.: 31).

The inalienability of things as gifts is a recurrent theme of Mauss' work (ibid.: 9–10, 18, 24, 31, 42, 112, etc.). He showed that "the indissoluble bond of a thing with its original owner" is a feature of gift exchange systems from all over the world. And he noted that because of the inalienable nature of the thing transmitted, "the alliance contracted is not temporary, and the contracting parties are bound in perpetual interdependence" (ibid.: 62). In other words, he argued that gift exchange is an exchange of inalienable things between persons who are in a state of reciprocal dependence.

It follows from these definitions of exchange that commodity exchange establishes a relationship between the objects exchanged, whereas gift exchange establishes a relationship between the subjects. In other words commodity exchange is a price-forming process, a system of purchase and sale. Gift exchange is not. As Mauss noted, "They replace our system of sale and purchase with one of gifts and return gifts" (ibid.: 30). With gift exchange, "It is wrong to speak . . . of alienation, for these things are loaned rather than sold and ceded" (ibid.: 42). An inalienable thing that is given away must be returned. Thus a gift creates a debt that bas to be repaid.

> Cuq could still say in 1910: "In primitive societies barter alone is found; in those advanced, direct sale is practiced. Sale on credit characterizes a higher stage of civilization; it appears first in an indirect manner, a combination of sale and loan." In fact the origin of credit is different. It is to be found in a range of customs neglected by lawyers and economists as uninteresting: namely the gift, which is a complex phenomenon especially in its ancient form of total presentation, which we are studying here. Now a gift necessarily implies the notion of credit. Economic evolution has not gone from barter to sale and from cash to credit. Barter arose from the system of gifts given and received on credit, simplified by drawing together the moments of time which had previously been distinct. (Mauss [1925] 1974: 34–35)

The gift economy, then, is a debt economy. The aim of a transactor in such an economy is to acquire as many gift-debtors as he possibly can and not to maximize profit, as it is in a commodity economy. What a gift transactor desires is the personal relationships that the exchange of gifts creates, and not the things themselves.

The problem that is most difficult for a European to understand is the obligation to give a thing as a gift. Mauss addressed himself to this problem, and in his treatment of it he raises a number of significant issues. First, gift exchange is peculiar to clan-based societies and not class-based societies. Secondly, "charity wounds him who receives" (ibid.: 63). In other words, gift-giving places the debtor in a subordinate position. Furthermore, "The person who cannot return a loan . . . loses his rank and even his status of a free man" (ibid.: 41). Thus gift exchange is a means by which the relations of domination and control are established in a clan-based economy. It should be remembered, too, that a clan-based economy is relatively egalitarian in the sense that there does not exist one group of people who live off the surplus product of another group of people. Of course clans may have a rigid hierarchical structure, with the chief's clan at the top. But, as Mauss notes, the exchange of things as gifts tends to be absent in such societies; it flourishes in those societies where there is an unstable clan hierarchy changeable from time to time (ibid.: 91, fn. 68). This is precisely the situation one finds in most areas of PNG today.

Another theme of Mauss' theory is the anthropomorphic quality of gifts. This property of gifts is an aspect of their inalienable nature. For example, speaking of an American Indian tribe, he noted that "The only domestic animal in these tribes is the dog. It is named according to the clan and cannot be sold. 'They are men like us,' say the Kwakiutl" (ibid.: 112). This is to be contrasted with Marx's theory of the "fetishism" of commodities. "Fetishism" refers to the reified nature of things as commodities and is an aspect of the alienability of a commodity (see Marx [1867] 1965: 76–87).

Mauss developed a "three-stage theory" of the evolution of the gift economy. The first stage is the system of "total prestations," where two clans oppose each other and exchange "courtesies, entertainments, ritual, military assistance, *women*, *children*, dances and feasts" (Mauss [1925] 1974: 3, emphasis added). An example is the hunting and gathering tribes of the Australian Aborigines. Total prestation "constitutes the oldest economic system we know. It is the base from which gift-exchange arose" (ibid.: 68).

The gift economy, then, is the second stage. The third stage is the commodity economy. Central to Mauss' theory is the concept "money," by which he meant any instrument of gift or commodity exchange. But money is not merely a physical thing, says Mauss (1914: 106); it is essentially a social relation. Mauss ([1925] 1974: 94) argued that

> At first it was found that certain things, most of them magical and precious, were by custom not destroyed, and these were endowed with the power to exchange. . . . In the second stage, mankind having succeeded in making things circulate within the tribe and far outside it found that these purchasing instruments could serve as a means to count wealth and make it circulate. . . . The third stage began in ancient Semitic societies which invented the means of *detaching* these precious things from groups and individuals and of making them permanent instruments of value measurement—universal, if not entirely rational—for lack of any better system. (emphasis added)

The next significant contribution to the theory of gifts was Lévi-Strauss' *The elementary structures of kinship*. Whereas Mauss was primarily interested in the exchange of things as gifts and mentioned the exchange of people as gifts only in passing, Lévi-Strauss made the latter the principal object of his analysis. He argued that women are the "supreme gift" ([1949] 1969: 65) and that if we can understand the principles governing the exchange of women as gifts, then we can understand the principles governing the exchange of things as gifts much better.

His principal contribution was to conceptualize marriage as a system of the gift exchange of women. This is how marriage is conceived of in European society. For example, in a Christian wedding ceremony it is the father who gives away the daughter, and not the mother who gives away the son. Marriage in European societies has limited economic significance and is usually ignored by economists. But "in primitive societies . . . marriage is of an entirely different importance, not erotic, but economic" (ibid.: 30). In clan-based societies the exchange of women at marriage is, among other things, an exchange of productive labor between clans.

Lévi-Strauss distinguished between "complex" exchange and "elementary" exchange: the former refers to marriage in European-type societies, the latter to marriage in non-European societies. He defined "elementary" structures as

those systems in which the nomenclature permits the immediate determination of the circle of kin and that of affines, that is, those systems
which prescribe marriage with a certain type of relative, or, alternatively,
those which, while defining all members of the society as relatives, divide
them into two categories, viz., possible spouses and prohibited spouses.
The term "complex structures" is reserved for systems which limit themselves to defining the circle of relatives and leave the determination of
the spouse to other mechanisms, economic or psychological. (Lévi-
Strauss [1949] 1969: xxiii)

This contrast may be seen as an attempt to develop Morgan's distinction between "descriptive" and "classificatory" kinship systems in terms
of Mauss' theory of the gift.

Lévi-Strauss limited himself to a discussion of "elementary" structures, and within this category he distinguished between "restricted" and
"generalized" exchange. He said:

Generalized exchange establishes a system of operations conducted "*on
credit.*" *A* surrenders a daughter or a sister to *B*, who surrenders one to *C*,
who, in turn, will surrender one to *A*. This is its simplest formula. Consequently, generalized exchange always contains an element of trust. . . .
There must be the confidence that the cycle will close again, and that
after a period of time a woman will eventually be received in compensation for the woman initially surrendered. (Lévi-Strauss [1949] 1969:
265, emphasis added)

Restricted exchange only involves two parties, *A* and *B*, who exchange
classificatory daughters or sisters. Lévi-Strauss argued that restricted exchange is the original form of gift exchange, that generalized
exchange is a more developed form of this, and finally that the gift
exchange of things is a yet more developed form. "Brideprice"[3] is an
intermediary form between the last two, "it is a process whereby the

---

3. "Bridewealth" is the preferred term nowadays. This is consistent with the
    conception of marriage as a gift exchange. As Dalton (1971: 193) notes,
    "To use the term 'brideprice' is to imply that payment at marriage is a mar-
    ket or commercial [i.e. commodity] transaction."

woman provided as a counterpart is replaced by a symbolical equivalent" (ibid.: 470).

Lévi-Strauss' theory of the evolution of the gift economy revolves around the interpretation of the phenomenon of incest taboo. He said,

> The prohibition of incest is less a rule prohibiting marriage with the mother, sister or daughter, than a rule obliging the mother, sister or daughter to be given to others. It is the supreme rule of the gift, and it is clearly this aspect, too often unrecognized, which allows its nature to be understood. (Lévi-Strauss [1949] 1969: 481)

It was man's desire to maximize the length of the kinship distance between himself and his wife that caused society to progress through the different stages of society (ibid.: Chap. XXVIII). For example, marriage with one's father's sister's daughter is better than marriage with one's sister, and marriage with one's mother's brother's daughter is better than marriage with one's father's sister's daughter from the point of view of kinship distance ([1949] 1969: 452).

A number of important contributions to the theory of the gift have been made since Lévi-Strauss' *The elementary structures of kinship* ([1949] 1969) and it is useful to review these quickly.

With the publication of *Trade and markets in the early empires*, edited by Polanyi, Arensberg, and Pearson (1957), the so-called "substantivist" school of economic anthropology emerged. Polanyi distinguished between the two meanings of economic, the "substantive" and the "formal." "The latter" (i.e. neoclassical economics), he argued (1957: 243), "derives from logic, the former from fact." He set out to build a "substantive" theory of economics from the historical and anthropological record. Perhaps the most significant advance made by this school is the theory of modes of exchange they have developed. Sahlins' *Stone Age economics* (1972) contains the most mature version of this theory. One of the important points he made was that the distinction between gift exchange and commodity exchange should not be seen as a bipolar opposition but rather as the extreme points of a continuum. The key variable in the movement from one extreme to the other is "kinship distance" (ibid.: 85–276): gift exchange tends to be between people who are relatives; as the kinship distance lengthens, and the transactors become strangers, commodity exchange emerges. This argument, which is based on a wealth of anthropological evidence, is a sophisticated restatement of Marx's distinction between commodity exchange and noncommodity exchange.

Another "school" to emerge is the neomarxist school.[4] Important theoretical and empirical contributions have been made by its founders, Meillassoux (1960, 1964, 1975) and Godelier ([1966] 1972, 1973 [1977]). For example, Godelier, who has carried out many years' fieldwork among the Baruya of PNG, makes the simple—but profound—point that a single object may exchange as a gift within a tribal community and as a commodity outside it ([1973] 1977: 128). In other words, he has shown how a single natural object (salt in the case of the Baruya) can assume different social forms depending upon the social context.

An important perceptual breakthrough was made by Baric (1964) in her analysis of the Rossel Island "shell-money" system of PNG. She made the point that "it is impossible to speak of Rossel currency in terms of values . . . "ranks" rather than "values" . . . represent the picture of relationships more accurately" (ibid.: 47). Bohannan (1959) made a similar point in his analysis of the Tiv gift economy of West Africa where he argued that a gift economy has multiple spheres of exchange while a commodity economy has only one sphere. This perception of the gift economy, which recognizes that objects of gift exchange are ordinally related rather than cardinally related, enables the analyst to see the gift economy in its own right rather than by using inappropriate categories such as "price," "money," and so on.

It is clear from the foregoing discussion of the theory of the gift and the theory of the commodity that while many divergent approaches exist, a common theme runs through it all. This common theme enables the identification of the political economy approach. There is a common method: concepts and distinctions are empirically based, being derived from the historical and anthropological facts; explanation involves explicating the logical history of a category. There is a common perceptual standpoint: the people/land relation is the central focus, giving the concept "clan" in the one case, "class" in the other.[5] The concepts, gifts

4. Copans and Seddon (1978) have produced a useful survey of this literature.
5. This distinction, which is drawn very sharply here, is modified in the next chapter.

and commodities, while different, are nevertheless complementary: the concept "commodity," which presupposes reciprocal independence and alienability, is a mirror-image of the concept "gift," which presupposes reciprocal dependence and inalienability.

ECONOMICS

The theory of modern goods

Contemporary economists, by appropriating Smith and Ricardo as "fathers," tend to blur the distinction between political economy and economics. However, the people who launched economics on its rise to dominance—Jevons, Walras, and Menger—were well aware of the paradigm shift they set in motion. They realized that the new conceptual framework, method, and perspective they were adopting were so radical as to warrant not only a new set of economic terms, but a new name for the subject. The change from "political economy" to "economics" epitomized this revolution.

In the 1860s, practitioners of the new approach realized that the term "political economy" did not describe what they were doing and there was much discussion about the problem. Hearn (1863), for example, rejected the term for three reasons: first, its etymology involved an inconsistency as one part referred to the family and the other to the state; secondly, to the extent that it referred to the management of affairs of state it was an art not a science; thirdly, and most importantly, the perspective of political economy was society and not the individual. Hearn (ibid.: 5) believed that the method of political economy, which involved an inquiry into public or national wealth before the inquiry into the principles of private or individual wealth, was an "inversion of the natural arrangement." He suggested the word "plutology" as an alternative. Jevons agreed completely with Hearn on principle but suggested the term "economics" instead (Jevons [1871] 1970: xiv, 273). This term was adopted by Jevons' followers.

Jevons' book—mistitled *Theory of political economy* ([1871] 1970)—was one of the first to lay down the principles of economics in a clear and precise manner. He contrasted the historical perspective of political economy——"the Science of the Evolution of Social Relations" (ibid.: 20)—with the forward-looking perspective of economics. He stressed that a principle of mind, which any true theory must take into account, was that of foresight. Things, he said, must be valued with a view to future utility, not past labor (ibid.: 164).

Jevons (ibid.: 18) pointed out that the basic concepts of economics are derived from subjective axioms which are known intuitively, and that the test of a theory is its ability to predict:

> The science of economics . . . is in some degree peculiar, owing to the fact, pointed out by J. S. Mill and Cairnes, that its ultimate laws are known to us immediately by intuition, or, at any rate, they are furnished to us ready made by other mental or physical sciences. That every person will choose the greater apparent good; that human wants are more or less quickly satiated; that prolonged labour becomes more and more painful, are a few of the simple inductions on which we can proceed to reason deductively with great confidence. From these axioms we can deduce the laws of supply and demand, the laws of that difficult conception, value, and all the intricate results of commerce, so far as data are available. The final agreement of our inferences with a posteriori observations ratifies our method.

While Jevons' book contains a precise statement of the basic principles of the new approach, his work, like that of many others that followed, is replete with terminological confusions. As Wicksteed (1910: 2) was to note, "Adhesion to the traditional terminology [of political economy] has disguised the revolution that has taken place." Jevons argued for the term "economics" yet called his book *Theory of political economy*, he used the term "commodity" instead of "good," and he confused use-value with utility. Menger ([1871] 1950: 52) was more precise in his use of terminology.

> Things that can be placed in a causal connection with the satisfaction of human needs we term *useful things*. If however, we both recognize this causal connection, and have the power actually to direct the useful things to the satisfaction of our needs, we call them *goods*.

However, he did not manage a complete terminological breakthrough and reserved the troublesome term "commodities" to describe intermediate goods (Menger [1871] 1950: 240). The terms "utility," "use-value," and "exchange-value" caused him and subsequent writers endless confusion. Clark (1886: 74) realized that "utility is never identical to value, either in use or exchange"; but it was some time before this became common knowledge and the terminology of the theory of commodities fell into disuse.[6]

Along with the change from "commodities" to "goods," from "logical history" to "prediction," and from "society" to "the individual," there was a change from "reproduction" to "scarcity." A fundamental distinction in political economy is the one between reproducible products, the quantity of which can be multiplied without limit by the expenditure of more labor, and scarce products. This distinction, which was drawn very precisely by Ricardo ([1817] 1951: 12), was disputed by Walras. "There are no products that can be multiplied without limit," he argued (Walras [1874] 1954: 399). "All things which form part of social wealth exist only in limited quantities." This view was generally accepted. The focus of economic analysis henceforth moved from the study of the social relations of reproduction to the study of individual choice. The economic problem was redefined as the problem of understanding how universal economic "man" allocated his scarce resources among his competing, and unlimited, wants.

The economics approach is the dominant orthodoxy today. The advances made by Samuelson ([1947] 1971) and Debreu ([1959] 1971) have merely refined and developed the concepts introduced by Jevons and others; they have not altered the basic premises. As their axiomatic mathematical theories illustrate, the unexplained data of the economics approach remain the subjective preferences of individuals; all the concepts used by contemporary economists—"goods," "marginal utility," "marginal product," and so on—derive their meaning from these subjective data.

---

6. This terminological revolution is an excellent illustration of the philosophical proposition that "conceptual changes show up as changes in language" (Pearce and Maynard 1973: x).

The theory of traditional goods

Economic theory continued to be primarily concerned with the analysis of economic behavior in European-type economies up until the Second World War. It was only after the war, as the political movements for decolonization gathered force, and the cry for "economic development" began to be heard, that attention turned to the analysis of the noncapitalist non-European economies. This immediately posed the theoretical problem of having to distinguish between different types of economic systems, and economics responded to this challenge, first, by asserting its own universality and, secondly, by developing a theory of "distortions" to explain the non-European economies.

The universal applicability of economics was vigorously argued by Knight (1941) in his now famous review of Herskovits' *The economic life of primitive peoples* (1940). His defense was nothing more than a restatement of principles laid down by Jevons seventy years before:

> The principles of economy are known intuitively; it is not possible to discriminate the economic character of behavior by sense observation; and the anthropologist, or historian seeking to discover or validate economic laws by inductive investigation has embarked on a "wild goose chase." Economic principles cannot even be approximately verified—as those of mathematics can be, by counting and measuring. (Knight 1941: 245)

This sparked off a debate that still rages in the anthropological journals (see Dalton 1969; Gudeman 1978), a debate that is, in essence, about political economy versus economics.

The theory of "distortions" is an attempt to account for the particular features of non-European economies in terms of a deviation from the "Pareto optimum." Individuals in a neoclassical world are assumed to maximize utility, subject to budget constraints. In the pure case—in effect the "modern" goods case—this establishes an equality between the marginal rate of transformation in production and the marginal rate of substitution in consumption. If there is a "factor market imperfection" (e.g. a wage differential between the rural and urban sectors), a "trade imperfection" (e.g. monopoly power in trade), a "consumption imperfection," or a "product market" imperfection, then this equality will not hold

(Bhagwati 1971). Imperfections of this type, it is argued, are to be found in the non-European countries. Thus "traditional" goods are produced with land, labor, or capital that has zero or negative marginal products or is consumed by individuals whose marginal utility for a good is zero. These propositions, it should be noted, only have meaning within the economics approach; they are totally meaningless from the perspective of political economy.

W. Arthur Lewis was one of the first to develop this line of approach. His classic article "Economic development with unlimited supplies of labor" (1954) is based on the assumption of unlimited supplies of labor. This he argued (ibid.: 141) "may be said to exist in those countries where population is so large relative to capital and natural resources, that there are large sectors of the economy where the marginal productivity of labor is negligible, zero, or even negative." Another premise of his theory was that capitalist sector wages are 30% or more above subsistence sector earnings (ibid.: 150).

Another seminal paper was Jorgenson's "The development of a dual economy" (1961). He adopted Lewis' wage distortion argument and argued that "output of the traditional or agricultural sector is a function of land and labor alone" (ibid.: 311), that is, that the marginal productivity of capital in agriculture does not even exist.

These theories emphasize distortions on the production side. Consumption-side distortions have been introduced by theorists who have tried to explain the gift economy of PNG. Consider Einzig (1948: 16):

> [T]he intellectual standard [of gift transactors] is inferior and their mentality is totally different from ours. We are, so to say, not on the same wavelength. Their attitude towards money differs fundamentally from ours in many respects. Unless we duly appreciate this difference, we have no means of understanding primitive money.

Thus, according to Einzig, the psychological preferences of gift transactors are distorted. This argument can be interpreted in marginal utility terms, a line of approach taken by Stent and Webb (1975). A traditional PNG consumer, they argued, is on the bliss point of his indifference curve (ibid.: 524). They also argued that the marginal product of land in PNG may be negative.[7]

The theory of traditional goods, and the distinction between traditional and modern goods on which it is based, is surrounded by terminological confusion. For example, the terms "backward," "rural," "peasant-owned," and "agriculture" are used as synonyms for "traditional"; the terms "advanced," "urban," "capitalistic," and "industry" are used as synonyms for "modern" (Dixit 1973: 326). But these terms describe quite different forms of activity. For example, a peasant/capitalist distinction is not necessarily identical to an agriculture/industry distinction, because some agricultural practices are capitalistic. This terminological confusion, unlike the terminological confusion that occurred in the early stages of the rise of the economics approach, is not due to a revolutionary development in underlying concepts. Rather, it is due to a fundamental contradiction in the theory of goods: a good is a universal category, whereas the objects of analysis—actual economic systems—are transitory historical phenomena whose essence can only be grasped by historically specific categories such as "gift" and "commodity."

---

7.   This theory is discussed further in Chapter V.

CHAPTER II

A framework of analysis

Having identified the respective conceptual, perceptual, and methodological bases of political economy and economics from an examination of the various theories of gifts, commodities, and goods, the task now is to develop the theory of gifts/commodities as a prelude to a critique of the theory of goods. Three stages in the development of the theory of gifts/commodities must be distinguished: first, the clarification of the general relations of production to consumption, distribution, and exchange; secondly, the specification of the social data necessary for the definition of particular economic relations within this general framework; thirdly, an analysis of the consequences of different social data for distinguishing between different economic systems.

In this chapter only the first two of these three steps are attempted. Marx's distinction between "productive consumption" and "consumptive production" is the starting point for analysis of the general relations of production to consumption, distribution, and exchange. This distinction is developed in the light of the concept of reproduction used by Lévi-Strauss. In the second part of this chapter, Marx's concept of "primitive accumulation," which defined the social data necessary for the definition of capitalism, is the starting point. Marx's discussion involves a distinction between class and nonclass society and the aim is to develop the latter category using Morgan's theory of clans.

THE GENERAL RELATION OF PRODUCTION TO
CONSUMPTION, DISTRIBUTION, AND EXCHANGE

Marx and Lévi-Strauss on reproduction

The term "reproduction" is used here to refer to the conditions necessary for the self-replacement of both things and people. As it is a holistic concept which includes production, consumption, distribution, and exchange as its principal elements, the concept of reproduction in general must weld eight elements—the production, consumption, distribution and exchange of things, on the one hand; the production, consumption, distribution, and exchange of people, on the other—into a structural whole. Marx's concept of reproduction does not quite succeed in doing this. Thus while the concept of reproduction developed by Marx is appropriate for analyzing certain aspects of European societies, it requires some modification before it is transferred to non-European ones such as PNG. In the latter, marriage—a human relationship not discussed explicitly by Marx—is of crucial economic importance. This omission could simply be tackled by developing a synthesis of Marx's concept of reproduction with that of Lévi-Strauss. However, such a synthesis would itself not be adequate, since certain important conceptual problems would still persist. Thus after pinpointing these, an attempt is made below to develop a modified synthesis which is appropriate for a type of society such as PNG.

Marx's model of reproduction in general is outlined in the "Introduction" to *Grundrisse* ([1857] 1973).[1] In this essay Marx's object is the general relations of material production, that is, the general relations of the production of things and people. He begins by criticizing the "bourgeois" economists' conception of material production. He attacks them for having "an independent Natural Individual" as the point of departure. The individual and isolated hunter and fisherman, with whom Smith and Ricardo begin, argued Marx, belongs among the unimaginative concepts of the eighteenth-century Robinsonades. He also attacks them for conceiving of the spheres of production, consumption, distribution, and circulation as independent, autonomous neighbors and for analyzing the relations between them in terms of a one-way avenue that has

---

1. See Carver (1975) for an exegesis of Marx's "Introduction."

production as the point of departure, consumption as the conclusion, distribution and exchange as the middle. Marx argued that production, consumption, distribution, and circulation must be grasped as members of a totality, distinctions within a unity, with production as the predominant moment. He pointed out that production is also immediately consumption because it necessarily involves the using up of materials and labor energies. This process he called productive consumption. But consumption is also immediately production, he argued, because in taking food, which is a form of consumption, the human being produces his own body. In other words, the consumption of things is a necessary condition for the production of human beings. This process Marx called consumptive production.

> In the former [productive consumption], the producer objectified himself, in the latter, *the object he created personifies itself*. Hence this consumptive production—even though it is an immediate unity of production and consumption—is essentially different from production proper. The immediate unity in which production coincides with consumption and consumption with production leaves their immediate duality intact. (Marx [1857] 1973: 91, emphasis added)

Distribution and circulation, "step between" production and consumption, argued Marx, and their structure is completely determined by production. But distribution is important because it defines particular forms of production. This comes about because distribution has a twofold character: it is (1) the distribution of products, and (2) the distribution of instruments of production. The latter defines historical forms of production, says Marx.

This dialectical approach to the analysis of production and consumption enabled him to grasp the relationship between these categories in a threefold way as identities, as opposites, and as composites. His rather awkward terms "production and productive consumption" and "consumption and consumptive production" capture this threefold relationship in a very precise way. However, because these concepts are constantly referred to in this book, the terms "methods of production" and "methods of consumption" will be used as respective shorthand expressions. The expressions "objectification process" and "personification process" will sometimes be used as alternatives in order to highlight this profound insight of Marx's into the nature of the production and consumption processes. The social significance of this insight will become apparent in subsequent chapters where particular production and consumption relations are examined.

If it is to be regarded at a general level, then there are two problems with Marx's account of reproduction as a whole. The first concerns the incompleteness of his notion of the methods of consumption. Marx discussed only the need for people but not the biological character of reproduction, that is, sexual relationships and parenthood. This omission led him to develop a one-dimensional concept of circulation, focused on things, rather than a two-dimensional one which brings in also the way people circulate. This naturally led simultaneously to the second general problem, that is, the extent to which it is legitimate as a general proposition to argue that the objectification process is the predominant sphere in all societies.

These two problems, however, derive essentially from the attempt to develop a conceptual framework appropriate for analyzing certain kinds of noncapitalist economies, and from the related attempt to abstract, at a general level, an overall framework which can be made specific for a wider range of societies than the capitalist ones with which Marx was concerned. Indeed, Marx's treatment of biological reproduction as an exogenous element may well have been appropriate given the historical conditions of his time and the particular historical characteristics of the type of society which he was analyzing.

A natural point of departure for exploring further the notion of consumption as the sexual reproduction of people is the work of Lévi-Strauss. For example, in *The elementary structures of kinship* he noted ([1949] 1969: 33) that food

> is more than just the most vital commodity it really is, for between it and women there is a whole system of real and symbolic relationships, whose true nature is only gradually emerging, but which, when even superficially understood, are enough to establish this connection.

He returned to this theme in *The savage mind*, where he noted ([1962] 1974: 104) an empirical connection between marriage rules and eating prohibitions. Among both the Tikopia of Oceania and the Nuer of Africa a husband abstains from eating animals or plants which his wife may not eat. The reason for this is that ingested food contributes to the formation of the sperm and he would otherwise introduce forbidden food into his wife's body during intercourse.

He continues (ibid.: 105):

Now, these comparisons are only particular instances of the very pro-found analogy which people throughout the world seem to find between copulation and eating. In a very large number of languages they are even called by the same term. In Yoruba "to eat" and "to marry" are expressed by a single verb the general sense of which is "to win, to acquire," a usage which has its parallel in French, where the verb "consommer" applies both to marriage and to meals. In the language of the Koko Yao of Cape York Peninsula the word *kuta kuta* means both incest and cannibalism, which are the most exaggerated forms of sexual union and the consumption of food.

Lévi-Strauss' argument that there is an empirical link between eating and sexual reproduction is uncontroversial. As Leach has pointed out (1964: 42), "Anthropologists have noted again and again that there is a universal tendency to make ritual and verbal associations between eating and sexual intercourse." This link can be seen as empirical support for Marx's conception of consumption as the production of human beings. However, it is also, simultaneously, an empirical critique of his conception of exchange (circulation), which takes no account of the circulation of people necessary for sexual reproduction. Lévi-Strauss' conception of exchange, as outlined in *Elementary structures*, can be seen as an attempt to overcome this problem in Marx. His principal contribution was to conceptualize marriage as the exchange of women between men.

Now while Lévi-Strauss' conception of exchange has an undisputed empirical basis, it fails to distinguish between exchange in general and exchange in particular. Marriage is a historically specific social relation that assumes different forms in different societies. It is not a necessary condition for the reproduction of people and is, therefore, not a general relation. Lévi-Strauss has confused sex with marriage (see Leach 1970: 103) and has, therefore, confused the general with the particular. Male dominance, too, is a particular rather than a general relation. Thus, at a general level of analysis, there is no *a priori* reason why woman should not exchange men for the purposes of sexual reproduction. The fact that it rarely happens is something that has to be explained with reference to particular historical conditions.

The principal conclusions that emerge from this brief discussion of Marx and Lévi-Strauss can be summarized as follows: (1) the production, consumption, distribution, and circulation of things and people are elements of a totality, not autonomous spheres; (2) neither the way in which things are produced nor the way in which people circulate is necessarily the "predominant phase," because the question of predominance is empirical rather than conceptual; (3) production is an objectification process that converts people's labor energies into things, while consumption is a personification process that permits the survival of people, first, by providing their nourishment and, secondly, through their sexual relationships; (4) particular historical processes of reproduction are defined by examining the appropriate historical evidence on the distribution of the means of production between groups of people.

A simple illustrative example

The concept of reproduction being advanced here is best illustrated by means of a simple example. Consider an extremely simple society which produces just enough to maintain itself. Suppose that it consists of two households and produces wheat as food and iron in the form of tools. Suppose further that the households are of equal size, each consisting of a husband, wife, son, and daughter, and that the means of production are equally distributed between them. How will this society organize itself to ensure self-replacement?

The objectification process. Consider first the relations necessary to ensure the self-replacement of things. Suppose that, for a given year, 280 quarters of wheat ($280W$) and 12 tons of iron ($12I$) are used to produce 600 quarters of wheat; while 120 quarters of wheat and 8 tons of iron are used to produce 20 tons of iron. If the total annual labor (L) is employed in each production process in equal proportions, then a year's operations can be tabulated as follows:

$$280W + 12I + \tfrac{1}{2}L \rightarrow 600W$$
$$120W + 8I + \tfrac{1}{2}L \rightarrow 20I$$

These relations are "the methods of production" (Sraffa 1960: 3); they describe an objectification process whereby labor-time is transformed into things. They record the quantities of wheat, iron, and labor that must be productively consumed to produce 600 quarters of wheat and 20 tons of iron. This productive consumption process, it should be noted, effects a redistribution of things between the processes: at the beginning of the year things (and labor) are distributed according to need, while at the end they are concentrated in the hands of their producer. An exchange is needed to effect a further distribution between the producers and consumers so that the process can be repeated. In this case the consumers (the householders) must get 200 quarters of wheat to consume unproductively; but this act of unproductive consumption is simultaneously also the consumptive production of people.

The personification process. An anthropologist such as Lévi-Strauss would depict the conditions of self-replacement of people in a kinship chart of the form of Figure 2.1. Here a male (M_1) from one household marries a woman (F_2) from another household and they produce a son (m_1) and a daughter (f_1), while M_1's sister (F_1) marries a male (M_2) from another household and they produce a son (m_2) and daughter (f_2).

This conception, while it captures the relations of reproduction necessary to ensure self-replacement, does not capture the essence of kinship as both a method of consumption and a personification process. This problem can be overcome by assuming that each household consumes 100 quarters of wheat and representing these relations as the mirror-image of the production relations as follows:

$$100W + M_1 + F_2 \rightarrow m_1 + f_1$$
$$100W + M_2 + F_1 \rightarrow m_2 + f_2$$

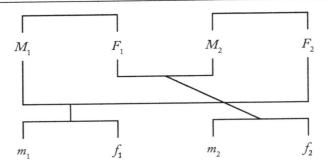

Figure 2.1. Kinship relations in a two-household society.

From this perspective, consumption is both the consumption of food and sexual relations; it is also an act of the consumptive production of children. The process as a whole is one of personification whereby things are converted into people. At the end of the consumptive production period, an exchange of people is needed in order to restore the initial distribution of people so that the process can be repeated. This exchange must take the form of brothers exchanging sisters or sisters exchanging brothers.

It is assumed here that the incest taboo is a biological relation, an approach that Lévi-Strauss ([1949] 1969: 24) is inclined toward.[2] However, recent researches have shown that the phenomenon of the incest taboo is not as universal as was once thought (see Hopkins 1980). The assumption that it is a biological relation is therefore invalid. However, the assumption has been retained here for purposes of exposition; in no way does it affect the conception of kinship as a consumption and personification process, or is it the basis of the subsequent analysis.

THE DEFINITION OF PARTICULAR ECONOMIES

The definition of particular economic systems within this general framework requires an examination of how, at given times and places, the means of production are distributed between groups of people. However, if the historical and anthropological record is examined, a bewildering array

---

2.   Compare Freud ([1913] 1919).

of data of this type is to be found. Fortunately, Jones ([1831] 1964) and Morgan (1877) have developed a simplified typology for classifying this evidence which, with minor modifications, is still useful today. Jones was concerned with the classification of the different forms of class society that existed at different times and places in Europe, while Morgan was concerned with the classification of the different forms of clan society that existed in various parts of the nineteenth-century non-European world (and continue to do so today). A synthesis of their approaches yields the following taxonomy:

I. CLAN-BASED SOCIETIES
    a. moiety
    b. phratry
    c. tribe
    d. nation
    e. confederacy

II. CLASS-BASED SOCIETIES
    f. slave
    g. serf
    h. metayer
    i. cottier
    j. proletarian

Given that land was the most important means of production until the rise of European capitalism, this list can be considered as an answer to the question: "How is land distributed between groups of people?" The answers "equally" and "unequally" provide the initial basis for the classification into clans and classes, because in a clan-based society the distribution of land between groups tends to be equal, while in a class-based society it tends to be relatively unequal.

An alternative way of deriving the bipolar opposition between clan and class is to ask: "What is the relation of the producer to the means of production?" In a clan-based society the relationship tends to be one of "unity," while in a class-based society it is "separation." Separation means that the subordinate class must exchange labor for food with the dominant class in order to survive; unity, on the other hand, means that a clan can produce its own food. It is clear that separation implies inequality, and that unity implies equality in the distribution of land between groups.

These distinctions define a rigid bipolar opposition between clan and class. The empirical reality is, of course, never so clear-cut, and the distinction must be seen as the dividing line on a continuum. At one end of the continuum there is the moiety or dual-clan system of organization, at the other end the proletarian or capitalist system of organization. As one moves from one extreme to the other, equality and unity give way to inequality and separation.

Consider now the subgroups within the category class. The divisions within this group can be considered as answers to the question: "How is productive labor transacted?" In a slave society, productive laborers have the same status as cattle, and are transacted in a similar way. Slaves, like cattle, are always the objects of exchange, never the transactors. In a serf society, surplus labor-time, for example three days per week, is exchanged for a small plot of land from which the worker produces his own food. Thus a serf, unlike a slave, is a transactor who pays a labor-rent for the land he occupies. This form of labor contract, as Jones ([1831] 1964: Chap. II) noted, prevailed in Eastern Europe in the early nineteenth century. A metayer is similar to a serf, with the difference that he exchanges his surplus product rather than his surplus-labor, that is, he pays a produce-rent for the land from which he obtains his food. The landlord also advances the metayer a small amount of stock in the form of seed and elementary tools. At the time Jones wrote, this form of labor contract was common in Western Europe, in Italy, France, and Spain. A cottier is similar to a serf, with the difference that he pays money-rents instead of produce-rents. He differs from the capitalist farmer in that he does not advance his own capital. Cottiers emerge on the periphery of the spreading capitalist frontier and Jones (ibid.: Chap. V) had the nineteenth-century Irish cultivator in mind when he developed this category. A proletarian differs from the serf, metayer, and cottier in that he exchanges his necessary labor-time (as distinct from surplus labor-time) for money wages. The proletarian is landless and must work as a wage-laborer in order to survive.

This taxonomy was developed by Jones by collecting historical data from different times and places and arranging it in logical-historical order. Thus labor-rents logically precede produce-rents, and produce-rents logically precede money-rents. Morgan has applied a similar method to anthropological data collected by various anthropologists to generate the subgroupings within the clan-based society category. A clan, Morgan (1877: 61–87) noted, has many defining characteristics. The two most important are the "exogamy rule"—the prohibition of marriage within a clan—and the possession of land in common. Rights over land are hierarchically arranged and the degree of complexity of this hierarchy varies with each subgrouping. A moiety is a dual-clan system where there is a simple division of members of a population, and the land upon which they live, into two groups. A phratry is a collection of moieties, a tribe a collection of phratries, a nation a collection of tribes, and a confederacy a collection of nations. This groups-within-groups structure goes the other way too: a moiety consists of a collection of subclans, a subclan a collection of sub-subclans, and so on. The structure of a clan-based society can therefore be extremely complex and anthropologists often run out of terms when attempting to describe the empirical situation. Furthermore, they often use different taxonomies and this creates endless terminological confusion (Fox [1967] 1974: 50).

A concrete example[3] of the clan structure of three highland PNG tribes is shown in Figure 2.2. The Kawelka and Tipuka tribes consist of ten clans. Some of these clans have the classic structure, for example clans p, q, r, and s; but others do not, for example clan o. There is a relatively egalitarian distribution of land between these clans, as the map shows. The population size of the clans varies quite a lot, from 61 in clan i to 741 in clan e. The variation in size of a clan is determined partly by its age: young clans are like infants, whereas old clans are like grandfathers and have many dependents. Warfare and conquest also affect the life and size of a clan. Thus the lifecycle of a clan varies from a few months to hundreds of years. Theoretically, a clan can last indefinitely if the relations of self-replacement can be organized properly. The four clans of the Trobriand Islands are organized in this way (see Chapter IV), but none of the highland clans are.

---

3. This is meant to be an illustrative example rather than a "typical" example. A tremendous variety of forms of clans are to be found in PNG. The abundance or scarcity of land is an important determining variable of the outward appearance the land/people relation assumes. Chapter VII considers some of these complications.

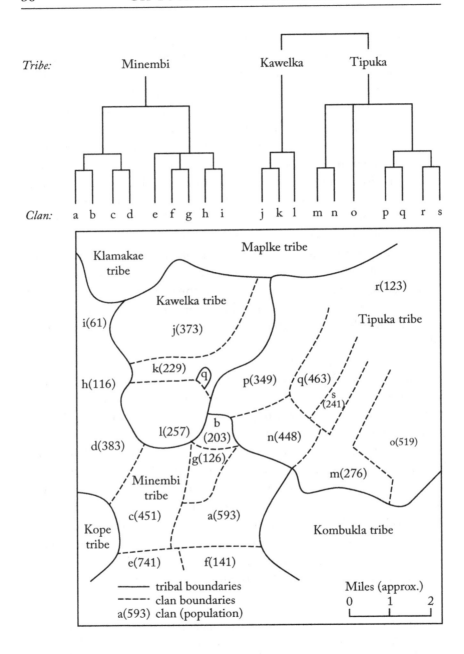

Figure 2.2. Distribution of land among three highland PNG tribes, 1965.
Source: A. J. Strathern (1971: 24, 61, 62; 1972: 65).

The notion of a clan as the "unity" of a producer with his means of production is illustrated by the linguistic evidence from these three tribes. In Hagen a clansman refers to himself as a "planted man" (*mbo-wue*) (A. J. Strathern 1972: 101).[4] Strathern adds:

> Whole groups are often referred to as of one stock (*mbo tenda*) or one root (*wamb pukl*), an idiom for common ancestry which is clearly derived from the model of vegetable growth of trees and plants in general, and which reflects the empirical importance of residing continuously and working in an area for making good one's claims to membership of the group which owns it. (A. J. Strathern 1972: 19-20)

At the clan level, the term "garden ditch" (*pana ru*) is used. This term emphasizes the definition of a clan as a relationship between people and land rather than as a biological relationship between people. The latter is important in determining clan membership but by no means the only determinant. In the past, clan members fought together to maintain or expand their boundaries. The losers in these wars lost their land and became refugees. Refugees, and their descendants, would eventually be absorbed into the clans of neighboring people, where they would be referred to as "taken and (re-)planted men" (*tepa rondi wue*) (A. J. Strathern 1972: 19).

The difference between a clan-based society and a class-based society can be summarized as the difference between "plantedness" and "uprootedness." This difference is the key to understanding the different social form things and people assume in different societies. The particular contrast to be focused on in subsequent chapters is between clan-based societies of the phratry and tribal type—the types to be found in PNG—and class-based societies of the capitalist type—the type imposed on PNG by the colonizers. This classification is taken as data for the purposes of subsequent analysis. The question of the origin of the various types of class and clan structure is an altogether different problem which requires an investigation of the historical process of separation. As Marx ([1857] 1973: 489) noted:

---

4. Note that the English word "clan" has its origins in the Latin word *planta*, sprout, scion.

It is not the *unity* of living and active humanity with the natural, in-organic conditions of their metabolic exchange with nature, and hence their appropriation of nature, which requires explanation or is the result of a historic process, but rather the *separation* between these inorganic conditions of human existence and this active existence, a separation which is completely posited only in the relation of wage labor and capital. In the relations of slavery and serfdom this separation does not take place; rather, one part of society is treated by the other as itself merely an *inorganic and natural* condition of its own reproduction.

The question of the origin of classes in Europe and clans in PNG is of no concern here. The historical existence of these social forms is taken as data. What is of concern is the consequences of this social data for understanding the principles governing the reproduction of things and people in PNG-type economies, a problem that is examined in detail in the next two chapters.

CHAPTER III

Gifts and commodities: Circulation

In a class-based society the objects of exchange tend to assume the alienated form of a commodity and, as a consequence, reproduction in general assumes the particular form of commodity reproduction. In a clan-based society the objects of exchange tend to assume the nonalienated form of a gift; reproduction assumes the particular form of gift reproduction. This comes about because the objectification process predominates in a commodity economy, while the personification process predominates in a gift economy: that is, things and people assume the social form of objects in a commodity economy while they assume the social form of persons in a gift economy. Furthermore, different types of class (clan) organization are associated with different types of commodity (gift) reproduction.

This chapter attempts to demonstrate some of these propositions by focusing on exchange (circulation).[1] It illustrates how commodity exchange establishes objective quantitative relationships between the objects transacted, while gift exchange establishes personal qualitative relationships between the subjects transacting. It also distinguishes a number of different types of commodity exchange and a number of

---

1. "Circulation is . . . exchange regarded in its totality" (Marx [1859] 1970: 204).

different types of gift exchange. Emphasis is given to the analysis of gift exchange because gift exchange of the PNG type is relatively unfamiliar.

THE DIRECT EXCHANGE OF THINGS

Exchange, in its simplest form, can be defined as a transaction involving two transactors, *A* and *B,* and two objects, *x* and *y.* The discussion here is limited to the case where *A* and *B* are individuals or groups, and where the objects are things.

The distinction between gifts and commodities manifests itself as a difference between the exchange relation established: gift exchange establishes a relation between the transactors, while commodity exchange establishes a relation between the objects transacted. This arises because of a difference in the social status of the transactors and a difference in the social status of the objects transacted.

The social status of transactors

The simple barter exchange of commodities presupposes, as Marx ([1867] 1965: 91) was first to point out, that transactors are in a state of *reciprocal independence*, that is, that the transactors are strangers, aliens. Such a state of reciprocal independence has no existence in a clan-based society based on communal property. In such societies people are related to one another and this brings with it rights and obligations of different kinds, that is, people in a clan-based economy are in a state of *reciprocal dependence*.

This distinction between dependence and independence should be seen as the extreme points on a continuum: as one moves from one extremity to another, the degree of dependence changes. In a clan-based society a measure of this dependence is "kinship distance" (Sahlins 1972: Chap. 5). This refers to "classificatory kinship distance" rather than the distance blood relations are apart. The meaning of this is best grasped by considering the position of an individual clansman in a tribal society of the ideal type. He is surrounded by a series of concentric circles each representing the ever-widening comembership spheres to which he belongs. The first circle contains his fellow clansmen, and the next his fellow tribesmen. A measure of kinship distance, then, is the radius of one of these circles. At the periphery, for example, individuals are almost complete strangers, while at the center they are very closely related. It is only at the periphery that exchange assumes the pure commodity form. In a gift economy of East Africa, for example, "there is a kind of continuum in exchange relations. Between strangers there is a strict pecuniary relationship; this aspect is less marked between neighbors and *tilia* (trading partners), and is least so between clansmen and best friends" (Schneider 1957: 286). This phenomenon seems common to all clan-based societies, as suggested by Sahlins' (1972: 231–46) survey of the evidence from Africa (Congo pygmies, !Kung Bushmen, Nuer, Tiv, Bemba), America (Washo, Eskimo, Shoshomi, Chuckchee), Oceania (Australian Aborigines, Maori), Asia (Semang, Andamans, Northern Tungas), and Melanesia (Busuma, Kuma, Siuai, Kapauku, Manus, Mafulu, Chimbu, Buka, Dobu, Trobriands, Tikopia).

This continuum of exchange relations defines a large number of different types of gift exchange. These can be classified as belonging to two broad types: interclan exchanges and intraclan exchanges. The principles governing these types of exchange are quite different. Broadly speaking, interclan gift-giving usually involves durable items such as shells and tends to be competitive, while intraclan giving usually involves food and tends to be noncompetitive.

The social status of objects

The material basis of a society not only determines the social status of the transactors, it also determines the social status of the object being transacted: commodities are *alienable* objects transacted by aliens; gifts are *inalienable* objects transacted by nonaliens.

In a commodity economy there is a marked distinction between things and persons. This distinction, which is "the very condition of part of our system of property, alienation and exchange" (Mauss [1925] 1974: 46), is not the basis of a gift economy.[2]

---

2. The system of "property, alienation and exchange" is familiar to gift transactors but is a subordinate and peripheral form of activity. See Malinowski ([1922] 1961: 189–90).

Leach's ([1954] 1977: 141–54) discussion of the distinction between Shan (commodity) "trade" and Kachin (gift) "trade" in Burma is a particularly good illustration of this. Shan trade is "mainly trade as we understand it—that is, the bartering of goods of ordinary economic value to achieve a profit" (ibid.: 107). In Shan trade the objects transacted are alienated so that, after the exchange, the receiver of an object is the owner. But the receiver is not the owner after a Kachin gift exchange:

> Kachins do not look upon movable property as capital for investment, they regard it rather as an adornment to the person. . . . Wealth objects other than ordinary perishable foodstuffs have value primarily as items of display. The best way to acquire notoriety as the owner (ruler) of an object is publicly to give possession of it to someone else. The recipient, it is true, then has the object, but you retain sovereignty over it since you make yourself the owner (*madu*) of a debt. In sum, the possessor of wealth objects gains merit and prestige mainly through the publicity he achieves in getting rid of them. (Leach [1954] 1977: 142–43)

This distinction between alienability and inalienability is just another way of talking about the presence or absence of private property. This point can be clarified by contrasting the concept of land as a gift with the concept of land as a commodity. Consider the following description of land tenure in the Siane of PNG, for example.

> [T]he system of land tenure is of the kind common in segmentary societies. An individual has different rights by virtue of his membership in various groupings, hierarchically arranged in order of increasing size. The totality of rights is . . . called overlapping stewardship. (Salisbury 1962: 73)

Here, an individual may possess a given piece of land but it is owned collectively, in ascending order, by the subclan, clan, tribe, and so on. When land is a commodity, by way of contrast, there is no "overlapping stewardship." In a commodity economy, an individual owns the lands he possesses, that is, there is private property of land. The concept of a thing-gift is an extension of the idea of overlapping stewardship to the products of land. Compare Siane land tenure with the Plateau Tonga (of East Africa) formulation of cattle ownership, for example.

I own cattle. I belong to a kinship group. Therefore my kinsmen have the right to demand my assistance. My rights over my cattle are subject to the obligation which I have to assist my kinsmen. (Colson 1951: 12)

The Siane have a similar concept of property. They make a distinction between the *merafo* of an object and the *amfonka* of an object.

The rights of a *merafo* are those of a trustee momentarily exercising control over goods the absolute title to which is vested in a corporation which exists perpetually. The ancestors made these goods at the beginning of time when they emerged from holes in the ground, and their descendants (or reincarnations) must be handed these goods in unimpaired condition in the future. The trustee justifies his position in terms of his descent from the ancestors, and validates the privileges he obtains from his trusteeship by the performance of rituals in honor of the ancestors. (Salisbury 1962: 66)

Objects become *amfonka* property by virtue of the work done in creating them; the relationship between a thing and its producer is likened to the relationship between a person and his/her shadow (ibid.: 62). The producer regards his/her product as part of his/her person. For example, "Pigs cannot be eaten by their *amfonka,* and such an act is treated with the same distaste and horror as is expressed at the idea of cannibalism" (ibid.: 65).

One of the social consequences of the inalienable relation between a thing-gift and its producer is the phenomenon of personification: things are anthropomorphized in a gift economy. In the highlands of PNG, pigs, the principal instruments of gift exchange, are regarded as humans (Modjeska 1977: 92). In the coastal areas, yams, the principal means of subsistence, are regarded as human beings in metamorphosed form; legends exist explaining how yams originated by metamorphosis from humans (Fortune [1932] 1963: 95). Gawa Island specializes in the production and exchange of the ocean-going canoes which are used for the famous *kula* gift exchange system. These canoes are traded as gifts rather than commodities. Thus, although the clan which produces a canoe loses possession of it, it is never alienated from the clan. Like other gifts, canoes are personified.

Canoes are adorned to make them beautiful. This adornment which Gawans compare to festive human adornment is concentrated primarily on the prowboards. . . . Verbal labels for human body parts are also playfully transferred to prowboard parts. Primarily through this adornment, the canoe acquires virtual properties of form that synthesize the non-human and human domains. (Munn 1977: 47)

Canoe origin myths also express this strong bond between things and persons. So too do the origin myths of people. Among the Umeda, for example, it is said that Umeda ancestors hunted and killed a cassowary in the forest. When it died on the present site of the Punda hamlet, its bones turned into men and its blood and flesh into women (Gell 1975: 226).

The personification of gifts provides a striking contrast to what Marx ([1867] 1965: 76–87) called the "fetishism" (i.e. objectification or reification) of commodities: the tendency for relations between people in a capitalist society to assume "the fantastic form of a relation between things." In a commodity exchange, the reciprocal independence of the transactors, and the alienability of the objects transacted, means that the exchange relation established is between the objects rather than the subjects. Thus commodity exchanges objectify social relations between people and they appear as a quantitative relation between the objects exchanged.

The spatial aspect of exchange

The social status of the transactors, and the social relation between a transactor and the object transacted, has a number of profound consequences for understanding the difference between exchange in general and particular forms of exchange. The first consequence is that one act of exchange, while representing only one commodity transaction, becomes two transactions for the particular case of gifts. This is because gift giving is unidirectional, a point that is best illustrated by a simple example.

Suppose two transactors, A and B, exchanged two things, x and y. When x and y are commodities this exchange appears as one transaction, as shown in Figure 3.1. Here A gives B commodity x in exchange for commodity y, and a quantitative exchange relation is established between the objects: one unit of commodity x equals one unit of commodity y.

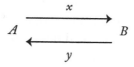

Figure 3.1. Commodity exchange.

However, when x and y are gifts this exchange appears as two transactions, as shown in Figure 3.2.

$$A \xrightarrow{\quad x \quad} B \xrightarrow{\quad y \quad} A$$

Figure 3.2. Gift exchange.

Here A gives B gift x. B now has possession of x but A has ownership because it is A's inalienable property. Thus a gift–debt relationship is established between A and B, with A the creditor, B the debtor. The relationship is complicated by the fact that B simultaneously gives A gift y. This creates a gift–debt relationship in the opposite direction, with B the creditor, A the debtor. The one exchange consists of two transactions and the transactors become mutually indebted to each other. Thus the exchange relation established is between the transactors rather than the objects, as is the case with commodity exchange.

Gift-debt of this type can only be cancelled by reversing the exchange, that is, by B returning x to A, and A returning y to B. Thus gift exchange is the exchange of like-for-like. Hill's (1972: 211) description of the important *biki* gift exchange system among the Hausa of Northern Nigeria illustrates this point.

> Contributions are not necessarily in cash, but may take such forms as clothes, threshed grain, bundles of grain, small livestock, food together with money, or enamelware; but like must always be "exchanged" for like, so that, e.g., a donor of threshed grain must be given such produce in return.

It is important to stress that it is not the natural attributes of the thing exchanged which determine whether or not an exchange is of the gift or commodity form. Paper money can assume a gift form in certain social contexts, as Hill's Hausa example illustrates.

Simple commodity exchange is different because it involves the exchange of unlike-for-unlike. Thus it is an exchange of heterogeneous rather than homogeneous things. When *A* gives *B* commodity *x*, a commodity-debt is established; but if *B* simultaneously gives *A* commodity *y* this debt is simultaneously cancelled because the alienability of the objects brings about a transfer of ownership.

The temporal dimension of exchange

The social data of an exchange also affect the temporal relationship established. Simple commodity exchange establishes a relation of equality between heterogeneous things at a given point in time while gift exchange establishes a relation of equality between homogeneous things at different points of time.

As an illustration, consider once again exchange in general where *A* and *B* exchange both *x* and *y*. This is simultaneous exchange but it can be split up into two parts that can be thought of as occurring at two different points in time. If this pair of temporally separated transactions is reproduced at a further two points in time, but in the reverse direction, the temporal outcomes of the debts thereby created will differ depending on whether the debt was of the commodity or the gift variety. This is illustrated in Figure 3.3.

Value and rank

The difference between a commodity exchange relation and a gift exchange relation can be summed up as the difference between "value" and "rank." Commodity exchange—the exchange of unlike-for-unlike—establishes a relation of *equality* between the objects exchanged. When *A* and *B* exchange *x* and *y* as commodities of equal value, a relation of the form $x = y$ is established. In a commodity economy, because of the operation of the law of value, two heterogeneous things are treated as equivalent and the problem is to find the common measure.

Gift exchange—the exchange of like-for-like—establishes an unequal relationship of *domination* between the transactors. This comes

Time	Exchange in general	Particular forms of exchange	
		Commodity transactions	Gift transactions
1	$A \xrightarrow{\ x\ } B$	A becomes creditor to B who receives x as a commodity	A becomes creditor to B who receives x as a gift
2	$B \xrightarrow{\ y\ } A$	B cancels debt to A who receives y as a commodity in return	B becomes creditor to A who receives y as a gift
3	$B \xrightarrow{\ x\ } A$	B becomes creditor to A who receives x as a commodity	B cancels his debt to A who receives x as a return gift
4	$A \xrightarrow{\ y\ } B$	A cancels debt to B who receives y as a commodity in return	A cancels his debt to B who receives y as a return gift
Outcome		Times (1 and 2) and (3 and 4) linked	Times (1 and 3) and (2 and 4) linked

Figure 3.3.

about because the giver usually is regarded as superior to the receiver (A. J. Strathern 1971: 10). This is a feature that is common to gift exchange systems all over the world. But as Strathern (ibid.: 10) notes: "Whether this superiority implies political control over the recipient or whether it merely indicates a gain in prestige on the part of the giver are matters in which individual systems vary." The precise meaning of "domination" is an empirical question; for the subsequent exposition it is sufficient that it implies that the giver has *some* kind of superiority.

Thus when A and B exchange x and y, A is superior to B because he gives him an x; but B is superior to A because he gives him a y. So who is superior to whom? This is the problem of rank and the answer to the question depends, in the first instance, on the rank of the objects, that is, their exchange-order. Objects as gifts have this exchange-order rather than exchange-value, because the relationship between them is ordinal rather than cardinal. This provides the key to understanding the shell-gift exchange systems (misleadingly called "shell-monetary" systems) of PNG, of which the so-called Rossel Island "monetary system" first described by Armstrong in the *Economic Journal* (1924) is the most famous example. This island then had, and still has, a highly developed shell-gift exchange system. Over twenty different ranks of shell-gifts are distinguished. The top-ranking shell-gifts are small, highly polished, and extremely rare, while the bottom rank of shell-gifts are large, rough in appearance, and in abundant supply. The relation between the top shells and the lower ones was first analyzed (incorrectly) in value terms; but as Baric (1964: 47) was later to observe, "'ranks' rather than 'values'. . . represent the picture of the relationships." Thus a shell-gift of high rank does not equal a number of shell-gifts of low rank. Leach ([1954] 1977: 154) provides a similar analysis of the instruments of exchange used in the Kachin gift economy. The central idea is that the objects are not interchangeable.[3] For example, in Malekula, pigs are ranked according to the size and curvature of their tusks. High-status pigs have long finely curved tusks; one of these pigs does not equate with two pigs of low status (Deacon 1934: 197).

When A and B exchange x and y as gifts, then, the objects have exchange-order. Suppose x (given by A to B) has higher rank than y (given by B to A). It implies that A is superior to B because he has given the higher-ranking gift.

The ranking of things as gifts varies from society to society. It involves the classification of things into what has been called "spheres of exchange" by Bohannan and Bohannan (1968: 227–33) in their discussion of the Tiv gift economy of West Africa. This economy had three spheres of exchange. The supreme sphere contained a single item: rights in human beings, especially dependent women and children. The middle or "prestige" (*shagba*) sphere included cattle, horses, *tugudu* cloth, brass rods, and, in former times, slaves. The lowest sphere contained subsistence products: chickens, goats, household utensils, craft products (mortars, grindstones, calabashes, baskets, pots, beds, and chairs), some tools, and raw materials. The inclusion of women in the top sphere is a common practice and it is the empirical basis of Lévi-Strauss' ([1949] 1969: 65) theory that women are the "supreme gift." The inclusion of subsistence products in the lowest sphere is also common practice. It is in this sphere that the distinction between gift exchange and commodity

---

3. The analogy with playing cards is often drawn. Just as a ten of clubs does not equal a pair of fives, a gift of high rank does not equal a number of gifts of low rank.

exchange becomes blurred, because the products of this sphere are often marketed outside the community.

Contrast the traditional hierarchy of gifts[4] among the Mae-Enga of highlands PNG given by Meggitt (1971: 200):

1. Pigs, cassowaries.
2. Pearl-shell pendants, pork sides, stone axes, cassowary-plume head-dresses, cowrie-shell headbands.
3. Cowrie-shell necklets, bailer-shell pendants, gourds of tree oil, packages of ash salt, net-bags and aprons, birds of paradise plumes, bows, spears, hand drums, fowls, possums, etc.
4. Conus-shell pendants, woven armlets and belts, bone head-scratchers, water gourds, rattan, bark fibre, tobacco, etc.
5. Vegetable foods:
   (a) Luxuries—pandanus nuts, taro, yams, ginger, sugarcane, bananas, sefaria.
   (b) Staples—sweet potatoes, beans, relishes.

The top-ranking gifts were exchanged between clans and subclans at competitive gift exchange ceremonies, mortuary ceremonies, and marriage ceremonies. The lower-ranking gifts were distributed within clans. The shells found their way into the highlands via the traditional trade routes.

It is clear that each rank of gift contains a heterogeneous collection of things. While things of different rank are not interchangeable, things of the same rank are. Thus the principle of like-for-like must be interpreted as rank-for-rank. A pig-gift can be followed by a pig or cassowary counter-gift in the Mae-Enga case. This adds a further complication because it means that some gift exchanges appear as commodity exchanges. The famous *kula* gift exchange system, which still exists, is like this. In the *kula*, armshells exchange for necklaces in a large interisland system of exchange. The necklaces move in a clockwise direction and the armshells in an anticlockwise direction around the islands. However, these shells have their own spheres of exchange. Austin (1945) collected data on the existence of ten spheres in Kiriwina. The largest, oldest, most colorful

---

4. Meggitt (1971: 200) incorrectly describes these as "commodities."

and attractive shells belong to the top rank; the smallest, newest, least colorful and attractive to the bottom rank. Only a top-ranking armshell can be exchanged for a top-ranking necklace, and a middle-ranking armshell for a middle-ranking necklace, and so on. Top-ranking shells do not equate to a number of a low-ranking shells.

The redefinition of like-for-like as rank-for-rank also calls for a redefinition of inalienability. While it is conventional to interpret this in a literal sense at the level of pure theory, in practice this must be modified and interpreted in more of a metaphorical sense. Strictly speaking, like-for-like exchanges are impossible because, for example, a particular pig will be one day older tomorrow and hence a different pig. Thus "likeness" is a social concept that varies from one gift economy to another.

To recapitulate: the distinction between value and rank epitomizes the difference between commodity exchange relations and gift exchange relations. The former emphasizes quantity, objects, and equivalence; the latter emphasizes quality, subjects, and superiority.

The motivation of transactors

The motivation of the gift transactor, some people believe (Pospisil 1963; Epstein 1968), is that of the capitalist, that is, profit maximization. This is a profound misunderstanding. The gift transactor's motivation is precisely the opposite of the capitalist's: whereas the latter maximizes net incomings, the former maximizes net outgoings. The aim of the capitalist is to accumulate profit while the aim of the "big-man" gift transactor is to acquire a large following of people (gift-debtors) who are obligated to him.

Table 3.1, which shows the shell-gifts given and received by Enona clan (Irian Jaya) in 1955, illustrates this point. On interclan account, Enona gave 2638 shells of a certain rank and received 759 in return, giving a net credit of 1879. However, the bulk of the transactions were carried out by household number 6, who had a net credit of 1210. This household, which has the most prestige and status in the village, is the big-man's household.

Table 3.1 also illustrates the way in which the motive "maximize net outgoings" must be qualified. This motive only refers to interclan gift transactions. Intraclan gift-giving is governed by altogether different principles. The principle that the giver is superior does not operate here.

Table 3.1
Shell-gifts given and received by Enona clan, Irian Jaya, 1955

Household number	Intra-clan transactions			Inter-clan transactions		
	Credit	Debt	Net credit	Credit	Debt	Net credit
1	0	10	-10	60	130	-70
2	120	186	-66	121	1	120
3	12	2	10	11	60	-49
4	241	191	50	60	0	60
5	9	83	-74	76	22	54
6	204	255	-51	1,340	130	1,210
7	244	123	121	120	105	15
8	2	0	2	20	0	20
9	3	167	-164	60	61	-1
10	62	5	57	1	64	-63
11	64	61	3	21	60	-39
12	265	210	55	20	0	20
13	63	0	63	133	6	127
14	120	136	-16	365	60	305
15	82	62	20	65	0	65
16	0	0	0	165	60	105
	1,491	1,491	0	2,638	759	1,879

Source: Pospisil (1963: Table 31).

For example, an intraclan gift from a son to a father reinforces, rather than reverses, the father's relationship of domination. Thus, the fact that household number 6 has a net debit on intraclan account in no way affects the status of this household within the clan.

Food is usually the primary instrument of intraclan gift-giving. Food acquired by a household unit from production or exchange is distributed according to clearly defined rules that vary from society to society. For example, the Thonga (Southern Africa) distribute an ox in the following way: a hind-leg to the elder brother, a fore-leg to the younger brother, the other two limbs to the eldest sons, the heart and kidneys to the wives, the tail and the rump to the relatives-in-law, and a piece of the loins to the maternal uncle (Lévi-Strauss [1949] 1969: 35–36). The distribution of food within a clan, and its shared consumption, is not simply concerned with biological nourishment; it serves as an important symbol of clan solidarity and identity (A. J. Strathern 1973). Among the Kaluli of the PNG highlands, for example, a sharp distinction is

made between the sharing of a meal and the exchange of food. Sharing
a meal implies a close brotherly relationship; giving food implies social
distance. For example, hosts do not eat with guests. They present a large
quantity of cooked food to their guests and, sitting apart, watch them eat
(Schieffelin 1977: 51).

The aim of an interclan gift transactor is not simply to maximize
the number of gifts of a given rank he gives away, but to give away a
gift of the highest rank. However, as these usually circulate amongst a
small group of big-men, a young ambitious man must begin by transacting gifts of low rank and work his way up the ladder of rank. Consider Berde's (1973: 193) description of the contemporary Rossel Island
system:

> On the lower end of the social ladder there are younger men and less
> talented older men desiring to borrow *ndap* (shell-gifts). These people
> must demonstrate qualities that inspire trust in order for a *lem* (big-man)
> to give them a *ndap* piece. What inspires trust in both *lem* and ordinary
> people is a demonstrated willingness to give goods and services to one's
> fellows when called upon. The underlying cultural foundation for this
> system is the understanding that no individual—*lem* or commoner—can
> avoid a need for the co-operation of and help from his fellows. Lending
> and helping, then, are really social investments redeemed at future occa-
> sions of personal need.

A young person is therefore faced with a dilemma: before he can give
away a gift of high rank he must receive it. Thus subordination is necessary before he can acquire status. Because a gift of high rank does not
equal a number of gifts of low rank, it is not sufficient for him to maximize his net outgoings of gifts of low rank. He must strive to maximize
his net outgoings of gifts of high rank.

The reason that the motivation of a gift transactor is often confused
with that of a capitalist is that incremental gift-giving appears to be
identical with the lending and borrowing of money at interest. If *A*
gives *B* 100 pigs today and *B* gives *A* 110 pigs one year later it seems
reasonable to argue that the increment of 10 pigs represents interest.
However, this argument overlooks an important difference between
gift-debt and commodity-debt: whereas commodity-debt increases

over time, gift-debt does not. When *A* gives *B* 100 pigs as a commodity at 10% interest per annum, a return of 110 pigs is necessary in order to *cancel* the debt. However, 100 pigs given as a gift requires a return of only 100 pigs to cancel the debt. If more are given, new gift-debt is created. Consider A. J. Strathern's (1971: 216) definition of *moka* gift exchange:

> One of the most striking features of the *moka* is the basic rule that to make *moka* one must give more than one has received. It is the increment that entitles a man to say he has made *moka;* if he returns the equivalent of what he was given initially, he is said to be simply returning his debts.

Moka is defined as the increment in excess of debt; it is this which brings prestige to the giver. The motivation to outgive sets in motion a theoretically never-ending series of exchanges: *A* gives *B* 100 pigs, *B* counter-gives 110 pigs (*moka* = 10 pigs), *A* counters with 30 pigs (*moka* = 20 pigs), *B* counters with 60 pigs (*moka* = 40 pigs), and so on. This sets up what Strathern (ibid.: 11) has called an "alternating disequilibrium" to capture the fact that the partners are superior to each other in turn.

In some areas of PNG, where the clan structure assumes a particular form, such that leadership is in the hands of elders rather than big-men, balanced rather than incremental giving is practiced. Among the Eastern Abelam of the Sepik District, for example, "men give their ceremonial exchange partners (equals) great quantities of displayed and decorated yams and receive exactly the same in return" (Forge 1971: 137). The balancing can be done simultaneously or over time and the principle of like-for-like is always adhered to. For example, the Wamira engage in a practice which involves the delayed exchange (i.e. intertemporal exchange) of female piglets: if *A* gives *B* a female piglet, then *B* is obligated to return the female offspring of that piglet to *A*. This practice binds a wide circle of people together in a web of gift-debt. Furthermore, because the one piglet may be exchanged three or four times, the accumulated debt often far exceeds the actual stock of pigs that are usually exchanged between close kin. Between more distant relatives, pork is exchanged in a more public and ceremonial way. However, the principle of balance and like-for-like is still preserved. If *A* gives *B* a hind-leg, *B* must repay a hind-leg two or three years later. The precise status of the transaction is clarified at the time of giving by shouting the words: "this pays off a debt" or "this creates a new debt" (see Kahn 1980: 171–74).

The difference between balanced and incremental gift-giving is one of form rather than substance, as the underlying motivation—to acquire relationships—is the same in both cases. The formal difference between them comes about because the gift in an incremental gift-giving sequence combines two gifts: one part of the return-gift cancels the original debt, the other part creates a new debt.

Table 3.2
Yam transactions (Urigubu),[a] *Trobriand Islands, PNG, 1950*

	Received	Given [c]	Surplus (+) or deficit (−)
Chief	76	3	+73
Village O[b]	31	32	−1
Village K	21	17	+4
Village T	31	19	+12
Village Y	32	35	−3
Village W	18	18	0

[a] Weiner (1976: 140) questions the correctness of the usage of this term to describe the yam transaction.
[b] O, K, T, Y, W designate the villages of Omarakana, Kasanai, Tilakaiwa, Yolawotu, and Wakailu respectively.
[c] The figures represent the number of people involved in the transaction. Multiplication by 750 lbs. of yams per person gives a rough indication of the quantity of yams involved. See Powell (1969a: 582-83) for more precise details.
Source: Powell (1969a: 589)

A third form of gift exchange that needs to be distinguished is "tributary" gift-giving. This occurs in tribes where leadership is in the hands of hereditary chiefs. Consider Table 3.2, which shows figures for the giving and receiving of yams on the Trobriand Islands, PNG, in 1950. It can be seen that while outgoings and incomings roughly balance for the commoners, the chief appropriates a sizeable surplus. However, this surplus is not invested by the chief in the production of more yams. Instead, it is ceremonially displayed in elaborately constructed yam houses as a symbol of his power and authority and ultimately redistributed to the people at various ceremonial distributions during the year (Powell 1969b: 588). The motivation of a chief in respect of gift-giving is the same as the big-man in that power, authority, and status are achieved by giving rather than receiving.

Consider Leach's ([1954] 1977: 163) account of tributary gift-giving among the Kachin:

> In theory . . . people of superior class receive gifts from their inferiors. But no permanent economic advantage accrues from this. Anyone who receives a gift is thereby placed in debt (*hka*) to the giver. The receiver for a while enjoys the debt (he has it, he drinks it: *lu*) but it is the giver who owns the debt (rules it: *madu*). Paradoxically therefore although an individual of high-class status is defined as one who receives gifts (e.g. "thigh-eating chief") he is all the time under a social compulsion to give away more than he receives. Otherwise he would be reckoned mean and a mean man runs the danger of losing status. For though Kachins hold that a man is born to high rank and do not acknowledge that social climbing is possible, they readily admit that it is possible "to go downhill" (*gumyu yu*)—i.e. lose class status.

The motivation of a transactor, then, is determined by the social context of the exchange. It varies in the first instance according to whether the society is class-based or clan-based, in the second instance according to the particular type of clan structure, and in the third instance according to whether the exchange is interclan or intraclan.

THE CIRCULATION OF THINGS

The analysis of the preceding section can now be extended to the more complicated case of circulation, that is, transactions involving three or more transactors.

Velocity of circulation

If the number of transactors exceeds the number of objects being exchanged, a series of transactions can only be brought about if some of the objects are used in two or more transactions, that is, they have a velocity of circulation greater than one. This phenomenon is general, but a clear distinction must be made between the velocity of circulation of instruments of commodity exchange and the velocity of circulation of instruments of gift exchange.

The circulation of commodities is described by the accounting identity $MV = PT$, where M is the quantity of money functioning as circulating medium, V the number of moves the money makes per unit of time, and PT the total value of the transactions involved. The formation of this identity presupposes alienation of the objects and reciprocal independence of the transactors. But where the objects are inalienable, and where the transactors are in a state of reciprocal dependence, objects have an exchange-order rather than an exchange-value. This means that the concept PT has no meaning and hence no equation of exchange is formed. What happens instead is that for a gift of a given rank, the gift-debt created by it exceeds the number of these gifts in circulation. Thus the velocity is a measure of the gift-credit multiplication. The relationship can be written $GV = D$, where G represents the number of gifts of a certain rank, V its velocity, and D the total gift-debt created by its circulation. There is a separate equation of this type for every rank of gift.

Table 3.3

Velocity of instruments of gift exchange used by Enona clan,
Irian Jaya for eight months ended August 1955

Type of gift		Stock (G)	x	Velocity (V)	=	Debt (D)
Indigenous cowrie	*(Km)*	918	x	5.32	=	4,888
Introduced cowrie	*(Tm)*	1,048	x	1.63	=	1,709
Introduced glass beads	*(b)*	2,577	x	1.89	=	4,875
Introduced small glass beads	*(Pag)*	313	x	0.20	=	64
Indigenous necklaces	*(Ded)*	137	x	0.25	=	34
Pigs		14	x	1.29	=	18

Source: Pospisil (1963: Tables 31 and 46).

Table 3.3 provides an empirical example of the velocity of the instruments of gift exchange used by Enona clan of Botukebo village (Irian Jaya) for the first eight months of 1955. The Kapauku had a number of ranked cowrie shells (*Km*), a number of ranked shell necklaces (*Ded*), and also pigs as its traditional instruments of gift exchange (Pospisil 1963: 301–5). As in other parts of the highlands, "white man's cowrie" (*Tm*) was introduced by the colonizers. However, the Botukebo were reluctant to accept this as a substitute for *Km* and passed it on to neighboring tribes as "counterfeit" (ibid.: 304). The colonizers also introduced two classes of glass beads: *b*, which was long and light blue in color; and *pag*, which was much smaller in size. The quantity of each of these instruments held by the Enona clan as at August 1955 is shown in Table 3.3 under *G*. There were 918 *Km*s in total; the numbers for each rank within this class are not given. There were 137 *Ded* and 14 pigs, the other highly valued instruments of gift exchange. The pig numbers were down because in 1953 Botukebo gave a large pig feast which considerably depleted the local herd (ibid.: 217). Glass beads were ubiquitous. Pospisil recorded 2577 *b* and 313 strings of the smaller variety *pag*. The number of introduced cowrie shells, *Tm*, stood at 1048. Pospisil has recorded the role that these instruments played in 179 transactions. These transactions were for *daba menii*, which he translates as "giving for no specific purpose" (ibid.: 350), and for marriage-gifts. These data enable us to calculate the velocities of circulation as shown. For the period under consideration, *Km* was clearly the most important instrument in circulation. It had a velocity of 5.32 and generated debt to the extent of 4888 *Km*. The glass beads, *b*, had a velocity of 1.89 and generated debt of 4875 *b*; the other instruments all had lower velocities.[5]

Roads of gift-debt

The outcome of the circulation of gifts of different rank with a velocity greater than one is to create "roads" of gift-debt which bind people together in a complicated web of gift-debt. Gifts of high rank create major "highways" that connect people of high rank, gifts of low rank create minor by-ways that connect people of low rank, while middle-ranking gifts connect the highways and by-ways to form an extremely complicated network of roads complete with major junctions, minor junctions, fly-overs, roundabouts, one-way avenues, and culs-de-sac. The big-man, if he is to be successful, must know this map. He must also know the timetable of the gifts which travel along the roads, and how to construct and destroy roads as a strategy for outmaneuvering rivals.

---

5. Contrast Dubbeldam's (1964) attempt to explain these data in terms of the equation $MV = PT$.

15th July 1964   19th June 1964   14th Aug 1964   11th July 1964

A ←——————— B ←——————— C ←——————— D ←——————— E

——————→   ——————→   ——————→   ——————→

11th Sept 1964   26th Sept 1964   10th Jan 1965   Sept 1974

Figure 3.4. The main 1964–1974 *moka* chain.

Consider Figure 3.4, which shows the main road of a highlands PNG *moka* gift exchange that took place between 1964 and 1974. This road linked five clans of three tribes: *A* Kengeke, *B* Kendike, *C* Kitepi/ Oklembo, *D* Mandembo, and *E* Komonkae/Ruprupkae. Pigs were the main item exchanged and a considerable number were transacted. For example, about 130 pigs were given by *D* in the August 1964 gift. In the September 1974 exchange over 600 pigs, as well as several thousand Australian dollars, were given. This example illustrates two principles of gift-giving: delayed exchange between any two transactors and a temporal sequence of giving along a road. The gift from *D* to *C* in August 1964 does not form a genuine sequence. What explains this apparent anomaly is that *D* had privately passed on a number of pigs long before August (A. J. Strathern 1971: 127).

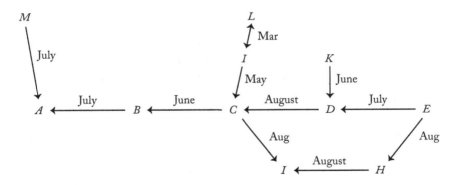

Figure 3.5. The minor 1964–1974 *moka* chains: initiatory sequence.

Figure 3.5 shows the minor roads that fed into the initiatory sequence of the main road, and Figure 3.6 shows the minor roads that fed into (and led off) the return sequence along the main road. What these figures

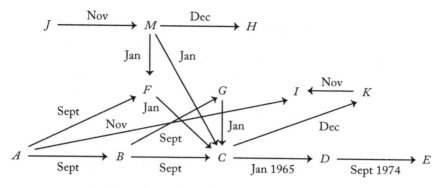

Figure 3.6. The minor 1964–1974 *moka* chains: return sequence.

illustrate is the importance of timing. For example, C was a major junction both on the initiatory and on the return sequence. C's initiatory gift to B was dependent on receipt of pigs from I, which in turn was dependent on receipt of pigs from L. Similarly, C's return gift to D in January 1965 was dependent on gifts from F, M, G, and J. Thus successful gift-giving involves much negotiation and the skillful coordination of large numbers of transactors. It also involves much anxiety because the more important transactors on the minor roads (e.g. F, I, and G) find themselves involved in many different roads with conflicting rights and obligations. The career of a big-man is critically dependent upon knowing those obligations to honor and those upon which to default.

Production and destruction[6]

The preceding discussion illustrated how a big-man can achieve eminence by gaining a dominant position in a network of exchange relations. This strategy, which A. J. Strathern (1969) has called the "finance" strategy, involves increasing the velocity of exchange of a given number of instruments of gift exchange. But there are other strategies, which focus on the stock of gifts rather than their velocity, that can be adopted. These can be called the "production" strategy and the "destruction" strategy.

---

6.   This section is an attempt to develop A. J. Strathern's (1969) stimulating discussion on "Finance and production: Two strategies in New Guinea highlands exchange systems."

In PNG today, shells, pigs, and money are the principal instruments of gift exchange but they are all difficult to produce: money must be earned through wage-labor or cash cropping; shell-gifts are made from a special type of shell which requires hundreds of hours of painstaking labor to fashion into an acceptable shape; pigs can only be produced if surplus land and labor is available. Another problem with pigs is that they take a long time to produce and they depend on the same staple food, the sweet potato, as do human beings, and consume it in much the same quantities (A. J. Strathern 1969: 43). In the highlands of PNG women tend to be the producers and men the transactors (Marilyn Strathern 1972). Reliance on the production strategy therefore places strains on the relationship between a man and his mother and/or wife. While the status of women is not high in the highlands, women are by no means the compliant slaves of men. Indeed, they exercise considerable power and often influence the course of important events (see, e.g., Feil 1978).

The important point to note with respect to the production strategy, then, is that "given certain features of New Guinea highlands subsistence methods and social structure, individuals or groups cannot expand their production beyond a certain point" (A. J. Strathern 1969: 43). This limitation of the production strategy must be seen in the light of its great advantage over the finance strategy. Whereas the latter involves coordinating the activities of hundreds of people, the production strategy is subject to the decisions of only a few people. A household head simply directs those over whom he has authority to produce more pigs by a certain date.

The destruction strategy is perhaps the simplest of them all. It involves the decision of one person and has the effect of reducing the stock of circulating gifts. The "potlatch" system of Kwakiutl is perhaps the most famous example of this. Consider Boas ([1897] 1966: 353):

> The rivalry between chiefs and clans finds its strongest expression in the destruction of property. A chief will burn blankets, a canoe, or break a copper, thus indicating his regard of the amount of property destroyed and showing that his mind is stronger, his power greater, than that of his rival. If the latter is not able to destroy an equal amount of property without much delay, his name is "broken." He is vanquished by his rival and his influence with his tribe is lost, while the name of the other chief gains correspondingly in renown.

This system is quite common in PNG although the destruction assumes a different ceremonial form. Among the Enga of highland PNG, pigs are the principal instruments of exchange. Every so often—about every four years in the ideal case—an exchange cycle culminates in a massive slaughter. The effect of this is precisely the same as the destruction of potlatch gifts: a reduction in the stock of circulating gifts.

The rationale of the destruction strategy has baffled many observers and its consequences have been incorrectly analyzed. For example, Codere (1950: 75), in her analysis of potlatch, argued that the destruction of blankets destroyed gift-credit. Meggitt (1974) put forward a similar argument in his analysis of Enga pig kills. However, the destruction of gifts leaves the actual gift-credit unaffected. It merely reduces the current stock of gifts and limits the *potential* gift-credit that can be created. For example, suppose pigs in circulation totaled 400. If big-man A, in an attempt to outsmart his rival B, destroyed 250 of these, then it is clear that B cannot outsmart his rival by killing more pigs because only 150 pigs are left in circulation.

The destruction strategy gives the gift transactor a third option to the two logically imposed by the "equation of gift exchange." From the equation $D = GV$, it can be seen that a transactor can increase gift-debt (D) by increasing the stock of gifts (G) with velocity (V) constant (the production strategy), or by increasing V with G constant (the finance strategy). The destruction strategy means that $D = GV$ no longer describes the historical record; it reduces G and makes it harder for an opponent to increase D. Suppose, for example, that for a given historical period, 40,000 (D) = 400 (G) × 100 (V). If 250 (G) are destroyed at the end of the period the equation does not become 15,000 (D) = 150 (G) × 100 (V) as Codere and Meggitt would have it. This is because gift-credit of 25,000 (D) are not destroyed when 250 (G) are destroyed. Instead, an inequality of the form 40,000 (D) ≠ 150 (G) × 100 (V) arises, that is, a gift transactor's actions are not constrained by the logic of a simple equation. The destruction strategy effects an "alienation of the inalienable." In other words, when gifts are destroyed no debt is created. This destruction may be symbolic as, for example, when a gift is made to a god but appropriated on his behalf by an intermediary. Where the gift has a number of use-values, for example pigs and money, such an arrangement can be quite beneficial to the intermediary. This type of gift exchange, because it involves alienation, is the only type capable of generating capital accumulation, that is, the accumulation of assets without the accumulation of liabilities (see Case 12, Chapter VII).

THE CIRCULATION OF PEOPLE

Work-commodities

The general principles discussed above concerning the exchange of things apply to the exchange of people. However, the extension of the argument to people is not a straightforward matter as many new issues are introduced. In the first place, a distinction must be made between an exchange of labor-time and an exchange of a stock of labor. In a commodity economy this is a distinction between transactions involving wage-laborers and transactions involving slaves. The buying and selling of wage-labor presupposes that various conditions be fulfilled. The first condition is that the transactor is able to alienate his own labor-time by placing it at the disposal of the buyer temporarily, for a definite period of time. He can only do this if there are no relations of dependence between buyer and seller; both must transact as equals in the eyes of the law. The second essential condition is that the laborer must be obliged to offer his labor-time for sale, that is, a proletariat must exist. These conditions are not met in a slave economy. Relations of dependence exist between master and slave and these people never meet as equals in the market place. The buyer of slave labor confronts as seller another master, never the slave, who is merely the object of the transaction. Thus a slave is transacted as a commodity in the same way that an ox is transacted, "rump and stump, once for all" (Marx [1867] 1965: 165).

Work-gifts

The distinction between an exchange of a stock of labor and the exchange of labor-time also applies to a gift economy. Labor-time is often given as a gift and it creates the obligation to return a work-gift at some future time. For example, cooperative work parties are very common in gift economies. A person who has a house to build or a cultivation site to clear enlists the aid of a number of friends so that the various tasks can be carried out simultaneously and efficiently. At the end of the day the workers are treated to food and drink but this is not regarded as the payment of the work. As Watson ([1958] 1964: 107) notes in his discussion of work parties among the Mambwe of East Africa:

> The basis of Mambwe co-operative work is reciprocity. A man who attends another's work-party obliges the other to work in his own fields in return. Beer is not pay: it is work which is reciprocated.

Thus the principle of like-for-like operates with work-gifts, too.

Women-gifts

The exchange of labor as a stock in a gift economy raises the very important question of marriage. The principle of clan exogamy—the prohibition of marriage within the clan—means that the creation of a new household at marriage involves the spatial exchange of either men or women. Historically, it has been the men who have exchanged women rather than the other way around. While the reasons for the origin of this practice are unknown, it is clear that the practice is a consequence of male dominance. Furthermore, the spatial exchange of women reproduces male dominance by separating women from their land, making it harder for them to exercise their rights over it. However, the spatial exchange of women at marriage does not alienate women from their land. They retain their links with their own clan, which means that gift-debt is established between the transacting clans, binding them together in a web of debt.

Consider Williams ([1936] 1969: 168):

> I suggest that the exchange of girls in marriage falls into line with . . . other exchanges. The unmarried girl is, so to speak, the supreme gift. The insistence on reciprocity is the same, and the transaction serves the same purpose, that of binding the contracting groups together in a bond of mutual restraint and fellowship. We have seen that groups united by marriage acknowledge this bond; that they maintain it by reciprocal services, and that the norm of conduct between them is one of respect and goodwill.

The notion that women are the supreme gift, that is, gifts of the highest rank, is a seminal one and, as noted above, was taken up and developed by Lévi-Strauss ([1949] 1969: 65). If the exchange of women-gifts at marriage is seen as the basis from which all other gift exchanges arise, then many of the puzzles presented by the gift exchange of things become comprehensible. In order to grasp this point it is necessary to distinguish three basic types of women-gift exchange: generalized, restricted, and delayed. These distinctions are best illustrated by taking concrete examples.

Generalized exchange of women-gifts. The generalized exchange of women-gifts involves the circulation of women among three or more transactors. For example, if *A* gives to *B* and *B* gives to *C*, then *C* must give to *A*. This creates a special kind of domination/subordination relationship between the three transactors: *A* is superior to *B* directly because of the gift from *A* to *B*, and superior to *C* indirectly because of the gift from *B* to *C*. However, because *C* gives to *A*, *C* is directly superior to *A*. Thus, from the perspective of the whole, a form of equality reigns.

Consider the process of exchange among the Kachin of Burma (see Leach [1954] 1977). In this society there are five clans, *A*, *B*, *C*, *D*, and *E*, and exchange, in the ideal case, is circular, as shown in Figure 3.7.

$$A \longleftarrow B \longleftarrow C \longleftarrow D \longleftarrow E \longleftarrow A$$

Figure 3.7. Generalized exchange.

The relations of domination and subordination established are named: *mayu* (domination), *dama* (subordination), *ji* (indirectly superior), and *shu* (indirectly inferior).[7] These relations can be depicted in matrix form as in Figure 3.8.

This matrix captures the twenty relations of exchange established by the generalized exchange of women-gifts between the five clans. Reading across the first row records the fact that *A* is directly superior to *E*, to

7. See Leach (1954 [1977]: App. IV). This case, and the following two cases, have been simplified here for the purposes of exposition. A fuller analysis of the terms is given in the next chapter.

		Receiver				
		A	B	C	D	E
Giver	A	0	1	4	3	2
	B	2	0	1	4	3
	C	3	2	0	1	4
	D	4	3	2	0	1
	E	1	4	3	2	0

Figure 3.8. The relations of generalized exchange. *Key:* 1 *dama* (inferior), 2 *mayu* (superior), 3 *ji* (indirectly superior), 4 *shu* (indirectly inferior).

whom a woman-gift is given, indirectly superior to *D*, indirectly inferior to *C*, and directly inferior to *B*, from whom a woman-gift is received. The matrix as a whole gives the relations of all-to-all and describes the particular type of social equality established by generalized exchange.

Restricted exchange of women-gifts. A different type of equality is established by the restricted exchange of women-gifts at marriage. Restricted exchange involves two transactors, *A* and *B*, who exchange clan sisters simultaneously. Thus *A* becomes superior to *B* at the same time that *B* becomes superior to *A*. Consequently, mutual superiority creates a relation of equality between the transactors.

Consider the exchange of women-gifts among the Kariara of Western Australia (see A. Brown 1913). Here the exchanging groups *A* and *B* are internally divided into seniors (1*A* and 1*B*) and juniors (2*A* and 2*B*) to give four groups. Exchange between them assumes the form shown in Figure 3.9.

$$1A \longleftrightarrow 1B$$

$$2A \longleftrightarrow 2B$$

Figure 3.9. Restricted exchange.

This creates twelve relations of exchange between the transactors. These are named and can be described in matrix terms as in Figure 3.10.

		Receiver			
		1*A*	1*B*	2*A*	2*B*
Giver	1*A*	0	3	1	2
	1*B*	3	0	2	1
	2*A*	4	5	0	3
	2*B*	5	4	3	0

Figure 3.10. The relations of restricted exchange. *Key:* 1 *mama* (superior), 2 *kaga* (indirectly superior), 3 *kumbali* (equal), 4 *mainga* (inferior), 5 *kuling* (indirectly inferior).

The relation of exchange between exchanging partners is called *kumbali*. If this matrix is compared to the one above (Figure 3.8), it is clear that this relationship collapses the domination relationship and the subordination relationship into one, while the direct relation of domination becomes internal to a group. Thus 1*A* is directly superior to 2*A* and 1*B* is directly superior to 2*B*.

Delayed exchange of women-gifts. An intermediate case between restricted and generalized exchange is delayed exchange. Figure 3.11 illustrates what this means in the case of exchange between the four clans in the Trobriand Islands of PNG (see Malinowski [1929] 1968: 433–51).

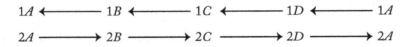

Figure 3.11. Delayed exchange.

It is generalized exchange from the perspective of the four senior groups (1*A*, 1*B*, 1*C* and 1*D*) or the four junior groups (2*A*, 2*B*, 2*C* and 2*D*) in that women move in a circle; it is restricted exchange in the sense that any two exogamous groups (e.g. *A* and *B*) exchange clan sisters directly; it is delayed exchange in the sense that 1*B* gives 1*A* a woman-gift this generation, while 2*A* returns the gift to 2*B* next generation. Another way of describing delayed exchange would be to say that if a mother is given, then her daughter must be returned.

Delayed exchange establishes yet another type of equality, as shown in the matrix of Figure 3.12.

		Receiver							
		1A	1B	1C	1D	2A	2B	2C	2D
Giver	1A	0	3	–	1	1	–	–	2
	1B	1	0	3	–	2	1	–	–
	1C	–	1	0	3	–	2	1	–
	1D	3	–	1	0	–	–	2	1
	2A	3	2	–	–	0	1	–	3
	2B	–	3	2	–	3	0	1	–
	2C	–	–	3	2	–	3	0	1
	2D	2	–	–	3	1	–	3	0

Figure 3.12. The relations of delayed exchange. *Key:* 1 *tama* (superior), 2 *kada* (indirectly superior/inferior), 3 *latu* (inferior).

In this case the relations of domination and subordination alternate over time: *B* is superior to *A* this generation after 1*B* gives to 1*A*, but inferior next generation when 2*A* gives to 2*B*.

In some cases, but not always, delayed reproduction involves the transfer of "bridewealth" at marriage. This is a direct exchange of thing-gifts for women-gifts and is sometimes called "brideprice," because it assumes the appearance of a commodity transaction. Exchanges of this type must be analyzed in an analogous way to the direct exchange of gifts of unequal rank. Women as gifts, like things as gifts, are never alienated from their clans, and when they are exchanged against thing-gifts mutual indebtedness, rather than prices, is the outcome. A reversal of the transaction is needed to cancel the debt created. Thus "bridewealth" is merely the first phase of two delayed exchange transactions. Consider M. Strathern (1972: 73):

In *moka*, pigs and shells are exchanged for each other, but ideally a reversal of the initial transaction should effect an eventual transfer of pigs for pigs and shells for shells. In the same way, while at each marriage bridewealth is given for a woman, a second woman should ultimately be given in return for the first, and thus a bridewealth for a bridewealth.[8]

Classificatory kinship terms and prices

The relations of exchange created by the exchange of the supreme gift are called "classificatory kinship terms" by anthropologists. However, from the perspective of the analysis given here they are analogous to prices, the relations of exchange established by the exchange of commodities. The difference is that prices describe value relations between objects transacted, while classificatory kinship terms describe rank relations between the transactors. Prices can be described in matrix terms. For example the *Financial Times* lists the prices of different currencies as shown in Figure 3.13.

	Pound Sterling	U.S. Dollar	Deutschemark
Pound Sterling	1.000	2.282	4.675
U.S. Dollar	0.438	1.000	2.049
Deutschemark	0.214	0.488	1.000

Figure 3.13. Prices of foreign currencies, 19th March 1981. *Source: Financial Times* (1981).

An altogether different notion of equality is involved here between an element of the matrix and its reciprocal. This can be written:

$$\frac{\text{price of } x}{\text{price of } y} = \frac{\text{quantity of } y}{\text{quantity of } x}$$

Thus if the US dollar price of a pound sterling is 2.282, then the quantity of pound notes given in exchange for one US dollar is 0.438, the reciprocal of 2.282. This relationship holds for all commodities, whether it be slaves, wage-laborers, or pigs. It is a cardinal relationship between

8. Strathern adds that for the Hagen case, marriage puts no individual or group under the specific obligation to find a woman in return. But while particular exchanges have little to do directly with the arrangements of marriages, there is a preference for marrying where links already exist (see Case 7, Chapter VII).

the objects transacted, unlike a gift exchange relationship, which is an ordinal relationship between the transactors.

CIRCULATION AND DISTRIBUTION

The argument advanced so far is summarized in Figure 3.14. At the highest level of abstraction there is a relationship between clan-based societies and gift exchange, on the one hand, and between class-based societies and commodity exchange, on the other. But what are of more interest are the divisions within these broad categories. The forms of exchange are arranged in logical-historical order and are related to the different types of land distribution with which they are principally associated, for example the purchase and sale of wage-labor with proletarians (i.e. landless workers). The logic of the commodity exchange classification is obvious and uncontroversial: barter (commodity (C) for commodity (C), C . . . C) is the original form of commodity exchange; next with the emergence of money (M), comes sale (C . . . M) and purchase (M . . . C); then trading for profit (M . . . C . . . M' where $M' > M$); and so on. The logic of the gift exchange classification is less obvious and more controversial and requires some explanation. The forms of exchange of women-gifts can be arranged in an order that goes: restricted → delayed → generalized. The logic behind this is simple to grasp and it has formed the basis of Lévi-Strauss' (1949 [1969]) theory of kinship. It merely involves classifying the forms of exchange in order from "simple" to "complex." The order: balanced → incremental → tributary can be achieved by following the same logic. However, the interlacing of the two types, and the relating of them to the different types of clan structure, is an exercise that requires theoretical elaboration and empirical verification. The propositions that emerge from this classification can be summarized as follows:

Proposition 1: moieties and phratries are associated with the restricted exchange of women-gifts, the balanced exchange of thing-gifts, and the leadership of elders.

Proposition 2: the incremental exchange of thing-gifts presupposes clan organization of the tribe and nation type, and is associated with delayed exchange of women-gifts and big-manship.

Distribution of land	Form of exchange	Example
I. Clan-based societies	I. Gift exchange	Personal relations
a. moiety	1. restricted exchange of women-gifts	$A \longrightarrow B \longrightarrow A$
b. phratry	2. balanced exchange of thing-gifts	$A \xrightarrow{10x} B \xrightarrow{10x} A$
c. tribe	3. delayed exchange of women-gifts	$1A \longrightarrow 1B \longrightarrow 1C,\ 2A \longleftarrow 2B \longleftarrow 2C$
d. nation	4. incremental exchange of thing-gifts	$A \xrightarrow{10x} B \xrightarrow{20x} A$
e. confederacy	5. generalized exchange of women-gifts	$A \longrightarrow B \longrightarrow C \longrightarrow A$
	6. tributary exchange of thing-gifts	$A \longrightarrow B \longleftarrow C$
II. Class-based societies	II. Commodity exchange	Objective relations
f. slave	7. barter exchange of commodities	$C \ldots C$
g. serf	8. buying and selling of commodities	$C \ldots M \ldots C$
h. metayer	9. merchant trade in commodities	$M \ldots C \ldots M'$
i. cottier	10. money lending	$M \ldots M'$
j. proletarian	11. buying and selling of wage-labour	$M \ldots C \ldots M'$

Figure 3.14. Relationship between distribution of land and forms of exchange.

Proposition 3: the generalized exchange of women-gifts, and the tributary exchange of thing-gifts, is associated with clan organization of the nation and confederacy type and chieftainship.

It should be noted that the hierarchy of gift exchange types involves a hierarchy of propositions that are nonreversible. For example, the incremental exchange of women-gifts presupposes the delayed exchange of women-gifts, but the delayed exchange of women-gifts does not necessarily imply incremental exchange; it may be associated with the delayed exchange of thing-gifts instead.

These propositions are based upon a number of subsidiary propositions, for example thing-gifts are symbolic substitutes for women-gifts, rather than women-gifts being symbols for thing-gifts. In order to understand these propositions, the sphere of exchange must be grasped as a part of a larger totality, that is, as part of the overall process of production, consumption, and distribution.

CHAPTER IV

Gifts and commodities: Reproduction

Commodity exchange relations are objective relations of equality established by the exchange of alienated objects between independent transactors. Gift exchange relations are personal relations of rank, established by the exchange of inalienable objects between transactors who are related. This distinction comes about because in a class-based commodity economy the methods of production predominate, while in a clan-based gift economy the methods of consumption predominate. In other words, commodity exchange relations are to be explained with reference to the methods of production, while gift exchange relations are to be explained with reference to the methods of consumption. Given the general definitions, in Chapter II, of production and consumption as objectification and personification processes, respectively, this proposition follows logically. However, the argument requires some elaboration for it leaves a number of questions unanswered, for example: Why does consumption predominate in a clan-based society? What particular forms does personification assume in the process of gift reproduction? Why does production predominate in a class-based society? What particular form does objectification assume in the process of commodity reproduction? What is the relationship between relations of exchange and relations of reproduction?

In this chapter an attempt is made to come to terms with these questions and, in the process, to pull together the threads of the argument about the nature of the political economy approach. It needs to be stressed once again that the concern is with the clarification of relations between "pure" categories. Thus, for example, the argument about the predominance of the methods of consumption in a gift economy abstracts from the historical fact that capitalist production relations predominate worldwide. Complications such as this are analyzed in the last two chapters, where the particular case of PNG is examined.

PRODUCTION OF COMMODITIES BY MEANS OF COMMODITIES

The methods of production

The aim of this section is to present a simple model of commodity reproduction so that simple models of gift reproduction may be compared with it. This is nothing more than a basic summary of Sraffa's (1960) argument that a necessary condition for self-replacement in a commodity economy is the quantification of the methods of production in certain proportions. This involves illustrating the classical economist's proposition that the relations of commodity exchange spring from the methods of production and productive consumption.

Industry	Inputs			Outputs
	Wheat	*Iron*	*Pigs*	
Wheat	240	12	18	450
Iron	90	6	12	21
Pigs	120	3	30	60

Figure 4.1. Commodity reproduction in heterogenous physical units.

Suppose that an economy produces wheat (W), iron (I), and pigs (P), and that, in one year, $450W$ was produced using $240W$, $12I$, and $18P$ as inputs; $21I$ was produced using $90W$, $6I$, and $12P$; $60P$ was produced using 120*W*, 3*I*, and 30*P.* The year's operations can be tabulated as in Figure 4.1.

This form of accounting is of no use to the capitalist because it provides no means for measuring profit: the heterogeneous physical units must be converted to a single value unit. Price formation brings this about. The economics paradigm holds that supply and demand determines prices (Harrod 1961). This proposition is false because such prices will not ensure self-replacement (Sraffa 1962). This can be illustrated by means of the example above which shows supply and demand in equilibrium: wheat supply of 450 is balanced by internal demand of 240, iron demand of 90, and pig demand of 120; iron supply of 21 is balanced by wheat demand of 12, internal demand of 6, and pig demand of 3; pig supply of 60 is balanced by demands of 18, 12, and 30. These supply and demand schedules can be represented in matrix terms as in Figure 4.2.

		Demand		
		Wheat industry	*Iron industry*	*Pig industry*
Supply	*Wheat industry*	240 *W*	90 *W*	120 *W*
	Iron industry	12 *I*	6 *I*	3 *I*
	Pig industry	18 *P*	12 *P*	30 *P*

Figure 4.2. Supply and demand matrix.

		Price ratios		
		W	*I*	*P*
Quantity ratios	*W*	1	0.133	0.533
	I	7.5	1	4
	P	1.875	0.25	1

Figure 4.3. Supply and demand prices.

A matrix of supply and demand prices can be derived from this. For example, the wheat industry supplies 90 units of wheat to the iron industry in exchange for 12 units of iron, giving an exchange rate of 7.5 units of wheat for one unit of iron. The other ratios are 6.66 units of wheat for one pig and four pigs for one unit of iron. This can be seen in matrix terms in Figure 4.3. Reading across the rows gives the quantitative exchange proportions while reading down gives the inverse relationship of relative prices, for example:

$$\frac{\text{quantity of wheat}}{\text{quantity of iron}} = \frac{1}{0.133} = \frac{\text{price of iron}}{\text{price of wheat}} = \frac{7.5}{1}$$

These prices are not the "correct" prices because they will not ensure self-replacement. Consider the wheat industry, for example. It gives $90W$ to the iron industry, for which it receives $12I$ (= 90 × 0.133) as required; but for the $120W$ given to the pig industry it receives $64P$ (= 120 × 0.533). This is far more than the $18P$ it needs and also more than the total production of pigs.

Reproduction prices in a simple economy of this type are determined by the labor-time required to produce the commodities. This can be seen by making the labor input explicit by supposing that the wheat input into each industry represents the real wages paid to units of homogeneous labor (L). If it is assumed that one unit of wheat exchanges for one unit of labor, then the labor-values of the commodities are determined by solving the following set of equations:

$$240 + 12p_i + 18p_p = 450p_w$$
$$90 + 6p_i + 12p_p = 21p_i$$
$$120 + 3p_i + 30p_p = 60p_p$$

where p_w, p_i, and p_p are the labor-values of wheat, iron and pig, respectively. The solution to this set of equations is $p_w = 10$ $p_i = 5_p$. This can be seen in matrix terms in Figure 4.4.

| | | Price ratios | | |
		W	I	P
Quantity	W	1	0.1	0.2
ratios	I	10	1	2
	P	5	0.5	1

Figure 4.4. Labour-values.

These prices are "correct" in that they ensure self-replacement. However, triangular trade, rather than bilateral exchange, is now required to effect the redistribution of commodities for self-replacement. This trade can be represented in matrix form as in Figure 4.5.

| | | Receiver | | |
		Wheat industry	Iron industry	Pig industry
Giver	Wheat industry	240 W	120 W	90 W
	Iron industry	12 I	6 I	30 W + 3 I
	Pig industry	18 P	12 P	30 P

Figure 4.5. Transaction matrix.

Thus, for example, the pig industry gets $90W$ directly from the wheat industry and $30W$ indirectly via the iron industry. This transactions matrix, which is determined by the production conditions, enables the initial conditions of production to be restored so that the process may be repeated.

The formation of these labor-value prices enables the production system to be expressed in value terms as in Figure 4.6. This example assumes that workers own their means of production and hence that surplus takes the undifferentiated form of wages. The example is easily extendable to more complex cases by assuming that workers and capitalists

Industry	Raw materials cost		Wages and profit	Total cost
	Wheat	Iron		
Wheat	120	90	240	450
Iron	60	60	90	210
Pigs	30	150	120	300

Figure 4.6. Commodity reproduction in value terms.

are opposed classes and that the latter earn a uniform rate of profit on their capital. In cases of this type, the proposition that labor-values determine prices has to be modified in a way that has been analyzed by Sraffa (1960). Such complications are of no interest here because they do not affect the simple point being made, namely that self-replacement in a commodity economy requires the transformation of the conditions of production from a heterogeneous physical form (Figure 4.1) to a homogeneous social form, that is, a value form (Figure 4.6).

The methods of consumption

The consumption sphere is very much a subordinate sphere under capitalism (Marx and Engels [1846] 1962: 28), and as such was not subjected to any systematic analysis by the classical economists.[1] A capitalist is only concerned to ensure that wage-laborers are reproduced as wage-laborers via the wage he pays them. It is of no concern to him how working-class families organize their marriages or their domestic labor arrangements.

 As such, the methods of consumption under capitalism are disorganized relative to the methods of production. This disorganization presents a striking contrast to a gift economy, where the methods of consumption are highly organized. The distinction is illustrated concretely in Figure 4.7, which compares the structure of an Australian working-class family with the structure of a PNG family. Contemporary working-class

---

1.   The subject has received much attention in recent years, however. See Himmelweit and Mohun (1977) for a review of some of the issues.

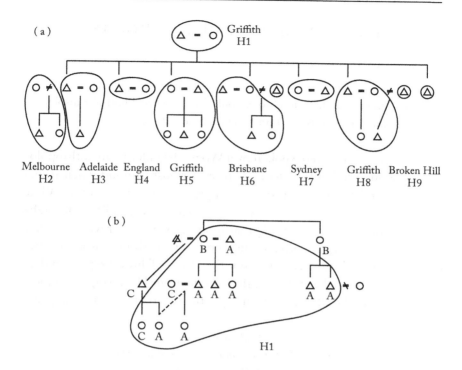

Figure 4.7. Family structures compared. (a) The structure of an Australian working-class family. (b) The structure of a Papua New Guinean family. *Key:* death, ↗ adoption, ↛ divorce, Griffith H1 location of a household, A clan membership.

families under capitalism tend to be atomistic and spatially dispersed[2] and this particular example illustrates this point well. The parents of the Australian household have seven children who have all set up their own households, with only two staying in the town of their birth. In the PNG family, by way of contrast, all the children of the parents, the children's children, and some relatives' children live under the one roof. But the most striking contrast is the fact that the PNG household members are classified by clan. This classification of people is a necessary condition for self-replacement in a gift economy; there is no quantification of things as there is in a commodity economy.

2.   This has not always been the case. See Humphries (1977) and Stone (1977).

CONSUMPTION OF GIFTS BY MEANS OF GIFTS

The methods of consumption

> Your fashion is to have food to eat only. We have food both for display
> and to eat. To you it is one thing; to us it is two things.

These words, which were spoken by a Wogeo Islander to an anthropologist (Hogbin 1967: 89), must be kept uppermost in mind when trying to understand the meaning of consumption in a gift economy. While the consumption of food is obviously a necessary condition for self-replacement, it is the other role that food plays which provides the key to understanding gift reproduction. Food as nourishment is a universal condition for self-replacement and, therefore, of little help in understanding the special nature of gift reproduction. However, the subject must be treated briefly before turning to the second role that food plays.

Table 4.1

*Estimates of food consumption per adult per day, Siane,
highlands district, PNG, 1959*

Item	Weight (lb)	Calories	
		No.	*%*
Sweet potato	4.20	1,890	65
Sugar cane	2.20	305	10
Yams or taro	0.33	135	5
Maize	0.25	105	3
Green vegetables	0.87	90	3
Cucumber	0.66	31	1
Pork and nuts	0.17	371	13
Total	—	2,927	100

Source: Salisbury (1962: 80).

Table 4.1 shows the estimates of daily food consumption of Siane adults. The diet is dominated by one staple, sweet potato, of which 4 lb is consumed per day. This compares with other societies in PNG where horticulture is practiced. In some areas yams are the principal staple, in others taro. Ecological factors are often the critical variables in deciding the principal staple. Taro, for example, requires abundant water supplies. In those societies more akin to hunting and gathering societies, sago is a popular food. However, there is a much greater variety in the diet of the "hunter/gatherer" tribes. Most of their calorie intake comes from the consumption of taro, yams, fish, coconuts, bananas of various types, and meat such as pig or wallaby.

The most important role that food plays is that of a symbol of marriage relations and sexual relations. As Kahn (1980: 268) notes in her discussion of the Wamira of coastal PNG, food "seems to take on a symbolic value which exceeds its immediate nutritional importance for sustenance and survival." She adds (ibid.: 267):

> [T]aro and pork are metaphors for communicating human powers of production and reproduction. . . . In the domestication of pigs and in the ingestion of pork and meat, symbolic statements are made about the sexual cooperation and antagonism that are necessary between female and male.

This symbolic association is not an artifact of anthropological theory; it is made explicitly by gift transactors themselves. Consider the following courting song, sung by men in the PNG highlands:

> You told me: "I'll cook your food in my oven"
> You told me: "I'll cook your food on my fire"
> But I haven't eaten
> Any of this food yet
> I'm in my men's house, far away,
> Girl Wakle, up in the place of Mbiltik
> With skin like that of a ripe banana
> Let me take you off to Kendipi Rapu
> (A. J. Strathern 1975: 191)

The reference to cooking food is, as A. J. Strathern notes (ibid.: 191), another way of saying, "I'll come and make love with you."

Because of the very important symbolic role that food plays, it is subject to various rules relating to its shared consumption. These rules, together with food taboos, serve to regulate the relations between groups of people. For example, the sharing of food often implies a close brotherly or sisterly relationship. Among the Siane it indicates common membership of a group (Salisbury 1962: 188). Similarly for the Daribi (PNG), who say, "We marry those with whom we do not eat meat" (Wagner 1967: 168). In the Trobriands, the sharing of food symbolizes the marriage bond between groups. Food is consumed in private by husband and wife. Yams are the staple and every yam consumed is cut in half and shared (Weiner 1976: 196).

While the sharing of food symbolizes togetherness, taboos on eating food symbolize separateness. Among the Kaluli tribe of the PNG highlands, for example, the bandicoot is a bush animal that is eaten by children of both sexes, middle-aged men, elders, widows, and widowers; but it is taboo for newly married men, fathers of small children, and menstruating women. In other words, the bandicoot is something that can only be eaten at the beginning and end of one's lifecycle. "The primary impact of these food restrictions among men," notes Schieffelin (1977: 64), "is to inhibit relationships between newly married men and their kinsmen and age-mates within the same longhouse community. At the same time they encourage pursuit of certain relationships outside it, namely, with affines."

Food taboos serve not only to regulate relations between individuals, but also to rank clans and subclans. In the Trobriand Islands, one of the few areas in PNG where a chieftainship system exists, food taboos are an important manifestation of rank.

The taboos of rank include numerous prohibitions in the matter of food, certain animals especially being forbidden, and there are some other notable restrictions, such as that prohibiting the use of any water except from waterholes in the coral ridge. These taboos are enforced by supernatural sanction, and illness follows their breach, even if it be accidental. But the real force by which they are maintained is a strong conviction on the part of the taboo keeper that the forbidden food is intrinsically inferior, that it is disgusting and defiling in itself. (Malinowski [1929] 1968: 26–27)

Taboos of this kind are highly formalized in India, where the principle of hierarchy is the dominant ideology (Dumont [1966] 1979: 83–91).

Consumption in a gift economy, then, is not simply the act of eating food. It is primarily concerned with the regulation of relations between people in the process of social and biological reproduction. These regulations often assume the form of highly formalized rules which are designed to ensure the self-replacement of clans. It is to a consideration of these systems of self-replacement that the discussion now turns.

Restricted reproduction. The most elementary form of clan structure is the dual-clan or moiety system. This divides the population and land into two equal parts, *A* and *B*. Each clan consists of males (*A, B*) and females (*a, b*). Self-replacement in such a society has the simple form of Figure 4.8.

Clan land	Father's clan	Mother's clan	Son's clan	Daughter's clan
A	*A*	*b*	*A*	*a*
B	*B*	*a*	*B*	*b*

Figure 4.8. Restricted reproduction.

On land *A*, the senior male members of clan *A*, together with their wives from clan *B*, produce children who belong to clan *A*; on land *B*, adult male members of clan *B*, together with their wives from clan *A*, produce children who belong to clan *B*. This consumptive production process effects a redistribution of people over the lands. To restore the original conditions of consumption an exchange of the form of Figure 4.9 is needed. In other words the junior men must exchange clan-sisters to enable the process to be repeated. This system is patrilineal because clan membership is determined by the father's line and patrilocal because sons live on their fathers' land.

$$A \xrightarrow{\quad a \quad} B \xrightarrow{\quad b \quad} A$$

Figure 4.9. Restricted exchange.

This process of clan self-replacement classifies individuals of a family in the way shown in Figure 4.10. This classification governs the relations between people and hence the biological process of reproduction that is the basis of clan self-replacement. In this case, a man (ego) of clan *A* may marry either his father's sister's daughter (*fzd*) or his mother's brother's daughter (*mbd*), for they are both classified as belonging to clan *B*. Different systems of clan self-replacement effect a different classification of these cousins, as will be seen below.

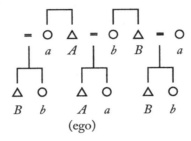

Figure 4.10. Restricted classification.

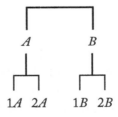

Figure 4.11.

Simple models of restricted reproduction of this type are not to be found. However, the basic principles operate in systems of a more complex type such as the phratry type of clan structure. This type of organization, as was seen in Chapter II, involves the subdivision of the clans into alternate generation groups 1*A*, 1*B*, 2*A*, and 2*B* as shown in Figure 4.11. Self-replacement in this example is more complex (see Figure 4.12). Here group 1*A* and their wives, group 1*b*, produce children who belong to group 2*A* and 2*a*. The men from 2*A* exchange "sisters" with the men from

2B, and reproduce, on land A, groups 1A and 1a. Thus, this case generates restricted exchange of the form of Figure 4.13.

Clan land	Father's group	Mother's group	Son's group	Daughter's group
A	1A	1b	2A	2a
A	2A	2b	1A	1a
B	1B	1a	2B	2b
B	2B	2a	1B	1b

Figure 4.12.

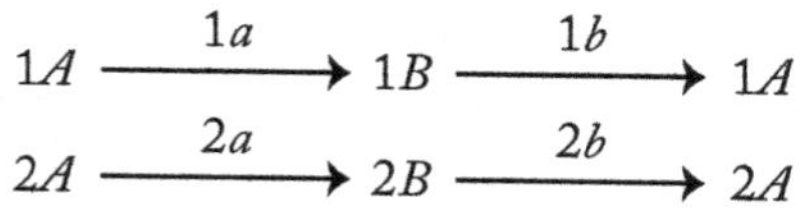

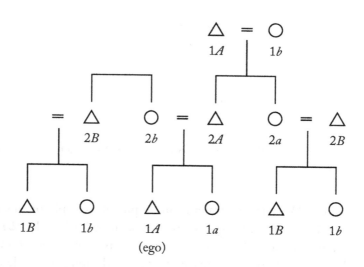

Figure 4.13.

Figure 4.14.

In this case a group is "reborn" every second generation, that is, it has a two-period self-replacement cycle. At the level of an individual family, this system of clan self-replacement effects the mode of classification of Figure 4.14. Thus a man (ego) and his grandfather belong to the same group, 1*A*, and men from this group can marry women from their own generation or two generations below who belong to group 1*b*.

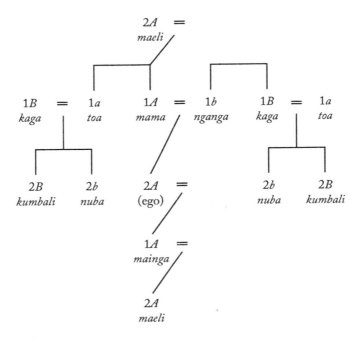

Figure 4.15. Kariara classification. *Source:* See Brown (1913) for a fuller description of this system.

The Kariara of Western Australia is an empirical example of this type (see Brown 1913). The four groups of this society, 1*A* Banaka, 2*A* Burung, 1*B* Palyeri, and 2*B* Karimera, belong to two moieties, *A* and *B*. Self-replacement of these groups was organized along lines identical to those discussed above. The classificatory kinship terms used by the Kariara, of which something has already been said in the last chapter, can be understood in terms of this model of self-replacement. Insofar as relations between individuals were concerned, they effected the classification shown in Figure 4.15.[3] These terms describe some of the relationships by which ego (2*A*) classifies his kinsmen. The interesting point to note is that they have a four-generation replacement cycle: ego calls his father's father and his son's son by the same term, *maeli*. This means that the phratry groups 1*A*, 2*A*, 1B, and 2B, have to be reproduced twice in order to reproduce the *maeli* group once. Thus, these classificatory kinship terms can be analyzed from a sociocentric perspective as relations of reproduction of a four-generation group model. As relations of reproduction they are also simultaneously relations of exchange and can be depicted in matrix form as shown in Figure 4.16. This matrix extends the analysis of the last chapter by considering the relationship between transactors and the transacted, as well as the relationships among the transacted. It illustrates, in concrete terms, the meaning of the concept "reciprocal dependence of transactors" (e.g. *kumbali*) and the concept "inalienable objects of exchange" (*mama* = domination relation).

		Receivers				Received			
		1*A*	1B	2*A*	2B	1*a*	1*b*	2*a*	2*b*
Givers	1*A*	0	3	1	2	12	13	1	2
	1B	3	0	2	1	13	12	2	1
	2*A*	4	5	0	3	8	4	12	13
	2B	5	4	3	0	4	8	13	12
Given	1*a*	14	13	8	6	0	9	7	6
	1*b*	13	14	6	8	9	0	6	7
	2*a*	10	11	14	13	11	10	0	9
	2*b*	11	10	13	14	10	11	9	0

Figure 4.16. Kariara exchange relations. *Read:* 1*A* from the first row is the *kaga* (2) of 2B from the fourth column. *Key:* 1 *mama*, 2 *kaga*, 3 *kumbali*, 4 *mainga*, 5 *kuling*, 6 *nganga*, 7 *yuro*, 8 *toa*, 9 *bungali*, 10 *kundal*, 11 *ngaraia*, 12 *kaja*, 13 *nuba*, 14 *turdu*.

Generalized reproduction. Dual-clan organization can become extremely complex as the subgroupings are continually subdivided. The self-replacement of these groups becomes exceedingly complex as a consequence (see

---

3. For the purposes of exposition the complete system is not shown. See Brown (1913) for a fuller description of the system.

Chapter VII). Nevertheless, the basic principle of restricted reproduction, and hence restricted exchange, operates no matter how complicated a dual-organization system becomes. The change in principle occurs with the move from a dual-clan system to one based on the three or more clans.

Clan land	Father's clan	Mother's clan	Son's clan	Daughter's clan
A	A	b	A	a
B	B	c	B	b
C	C	a	C	c

Figure 4.17. Generalized reproduction.

Suppose now there are three clans *A*, *B*, and *C*, and that the system of reproduction is patrilineal and patrilocal. In this case self-replacement assumes the form of Figure 4.17. At the end of the period of consumptive production both males and females are on their own land. The original conditions are restored if exchange assumes the form of Figure 4.18. This system of reproduction classifies individuals as shown in Figure 4.19. Insofar as ego is concerned, this places his *mbd* (b) in the marriageable category and his *fzd* (c) in the taboo category.

$$A \xrightarrow{a} C \xrightarrow{c} B \xrightarrow{b} A \xrightarrow{a} C$$

Figure 4.18. Generalized exchange.

The Kachin of Burma (see Leach [1954] 1977) is an empirical example of this type of clan self-replacement. A five-clan model is needed to illustrate the basics of their system of classifying people (Figure 4.20).[4] These relations can be represented in matrix form as shown in Figure 4.21. This matrix only shows the relations within ego's generation. A matrix twice the size is needed to show the relations over two generations, a matrix three times the size for three generations, and so on.

---

4.   See Leach (1954: 305) for a fuller description of this system.

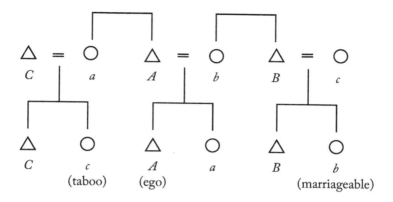

Figure 4.19. Generalized classification.

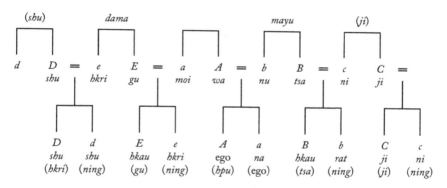

Figure 4.20. Kachin classification. *Source:* See Leach (1954: 305) for a fuller description of this system.

Delayed reproduction. The intermediate case between restricted and generalized reproduction involves a clan structure of the form of Figure 4.22. If the system is patrilineal and patrilocal, then the relations of self-replacement must assume the form of Figure 4.23. At the end of the period the initial conditions are restored if exchange assumes the form of Figure 4.24. Thus a clan gives away a woman and receives her daughter in return. This contrasts with restricted exchange, where a sister is exchanged for a sister, and generalized exchange, where the return gift is a more distant relation.

		Receivers					Received				
		A	B	C	D	E	a	b	c	d	e
Givers	A	0	1	3	2	1	10	14	13	12	11
	B	1	0	1	3	2	11	10	14	13	12
	C	2	1	0	1	3	12	11	10	14	13
	D	3	2	1	0	1	13	12	11	10	14
	E	1	3	2	1	0	14	13	12	11	10
Given	a	4	8	7	6	5	0	9	9	9	9
	b	5	4	8	7	6	9	0	9	9	9
	c	6	5	4	8	7	9	9	0	9	9
	d	7	6	5	4	8	9	9	9	0	9
	e	8	7	6	5	4	9	9	9	9	0

Figure 4.21. Kachin relations of exchange. 1 *hkau*, 2 *ji*, 3 *shu*, 4 *na*, 5 *rat*, 6 *ni*, 7 *shu*, 8 *hkri*, 9 *ning*, 10 *hpu*, 11 *tsa*, 12 *ji*, 13 *hkri*, 14 *gu*.

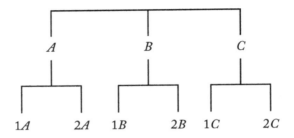

Figure 4.22.

Clan land	Father's group	Mother's group	Son's group	Daughter's group
A	1*A*	1*b*	2*A*	2*a*
A	2*A*	2*c*	1*A*	1*a*
B	1*B*	1*c*	2*B*	2*b*
B	2*B*	2*a*	1*B*	1*b*
C	1*C*	1*a*	2*C*	2*c*
C	2*C*	2*b*	1*C*	1*c*

Figure 4.23. Delayed reproduction.

$$1C \xrightarrow{1c} 1B \xrightarrow{1b} 1A \xrightarrow{1a} 1C$$

$$2C \xleftarrow{2b} 2B \xleftarrow{2a} 2A \xleftarrow{2c} 2C$$

Figure 4.24. Delayed exchange.

Delayed reproduction classifies individuals as shown in Figure 4.25. This classifies ego's *fzd* into the marriageable category and his *mbd* into the taboo category, precisely the opposite to what happens in the generalized reproduction case.

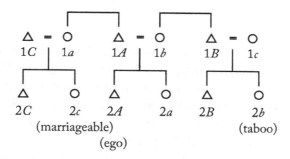

Figure 4.25. Delayed classification.

An example of reproduction of this type comes from the Trobriand Islands of PNG. It is worthwhile considering this example in full, because the system is matrilineal and "avunlocal," that is, upon marriage a man and his wife move to the land of the man's mother's brother. This provides a contrast to the patrilineal/patrilocal systems that have been analyzed to date.

On the Trobriands there are four clans, *A* iguana, *B* dog, *C* pig, and *D* snake, and the preferred marriage is between a man and his *fzd* (Malinowski [1929] 1968: 416–52). It follows from these facts that clan self-replacement assumes the form shown in Figure 4.26. In order to understand this system it is best to focus on one element: the reproduction of *1A* iguana. He resides on his own land and marries *1b* Dog and they

Clan land	Father's clan	Mother's clan	Children's clan	
A Iguana	1A Iguana	1b Dog	2B	2b Dog
A Iguana	2A Iguana	2d Snake	1D	1d Snake
B Dog	1B Dog	1c Pig	2C	2c Pig
B Dog	2B Dog	2a Iguana	1B	1a Iguana
C Pig	1C Pig	1d Snake	2D	2d Snake
C Pig	2C Pig	2b Dog	1B	1b Dog
D Snake	1D Snake	1a Iguana	2A	2a Iguana
D Snake	2D Snake	2c Pig	1C	1c Pig

Figure 4.26. Trobriand reproduction.

produce 2B and 2b dog. The male offspring, 2B dog, moves to his own land, marries 2a iguana, and reproduces 1A and 1a iguana. All the other male elements make similar moves. Consider now the female offspring, 2b dog. She moves to pig land where she marries 2C pig. The offspring of this union is 1B and 1b dog. Now by comparing the movement of 2B dog with his "sister," 2b dog, it is clear that the former moves to take up residence on his own land whereas the latter never resides on her own land either as an infant or as an adult. Thus both transactor and transacted move, but in such a way as to ensure that the male ends up residing on his own land whereas the female does not end up residing on her own land. By considering the reproduction of all the other elements it can be verified that similar movements happen.

Thus to restore the original conditions of consumption there must be a spatial exchange of males and females. The former takes the form of Figure 4.27. The redistribution of women over land takes the form of Figure 4.28.

The diagrams illustrate two important features of the system: at birth neither males nor females reside on their own land while females move to the land their mothers were born on. This is clearly an ingenious system for reproducing male dominance because it means that females never reside on their own land if these rules are followed. The standard

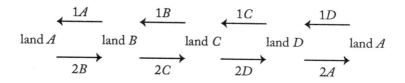

Figure 4.27. Trobriand spatial exchange of men.

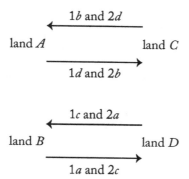

Figure 4.28. Trobriand spatial exchange of women.

feature of intermediate systems—the delayed exchange of women-gifts—is present in this system too. If attention is focused on the male transactors the pattern of exchange shown in Figure 4.29 emerges.

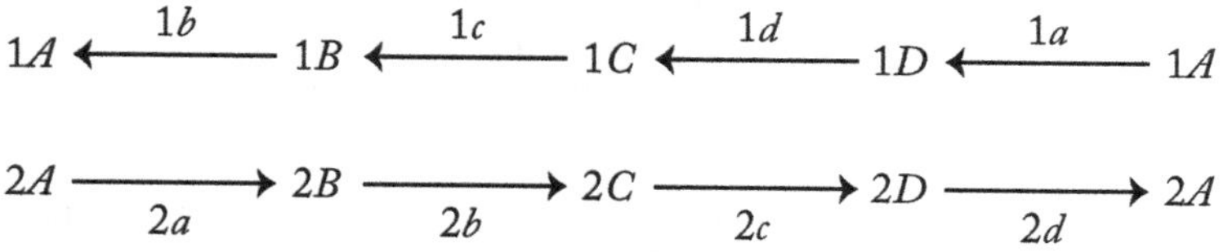

$$1A \xleftarrow{\quad 1b \quad} 1B \xleftarrow{\quad 1c \quad} 1C \xleftarrow{\quad 1d \quad} 1D \xleftarrow{\quad 1a \quad} 1A$$

$$2A \xrightarrow[\quad 2a \quad]{} 2B \xrightarrow[\quad 2b \quad]{} 2C \xrightarrow[\quad 2c \quad]{} 2D \xrightarrow[\quad 2d \quad]{} 2A$$

Figure 4.29. Trobriand delayed exchange.

The full set of classificatory kinship terms used on the Trobriands to distinguish these relations is shown in Figure 4.30.

The matrilineal/avunlocal system of the Trobriands, therefore, achieves the same objectives as a patrilineal/patrilocal system, albeit in a

(a)

	Receivers								Received							
	1A	1B	1C	1D	2A	2B	2C	2D	1a	1b	1c	1d	2a	2b	2c	2d
1A	7	5	–	1	3	1	4	–	6	4	–	1	3	1	4	–
1B	1	7	5	–	–	3	1	4	1	6	4	–	–	3	1	4
1C	–	1	7	5	4	–	3	1	–	1	6	4	4	–	3	1
1D	5	–	1	7	1	4	–	3	4	–	1	6	1	4	–	3
2A	–	–	–	–	7	1	–	5	–	–	–	–	6	1	–	4
2B	–	–	–	–	5	7	1	–	–	–	–	–	4	6	1	–
2C	–	–	–	–	–	5	7	1	–	–	–	–	–	4	6	1
2D	–	–	–	–	1	–	5	7	–	–	–	–	1	–	4	6
1a	6	5	–	4	2	4	–	2	7	4	–	4	2	4	–	2
1b	4	6	5	–	2	2	4	–	4	7	4	–	2	2	4	–
1c	–	4	6	5	–	2	2	4	–	4	7	4	–	2	2	4
1d	5	–	4	6	4	–	2	2	4	–	4	7	4	–	2	2
2a	–	–	–	–	6	4	–	5	–	–	–	–	7	4	–	4
2b	–	–	–	–	5	6	4	–	–	–	–	–	4	7	4	–
2c	–	–	–	–	–	5	6	4	–	–	–	–	–	4	7	4
2d	–	–	–	–	4	–	5	6	–	–	–	–	4	–	4	7

Givers label applies to rows 1A–2D; *Given* label applies to rows 1a–2d.

(b)

	Receivers								Received							
	1A	1B	1C	1D	2A	2B	2C	2D	1a	1b	1c	1d	2a	2b	2c	2d
1A	–	9	–	9	–	–	10	–	–	13	–	–	10	–	–	–
1B	9	–	9	–	–	–	–	10	–	–	13	–	–	10	–	–
1C	–	9	–	9	10	–	–	–	–	–	–	13	–	–	10	–
1D	9	–	9	–	–	10	–	–	13	–	–	–	–	–	–	10
2A	3	–	–	5	–	9	–	9	5	–	–	4	–	14	–	13
2B	5	3	–	–	9	–	9	–	4	5	–	–	13	–	14	–
2C	–	5	3	–	–	9	–	9	–	4	5	–	–	13	–	14
2D	–	–	5	3	9	–	9	–	–	–	4	5	14	–	13	–
1a	–	–	–	14	–	10	–	–	–	12	–	12	–	–	–	10
1b	14	–	–	–	–	–	10	–	12	–	12	–	10	–	–	–
1c	–	14	–	–	–	–	–	10	–	12	–	12	–	10	–	–
1d	–	–	14	–	10	–	–	–	12	–	12	–	–	–	10	–
2a	3	–	–	5	–	14	–	–	5	–	–	4	–	12	–	12
2b	5	3	–	–	–	–	14	–	4	5	–	–	12	–	12	–
2c	–	5	3	–	–	–	–	14	–	4	5	–	–	12	–	12
2d	–	–	5	3	14	–	–	–	–	–	4	5	12	–	12	–

Givers label applies to rows 1A–2D; *Given* label applies to rows 1a–2d.

Figure 4.30. Classificatory kinship terms, Trobriand Islands. (a) Pre-exchange terms. (b) Post-exchange terms. *Read:* 1A (row 1) is the *latu* (5) of 1B (col. 2) prior to the exchange and *lubou* (9) after the exchange. Key: 1 *tama* (F), 2 *ina* (M), 3 *kada* (MB), 4 *tabu* (FZD), 5 *latu* (S, D), 6 *lata* (Z), 7 *tuwa/bwada* (B), 8 *kwava* (W), 9 *lubou* (WB, ZH), 10 *yawa* (WF, WM), 11 *mwala* (H), 12 *ivata* (HZ), 13 7 + 11, 14 7+ 8, A iguana clan, B dog clan, C pig clan, D snake clan.

more roundabout way: men take up residence on their own clan land as adults, and exchange women in such a way as to ensure that they never reside on their own land. Only a matrilocal system can upset this arrangement. However, such systems are extremely rare.

Symbolic reproduction. Gift reproduction, and the exchange of women-gifts it implies, creates a web of gift-debt that binds all members of the society together. However, because it takes a generation to reproduce people, these roads of gift-debt run the risk of deteriorating. The process by which men and women are replaced by symbolic substitutes can be seen as an attempt to alleviate this problem. Food takes comparatively little time to reproduce. The sharing of food within a clan, and its exchange between clans, occurs on a daily basis. These daily acts constantly reproduce intraclan solidarity and interclan alliances. Not only do they keep the marriage roads open, they also serve to create new gift-debts. The marriage roads do not determine the structure of these new debts, but they do provide the basis. Thus the balanced exchange of thing-gifts is associated with restricted reproduction, delayed and incremental exchange is associated with delayed reproduction, and tributary gifts are associated with generalized exchange.

The personification of things in a gift economy is not simply an attempt to overcome the time problem in the process of reproducing people; it is an aspect of the predominance of the methods of consumption which are, as has been constantly stressed, a personification process: the act of consumption converts things into people. In gift economies this process is constructed metaphorically in a variety of ways. For example, among the Kewa (PNG), a husband regularly gives his wife's brother shell-gifts. The latter reciprocates by giving pork (LeRoy 1979). This appears as a commodity exchange (2 shells = 1 pork side), but this interpretation ignores the inalienable and personified value of the objects. Shells are the objects by which men individuate themselves; pork the women. Shells are given "to eat pork" (ibid.: 189), that is, the act of exchange symbolizes copulation, a necessary condition for reproduction. The same is true of the *kula* gift exchange system, where armshells are conceived of as female and necklaces as male. "When two of the opposite valuables meet in the *kula* and are exchanged, it is said that these two have

married" (Malinowski [1922] 1961: 356). Examples like this can be end-
lessly multiplied.

Thing-gifts can only enter the sphere of consumption and be exchanged as symbols if they have been produced. But they do not acquire
the status of symbols only in the sphere of consumption. They are produced as symbols and this gives the method of gift production a particular social form.

The methods of production

The sphere of production is the source of profit in a capitalist economy
and thus is the source of motivation for the society as a whole. In a gift
economy, by way of contrast, profit maximization is not the motivating
force. It is the method of consumption of gifts that provides the key
to understanding production and exchange. Thus the motivation underlying self-replacement springs from the sphere of consumption rather
than the sphere of production. The methods of production of thing-gifts
are therefore governed by the ideology of consumption: land, labor, and
the products of land are personified in terms of metaphors drawn from
this sphere, not objectified as "wages," "profits," and "prices." Gift production must be understood as the process of production of symbols
for use in the sphere of consumption. It has a twofold aspect: on the
one hand it is the production of food for intraclan consumption; on the
other hand it is the production of things for interclan gift exchange. The
physical nature of the latter often differs from the former in its durability. In the PNG highlands, for example, sweet potatoes are produced
for private daily consumption, while pigs are produced for exchange
(M. Strathern 1972: 35). In the coastal areas such as Milne Bay, on the
other hand, yams are produced both for consumption and for exchange.
However, the distinction between yams produced for consumption and
yams produced for exchange is carefully preserved. Special gardens are
often set aside for the latter. Only the best yams are given away. Special
large growing varieties are often planted for this purpose (Malinowski
[1929] 1968: 104–5; Weiner 1976: 137, 168).

The proposition that the methods of production are subordinated to
the methods of consumption is illustrated by the gardening practices followed on Woodlark (Muyuw) Island of PNG. On this island the layout

of a garden is governed by a number of rules, and it is believed that unless these rules are followed the food will not grow. The garden must have a specific spatial orientation. It must be rectangular and must run in an east/west direction. The western end is called the "eye" (*matan*) and the eastern end the "basis" (*wowun*). The garden is divided by two paths: an *atakot* path, which must "follow the sun," that is, go east/west, and a *katubal* path, which must go north/south. The intersection of these two paths is called the "navel" (*pwason*) of the garden. The Woodlark people have four clans and these are positioned about the navel in a specific manner: *dawet* clan faces north, *kwasis* clan south, *kubay* clan west, and *malas* clan east. Marriages are discussed by utilizing a diagrammatic form of this garden plan. Yams are the principal crop and two main types are grown. One type, called *kuv*, which produces one large tuber and grows rapidly, is likened to men; the other, called *parawog*, which produces a whole cluster of tubers and grows slowly, is likened to women. The people believe that yams are only really productive when they are planted together. The vines from different plantings should climb up the same stake, the *kuv* vines circling to the right, the *parawog* to the left. The intermingling of the vines is likened to sexual intercourse among people (Damon 1978: 199–215, 220–29). Variations on this theme are to be found everywhere. In the PNG highlands crops have gender. There are some crops which only men may plant and tend; others which only women may plant and tend; plus a third category which both sexes may cultivate (Sillitoe 1981). In the Sepik District of PNG, sago, one of the main staples, is classified as feminine. Before men can eat sago it must be made "masculine." This state can only be achieved if a man performs the final act of its transformation into food—the leaching process—himself (Williamson 1979).

A very important input into the production process is magic. The aim of magic, it has been noted, is to attract as much soul as possible into the crops because it is believed that only crops with a soul will grow. For example, the Wamira believe that magic makes their taro grow. Failure of a crop is attributed to the ritual incompetence of the cultivator or the sorcery of an enemy. Every step in the process of cultivation, except harvest, is accompanied by ritual incantation. Men possess the magic for planting taro; women own magic which is used during the later stages of cultivation (Kahn 1980: 129). On Dobu Island, where yams are grown, magic is bequeathed with a bequest of seed-yams within a matrilineage. It is believed that only magic and seed acquired in this way will produce food. Thus seed-yams acquired by barter exchange, for example, are regarded as useless (Fortune [1932] 1963: 70–71). The consumption of yams on Dobu is a private family affair. Visitors are never invited to share a meal; if they are given food they eat it with their backs turned to the givers (ibid.: 74). Thus the methods of production and consumption of yarns serve to keep the soul of the yam within the family line. The power of the magic derives from knowing the names of the first ancestors who changed themselves into yams, or who begat children that were yams. This knowledge is not freely given and is a source of power for those who possess it (ibid.: 95). Likewise, among the Garia (PNG), the monopoly of ritual knowledge gives the leaders their authority; hard physical labor without ritual is regarded as useless (Lawrence 1967: 100).

It is clear from this brief summary of the literature that the social organization of the reproduction of thing-gifts is governed by the methods of reproduction of people. The latter is a personification process which gives thing-gifts a soul and a gender classification; thus the reproduction of thing-gifts must be organized as if they were people.

In a gift economy the profit motive is absent: there is no drive to accumulate capital and to increase productive efficiency. The productivity of land and labor is therefore much lower in a gift economy than it is in a capitalist economy. Within a gift economy, differences between the productivity of land and labor appear to be related to the type of reproduction. Restricted reproduction is usually associated with hunting and gathering, while generalized reproduction is associated with more intensive methods of food production. The Australian Aborigines, among whom restricted reproduction was practiced, were hunters and gatherers. The home of generalized reproduction, according to Lévi-Strauss ([1949] 1969: 460–61), was Asia, where food production techniques were technologically superior to the Aborigines'. This rather clear-cut distinction becomes somewhat blurred in Melanesia, where intermediate forms of reproduction are found. There is no pure generalized exchange of women-gifts in PNG (Forge 1971: 139). Exchange tends to be either of the restricted or of the delayed type and it is impossible to associate these with different techniques of production in any unambiguous way. Most societies tend to employ a variety of techniques of production simultaneously.

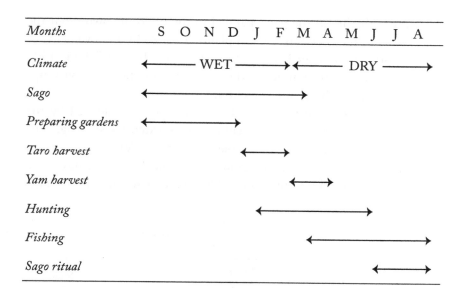

Months	S O N D J F M A M J J A
Climate	◄—— WET ——►◄—— DRY ——►
Sago	◄————————————►
Preparing gardens	◄————————►
Taro harvest	◄————►
Yam harvest	◄————►
Hunting	◄————————►
Fishing	◄————————►
Sago ritual	◄————►

Figure 4. 31. The annual cycle, Umeda, Sepik District. *Source:* Gell (1975: 161).

Consider Figure 4.31, which shows the annual cycle of the Umeda, Sepik District, PNG. The pattern of economic activity here bears a resemblance to the life of hunters and gatherers (Gell 1975: 15–18). The year is divided into two seasons: a wet season, which begins in September or October and ends around February or March, and a dry season, which takes up the remaining months. Sago preparation is the main activity in the wet season, and the sago which is not consumed during the wet season is stored for the dry season. Gardens are prepared for the taro and yam harvest during the wet season. These crops are harvested during the dry season, but it should be noted that only yams can be stored. Taro does not keep for more than a few days and must be eaten as soon as it is harvested. Other activities such as hunting and fishing take place in the dry season. The wet season is a period of dispersion: families live alone in the bush processing sago and subsisting on a fairly monotonous diet. The dry season, on the other hand, is the period when the whole village comes together. It is marked by the consumption of a large range of high-value foods and much collective activity, of which the sago fertility ritual is one of the most important. It is also interesting to note that "not only is the life of the palm parallel to the life of its owner but the movements of the coconuts used in planting parallel the movements of women going in marriage between the component hamlets" (ibid.: 150). This is another illustration of the thesis that the methods of consumption govern the methods of production.

A much more intensive method of production is practiced by the Kapauku, where three methods of cultivation—"extensive shifting," "intensive shifting," and "intensive complex"—are used. What is involved in these distinctions can be seen by examining Table 4.2, which shows the labor time spent on the cultivation of 900 square meters of sweet potato.

Table 4.2
Time spent on cultivation of 900 m² sweet potato, Botukebo,
Irian Jaya, 1955

Type of work	Extensive shifting (%)	Intensive shifting (%)	Intensive complex (%)	Sexual division of labour
Stage I				
clearing underbrush	19	27	18	M/F
felling trees	13	—	—	M
total	32	27	18	
Stage II				
fence building	29	16	10	M
digging ditches	—	10	7	M
making beds	—	—	31	M
total	29	26	48	
Stage III				
planting	2	2	8	F
weeding	12	20	5	F
harvesting	25	25	21	F
total	39	47	34	
Total (%)	100	100	100	
Total hours	263	299	455	
Yield (kg m⁻²)	0.81	1.38	1.69	

Source: Pospisil (1963: Tables 12 and 24).

Three stages in the cultivation of the land are distinguished: clearing, preparation, and cultivation. "Extensive shifting," a long fallow method of cultivation, used 32% of its total labor requirement in Stage I. With "intensive complex," a short fallow method, only 18% of the total labor-time was used in the first stage of the cultivation process. Trees do not grow on the land cultivated by this method, nor do they grow on the land used for "intensive shifting"; but this method is an intermediate fallow period method, as evidenced by the fact that 27% of the total labor-time was expended during Stage I.

Consider Stage II. A short fallow period method of cultivation requires the use of fertilizers if the soil is to be productive. This is achieved by making beds. The soil is arranged in

mounds 6 to 10 feet square, surrounded by ditches, which may be more than 3 feet deep. When the land is cleared prior to constructing the mounds, the tall grass is uprooted and placed in heaps on the site of each mound. Then the grass is left to grow again and use is made of the second growth, which is cleared and placed on top of the first. Ditches are then dug around each pile of straw, and earth and mud are thrown upon the rotting straw. The organic mud obtained from periodic clearing of the ditches is regularly added to the tops of the mounds. This type of agriculture, with true composting, is highly developed from the technical viewpoint. (Barrau 1958: 29)

From Table 4.2 it can be seen that 31% of the time involved in the "intensive complex" method was taken up making beds. This operation was absent from the "intensive shifting" method, but digging ditches was not. Neither operation was required for the "extensive shifting" method. In Stage III the "intensive complex" method required more time than the other methods in the planting process but less time in weeding. The "intensive shifting" method was most expensive of time in the weeding process. This took up 20% of the total time for this method compared with 12% for "extensive shifting" and 5% for "intensive complex."

The economic importance of women in the production process is also revealed in Table 4.2. Stages I and II of all three processes are done almost entirely by men. Men fell trees, build fences, dig ditches, and make the garden beds. The only role women have in the first two stages is helping to clear underbrush. In this task they share the work equally with the men. Stage III—planting, weeding, and harvesting—is almost 100% women's work.

The sweet potato yield from these three methods was 0.81 kg m^{-2} for the "extensive shifting" method, 1.38 kg m^{-2} for the "intensive shifting" method, and 1.69 kg m^{-2} for the "intensive complex" method.

Table 4.3

Input-output coefficients for sweet potato production, Botukebo, Irian Jaya, 1955

Method of cultivation	Land (m²)	+	Male labour (h)	+	Female labour (h)	→	Sweet potato (kg)
'Extensive shifting'	1.23	+	0.18	+	0.18		1
'Intensive shifting'	0.72	+	0.10	+	0.14		1
'Intensive complex'	0.59	+	0.17	+	0.13		1

Source: Pospisil (1963: Tables 12 and 24).

These data enable calculation of the land and labor coefficients for sweet potato production by the three methods. These figures are shown in Table 4.3. The factor that distinguishes the methods is the land intensity. The "extensive shifting" method is the most land-intensive method of production and the "intensive complex" is the least land-intensive. (There is a problem of description here. Whilst it is true that the most land-intensive method of cultivation is also the most land-extensive in the spatial sense, it is preferable to describe the methods in terms of the land used per unit of output. Instead of being limited to three rather awkward terms, the different methods can be thought of as belonging to a continuum, with the high land-intensive methods of production at one end, and the low land-intensive methods at the other.) As the land intensity falls, the skilled labor input must rise, if output is to be maintained. If one compares the two extreme cases in Table 4.3 it is clear that the low land-intensive method ("intensive complex") is labor-saving in terms of homogeneous hours: 0.36 compared with 0.30. Note that most of the labor saved is female labor and that the men do the skilled labor involved in the low land-intensive process.

Table 4.4 shows how the different methods were used to produce different crops: 90% of the total land area was taken up with the cultivation of sweet potato; 90% of this land area was cultivated by the "extensive shifting" method and accounted for 81% of the sweet potato crop; 1% was cultivated by the "intensive shifting" method and accounted for 2% of the sweet potato crop; 9% was cultivated by the "intensive complex" method and accounted for 17% of the sweet potato crop. Most of the secondary crops were cultivated using the "intensive shifting" method. It should be noted that the "extensive shifting" method was used mostly in the mountains behind the village whilst the other methods were used in the valley floor.

Table 4.4
Land required to produce different products, Botukedo, Irian Jaya, 1955

| Product | Land area (%) | Method of cultivation | | | Total |
		Extensive shifting (%)	Intensive shifting (%)	Intensive complex (%)	
Sweet potato	90	90	1	9	100
Sugar cane	5	—	100	—	100
Taro	2	—	100	—	100
Idaja	1	—	72	28	100
Pego	1	—	100	—	100
Others	1	—	97	3	100
	100				
Total area	172,482				

Source: Pospisil (1963: Tables 12 and 13).

Pospisil's (1973) data have been reanalyzed by a number of people who have tried to come to terms with the choice-of-technique question that these data pose. Why was the "extensive shifting" method used at the expense of the other more productive techniques, which required less labor per unit output? Elaborate hypotheses have been put forward by Moylan (1973). However, the answer is quite a simple one and has been given by Pospisil: when there is heavy rain the valley crops rot. So, in order to avoid the disastrous consequences of a total crop failure, different crops are planted in different places requiring different techniques. Another reason is the one given above: there is no drive to maximize yield per unit of land and labor in a gift economy.

The self-sustaining nature of the clan from the perspective of food production is illustrated by the data in Table 4.5, which show the

Table 4.5
*Production and distribution of sweet potato in Botukebo village,
January to August, 1955*

Production	Kg	%
Enona clan (16 households)	133,173	96
Outsiders	5,657	4
Total	138,830	100
Distribution		
Household consumption	86,193	62
Pig feed	37,200	27
Chicken feed	47	
Food for anthropologist and 21 assistants	13,830	10
Exports	2,774	
	140,044	
Minus imports	1,314	1
Statistical error	138,730	
	100	
Total	138,830	100

Source: Pospisil (1963: 395, 459).

production and distribution of sweet potato among one clan for an eight-month period. The clan, made up of 181 people divided into 16 households, produced 138,830 kg of sweet potato. Sixty-two per cent of this was consumed, giving an average daily consumption of 2.89 kg (6.35 lb) per standard consumption unit. Of the remaining 38%, 27% was used as pig feed and 10% to feed the anthropologist and his assistants.[5] Only an insignificant 1% was the net exchange with other clans. Not only is a clan self-sustaining from the perspective of food production, but the household units that make it up are also self-sustaining, or at least should be. The Siuai of Bougainville, for example, expect a household to be able to provide adequately for its own minimal subsistence

5. Sahlins (1972: 115–23) seems to have overlooked this point in his analysis of Pospisil's data. If pigs are included (ibid.: 121 fn. 9), the "surplus product" of the village is the food necessary to feed the anthropologist and his assistants. Sahlins' hypothesis that a "bifurcate, 'fish-tail' distribution of domestic labor intensity will be generally found in the Melanesian big-man systems" (ibid.: 117) must therefore be rejected.

and ceremonial needs and to carry out its traditional social obligations (Oliver 1955: 337). Among the Enga of PNG each woman is concerned to produce food for her own nuclear family unit, that is, for her husband, herself, and her unmarried children (Meggitt 1965: 236).

The self-sustaining nature of the food-producing unit is one of the reasons the sphere of production is subordinate. The principal economic problem is not the reproduction of food but the reproduction of labor and the establishment of secure tenure over land. This means that clans, and the reproduction of relations between them, become the principal concerns of the society.

SUMMARY

The argument of the preceding three chapters can be summarized in terms of the following propositions:

1. All societies must produce, consume, distribute, and exchange things and labor if they are to reproduce themselves. It follows therefore that certain economic categories have general applicability. The distinction between "production and productive consumption" and "consumption and consumptive production" provides the framework for capturing the interrelationship between these general categories.

2. In historically specific situations, things and labor acquire particular social forms and the principles which govern the reproduction of these particular social forms vary from society to society. The key to understanding these principles is to be found in the distribution of the means of production between people.

3. Things and land assume the commodity form in class-based socie- ties. Classes are formed when the producer loses control of his means of production. Capitalist commodity reproduction is a particular form of commodity economy whose condition of existence is the emergence of a property-less working class who offer their labor- power for sale freely, that is, labor assumes a commodity form in a capitalist society.

4. Things, land, and labor assume the gift form in clan-based societies. This is a particular form of unity of the producer and the means of production. A clan is a group of households who appropriate a piece of land, marry outside the clan, and who are defined in relation to other clans. This social group is to be contrasted with a working class who are a group of households without land, and who are only defined with reference to the property-owning capitalist class.

5. Commodity exchange is an exchange of alienable objects between people who are in a state of reciprocal independence that establishes a quantitative relationship between the objects exchanged. This relationship springs from the methods of production and productive consumption, which means that the principles governing the production and exchange of things as commodities are to be explained with reference to control over productive labor.

6. Gift exchange is an exchange of inalienable objects between people who are in a state of reciprocal dependence that establishes a qualitative relationship between the transactors. This relationship springs from the methods of consumption and consumptive production, which means that the principles governing the production and exchange of things as gifts are to be explained with reference to control over births, marriages, and deaths.

7. Gift reproduction can be of the restricted, delayed, or generalized type. Restricted reproduction generates the restricted exchange of women-gifts and is associated with the dominance of elders. Delayed reproduction (in PNG) generates delayed exchange of women-gifts and may be associated with the delayed incremental exchange of things and the dominance of big-men.

CHAPTER V

Traditional and modern goods: A critique

The economics approach perceives reality differently, employs different concepts, and uses different methods of analysis from the political economy approach. There is, therefore, no common ground on which the two approaches may be compared and evaluated: a constructive critique of one approach must be from the perspective of the other, that is, it must be external.[1] A critique of the economics approach must demonstrate the superiority of the concepts, perceptions, and methods of the political economy approach using the criteria of the latter. This is the purpose of this chapter. It identifies three problems within the economics approach. The first, which can be called the "conceptual problem," focuses on the general relations of production to consumption, distribution, and exchange. In the economics approach these categories are analyzed in a one-sided way as independent autonomous neighbors. Thus, for example, there is no conception of production being simultaneously consumption, and vice versa, that is, no productive consumption and no consumptive production. In some cases, as will be seen, there is no

---

1. A critique may also be internal. This involves demonstrating the logical inconsistency of an approach in its own terms. The "capital controversy" (see Harcourt 1972), which is concerned with the adequacy of the concept "capital," used by neoclassical economists, involves a critique of this type. The validity of this critique is taken as data for the purposes of this book.

exchange and distribution. The second problem, which can be called the "perceptual problem," focuses on the way "good" theorists (neoclassical economists) perceive gift exchange. Their categories either blind them to the phenomenon of gift exchange or force them to perceive it in terms of commodity exchange. The third problem, which can be called the "methodological problem," focuses on the social data of neoclassical economic analysis. These data take the form of an individual's subjective preferences and it renders all the concepts of neoclassical economics inherently subjective. As a consequence, neoclassical economists have no objective way of distinguishing between different economic systems.

The ultimate test of an approach is its ability to explain economic events that have occurred at a given place over a specified time period. This test enables a fourth problem in the economics approach to be identified. This problem, which can be called the "explanation problem," is dealt with in subsequent chapters.

THE CONCEPTUAL PROBLEM

The standard neoclassical conception of the general relations of production to consumption, distribution, and exchange can be represented diagrammatically as in Figure 5.1. Production, represented by firms, stands opposed to consumption, represented by households. This relation is mediated by exchange (the product market) and distribution (the factor market): households supply labor and demand consumption goods; firms demand labor and supply consumption goods.

This conception of the general relations of production to consumption stands in striking contrast to the picture presented in Chapter II, where "production and productive consumption" was opposed to "consumption and consumptive production." The first contrast to be noted is that the four elements of Figure 5.1 are treated as independent autonomous neighbors. Marx ([1857] 1973: 89) noted that the "bourgeois" economists of his day perceived of these categories in this way and criticized them for "crudely separating interconnected events" and for failing to consider the elements as part of an interdependent whole. This criticism is still valid today and has been made by Sraffa (1960: App. D). Sraffa likens the picture presented by modern theory to a "one-way avenue" that leads from "factors of production" to "consumption goods."

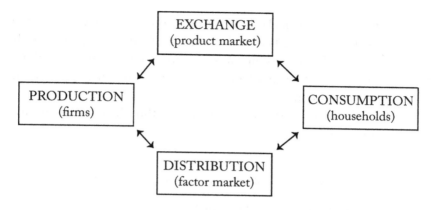

Figure 5.1. The neoclassical conception of the economy in general.

He contrasts this to the original picture of the economy, presented by Quesnay, as a circular process, that is, as a productive consumption process where some outputs are also inputs and where exchange distributes some products between production units and distributes other products (the surplus) between the various social groups that make up the society.

Sraffa's critique raises a second issue: the one-sidedness of the conception of consumption. Just as production fails to be grasped as a consumption process, so too does consumption fail to be grasped as a production process. In other words, production is grasped one-sidedly as a creation process and consumption is grasped one-sidedly as a destruction process. This is brought out clearly in Figure 5.2, which illustrates Sraffa's "one-way avenue" argument.

Figure 5.2.

Consumption, when viewed from this perspective, has inputs but no outputs. The missing element is consumptive production, that is, the reproduction of people process. Consumption, as has been seen in Chapter II, is a personification process by which things (food) are converted into people. At the general level this raises the question of sexual reproduction; at the particular level the question of marriage. One of the few neoclassical economists to realize this oversight is Becker (1974). It is useful to consider his attempt to overcome the problem, for it illustrates a number of other problems with the neoclassical conception of the economy in general.

Becker's theory of marriage is developed within the familiar optimization framework:

maximize $\quad Z = f(x_1, \ldots, x_m; t_1, \ldots, t_k; E),$

subject to $\quad \sum^m p_i x_i = \sum^m w_j l_j + v,$

where Z represents an aggregate measure of household-produced goods and includes "the quality of meals, the quality and quantity of children, prestige, recreation, companionship, love, and health status" (ibid.: 301); x_i the various market goods and services and p_i their price; t_j the time inputs of different household members; E the environment variables; w_j the wages rate of the jth household member and l_j the time he spends working in the market sector; v property income. Becker's innovation was to "assume that utility depends directly not on the goods and services purchased in the market place, but on the commodities produced 'by' each household" (ibid.: 301). Thus to maximize Z is to maximize utility.

This model is only relevant to a single male (M) or female (F). However, Becker does extend his analysis to cover the case for many males and females. Each is assumed to know the relevant entries in a payoff matrix showing the maximum household output that can be produced by any combination of M and F. The marriage market, he argued, will choose not the maximum household output of a single marriage but the maximum sum of the outputs over all marriages, "just as competitive product markets maximize the sum of the outputs over all firms" (ibid.: 310). He gives as an illustration the following matrix of payoffs:

	F_1	F_2
M_1	8	4
M_2	9	7

The optimal sorting is M_1 to F_1 and M_2 to F_2, even though the maximum output for any marriage is M_2 to F_1. This model, argued Becker (ibid.: 300), is relevant to all societies.

This theory illustrates a problem that is implicit in Figure 5.1, the tendency to universalize particulars. Firms, markets, wages, profits, prices, and so on, are treated as economic forms common to all societies. In other words, categories that are particular to the commodity economy are confused with general categories. But as has been pointed out in previous chapters, commodity forms are historical transitory forms which presuppose certain conditions for existence. For example, prices presuppose commodities, which in turn presuppose alienation and reciprocal independence. Neoclassical economists take the categories with which they are familiar in their own lives and impose them on all other societies. Their mistake is to assume that capitalism is a natural form of economic organization. This tendency to universalize particulars means that no distinction is made between the general and the particular and, as a consequence, that no distinction is made between one particular and another. Becker's theory of marriage, for example, confuses sex (the general) with marriage (the particular). Furthermore, the important distinctions between different types of marriage are obliterated. In PNG, marriage often involves a transfer of money in opposition to the bride (bridewealth), while in India the money goes with the bride (dowry). Even at the most superficial level, then, there is no way that these two different forms of marriage could be analyzed in the same terms. At the deeper level bridewealth is a form of gift exchange while dowry is a form of commodity transaction (inheritance) (Goody and Tambiah 1973). Such fine distinctions are impossible within the economics paradigm because of the universalization of the commodity economy.

The tendency to universalize particulars creates special problems for the category "exchange." Neoclassical theorists familiar with the PNG economy adopt contradictory positions on the question of exchange. Some say that it exists in general as commodity exchange and in the particular case of PNG as "primitive capitalist exchange." Others say that it does not exist in general because it does not exist in the particular case of PNG.

Epstein (1968) adopts the former position. She argues that Melanesian big-men were "primitive capitalists" who displayed "an overruling passion for accumulation." They used "shell money" (*tambu*) for purchases, sales, and lending and borrowing at interest.

"[B]ig men" in an attempt to increase their wealth often distributed
presents such as different kinds of crops, spears, clubs and ornaments
among their kin and neighbors who then had to pay for these gifts on
the occasion of a special feast, *vuvue*, arranged for the purpose. For the
vuvue the big man organized the erection of a special hut, which was
decorated with colorful feathers. Many people turned up for the feast,
dressed for the occasion. A number of them performed dances. After-
wards each man who had received a present paid for it in *tambu*, usually
a little more than its worth. The *ngala* remembered exactly the value of
each of the presents he had previously distributed and made sure the
return gift exceeded the value of the original present. Then there was
a big feast for all guests. On one such occasion expenses amounted to
300 fathoms *tambu* whereas the return totaled as much as 420 fathoms.
(Epstein 1968: 27–28)

It is clear from this example that Epstein has confused incremental gift-
giving with interest-bearing investment on capital. A gift of 300 fathoms
countered by a return gift of 420 creates a new gift-debt of 120. Epstein
has overlooked this point and has therefore confused commodity-debt
with gift-debt. As the basis of this distinction has been elaborated in full
in Chapter III, it will not be explained once again here.

The opposite position—that exchange in general does not exist because it does not exist in the particular case of PNG—has been adopted
by Stent and Webb (1975). They argue that in PNG the

economic unit . . . is small, roughly of family size, although it may on
occasions be· larger and involve a sub-clan or even an entire small village.
The unit is totally self-sufficient; it employs only its own labor and en-
gages in no trade with other units. There is no saving and no waste; *thus
production and consumption are identically equal.* (Stent and Webb 1975:
523–24, emphasis added)

From this perspective the general relations of production and consumption appear as in Figure 5.3. With this conception of the economy
in general, exchange and distribution drop out of the picture, leaving
production identical with consumption. As a description of the PNG
economy, and as a conception of exchange in general, Figure 5.3 is a

complete distortion of reality because exchange mediates production and consumption, both in general and in the particular case of PNG. What the neoclassical conception fails to do is to grasp simultaneously the fact that production is identical to consumption in one sense and opposite to consumption in another sense.

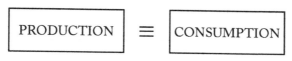

Figure 5.3.

THE PERCEPTUAL PROBLEM

Myrdal (1968: 16–20), in his critique of the application of neoclassical economics to the analysis of non-European economies, noted that a conceptual scheme can imprison the observer, allowing him to see only that which the scheme directs him to see and ruling out other interpretations of data. In other words, conceptual problems cause perceptual problems. For example, the confusion of exchange in general with commodity exchange inevitably leads to perceiving gift exchange as "primitive capitalism." But the consequences of assuming that production is identical to consumption, and therefore failing to perceive that exchange exists at all, are quite different. How does one analyze gift exchange using a conceptual framework that excludes exchange? This is what Stent and Webb have tried to do and it is instructive to examine how they overcome this problem.

According to them a key feature of PNG agriculture

> is that gardeners do not consider their work, hard though it often is, to be sheer drudgery. Thus it would be misleading to assume that work is necessarily a source of disutility; up to a point it is generally a source of pleasure. In Western terms, a Papua New Guinean's attitude towards his gardening is more like that of an amateur rose-fancier than, say, that of a commercial market gardener. (Stent and Webb 1975: 523)

Thus production for gift exchange is likened to amateur rose fancying. This metaphor is then developed in terms of an extremely elaborate three-dimensional geometrical model, and they arrive at the conclusion that the marginal product of land may be negative. It is this particular concept that overcomes the logical problem of analyzing gift exchange in terms of a model of a "single untraded product"; its meaning is illustrated in Figure 5.4.

Land (acres)	Total product (tons of yams)	Marginal product (tons of yams)
10	20	
20	40	+ 20
30	20	- 20

Figure 5.4. The negative marginal product of land in PNG.

The required amount of yams for consumption is 20 tons, which can be grown using 10 acres. But, because PNG gardeners are like rose fanciers, they use 30 acres of land instead of 10 acres. This amount of land also produces the required output of 20 tons. This anomalous situation comes about because, while the use of 20 acres of land involves a marginal product of plus 20, the use of 30 acres involves a negative marginal product of minus 20. Thus the use of the marginal 20 acres leaves total product unchanged. In reality, of course, if 30 acres of land was used the total product would be (say) 60 tons. This gives a surplus over consumption of 40 which can be used for gift exchange purposes. So, by inventing the concept "negative marginal product of land," Stent and Webb make the surplus product of 40, and hence the phenomenon of gift exchange, disappear.

Fisk, who adopts a similar conceptual framework to Stent and Webb, overcomes the problem in a rather different way. Consider the following:

Certain forms of ceremonial activity are of the greatest importance in the social system of the majority of the indigenous tribes of the New Guinea Territories. In this paper we are concerned with economic activity, and in our model we shall treat economic activity and ceremonial activity as distinct and separate. Ceremonial activity and the preparations therefore we shall treat in the category of leisure activity, and as affecting economic activity only to the extent that certain amounts of leisure activity are socially regarded as necessary, and that the amounts of labor available for economic activities are socially limited thereby. With one major exception, this assumption presents little difficulty, for the exchange of valuables that forms such an important part of most ceremonial activities has little or no relation to the normal economic production activities of the units involved. The exception is the pig. The pig is a complicating factor because, although its consumption is virtually confined to ceremonial, its production has a very direct relationship to the normal economic activities of the subsistence unit. . . . [I]n many parts of New Guinea they are . . . hand-fed from the produce of the cultivated gardens, and therefore towards the end of what is known as the "pig-cycle," when the number of adult pigs is approaching its maximum, there will be considerable increase in the demand for cultivated garden produce for feeding pigs. . . . [I]t is highly desirable that the complication of this cyclical variation in demand for garden produce be eliminated. To do this with a small subsistence unit would be virtually impossible without invalidating the model. However, the saving grace of the pig feast ceremonies, from our point of view, is that they tend to form a pattern in which the obligation to provide a major feast moves in regular sequence from sub-unit to sub-unit, within a given group of clans and tribes. Each sub-unit will therefore suffer considerable variations in demand for garden produce at different stages of its "pig cycle," but provided we take a sufficiently large group in our definition of the subsistence unit, the total garden production for pig food, the total number of pigs, and the total consumption of pig meat in ceremonial activity, will be reasonably constant. Therefore, by assuming that our pure subsistence unit is of substantial size, comprising a large number of sub-units participating in these ceremonial exchanges, we can consider pig-rearing as a normal and constant part of the production of food, and as part of the normal economic activity of agricultural production. (Fisk 1962: 464–65)

What Fisk does, then, is to create a distinction between "ceremonial activity" and "economic activity" and assume away the former. This assumes away the problem of gift exchange but not the phenomenon of *production* for gift exchange, as the so-called exception of the pig illustrates. The pig is not the exception, however. In the coastal areas yams are produced both for consumption and for gift exchange. Stent and Webb, to their credit, attempted to confront this problem head on.

These two cases illustrate in a rather dramatic way Myrdal's thesis that a conceptual scheme can imprison the observer, allowing him to see only that which he wants to see.

THE METHODOLOGICAL PROBLEM

Every theory must have its unexplained data. These data, which enable the problem of infinite regress to be overcome, are the basis from which the concepts and theories derive their meaning. In the political economy approach, historical data on the distribution of land between groups form the starting point. These define "classes" and "clans" and the various subdivisions within these groups. With the economics approach, on the other hand, the distinction between classes and clans is of no consequence; the preferences of utility-maximizing individuals provide the data of the analysis. Data of this kind are subjective and psychological and, therefore, non-observable. As a consequence of this, it becomes impossible to distinguish in any objective way between different economic systems. For example, Einzig's (1948: 16) claim that the intellectual standard of gift transactors is inferior and their mentality totally different from ours, and the Stent/Webb (1975: 524) assertion that PNG gift transactors are on the "bliss" point of their utility curves, are subjective statements that can be neither confirmed nor denied. Thus the distinction between "traditional" and "modern" goods is a purely subjective distinction which varies from one theorist to another.

Attempts to distinguish between different systems on the basis of the relative size of the marginal products for "factors of production" also fail. This is because of the confusion between particular categories and general categories, as mentioned above. Apart from the confusion between commodity markets and "exchange," another common confusion is between "capital" and "means of production." Jorgenson (1961: 311), for example, argues that in "the theory of a dual economy the output of the traditional sector is a function of land and labor alone; there is no capital accumulation." Salisbury (1962: 4), on the other hand, argues that "the traditional western economic concept potentially most applicable and useful in understanding the Siane material is that of 'capital.'" Thus Jorgenson argues that, because there is no capital in a gift economy, there are no means of production, while Salisbury argues that there is capital because there are means of production. Both are wrong. There are means of production (a general economic category) but there is no capital (a historically specific category).

These examples are sufficient to illustrate that economics contains many conceptual confusions and contradictions when compared to political economy. At the general level, production, consumption, distribution, and exchange are treated as isolated categories. These general categories are confused with the particular categories of the commodity economy. This confusion leads to the perception of a gift economy as "primitive capitalist" in some cases, or, in other cases, as a "subsistence economy" that has neither exchange nor distribution. The ahistorical, subjectivist approach of the economics paradigm focuses attention on the individual rather than classes and clans. This prevents the objective definition of different economic systems, a problem that is compounded by the inability to distinguish the general from the particular. Thus conceptual, perceptual, and methodological problems are interrelated. They also give rise to another problem, the explanatory problem, which is considered in the next chapter.

PART TWO

Theory

CHAPTER VI

The transformation of gifts into commodities in colonial Papua New Guinea

THEORIES OF CHANGE IN PNG

The previous chapters have contrasted the conceptual and methodological approaches of the economics and the political economy approaches in logical time. The task is now to demonstrate the relative superiority of the latter approach to the description, classification, and analysis of a concrete situation in historical time. As the subject of analysis, colonial PNG, covers a long time period (almost a hundred years) and a complex ecological and social area, it is necessary to define some limits of the analysis. This can be done by comparing the answers of the respective approaches to four basic questions that any theory of change must come to terms with: How is the indigenous economy conceptualized? How is the colonizing economy conceptualized? How is the interaction of these two economies theorized? What special problems does colonization pose for the theory of wages? The answers neoclassical economists give to these questions can be summarized as follows:

Indigenous economy: A "backward," "traditional" economy that produces subsistence goods, has a large pool of surplus labor and an inefficient allocation of resources.

Colonizing economy: A "dynamic," "modern" economy that produces goods for sale and uses resources efficiently.

Theory of change: The "modern" economy is the engine of growth which transforms the "traditional" sector into a "modern" sector. This transformation process proceeds in a linear step-like fashion, and stagnation may result when the traditional economy gets caught on one of these steps. Policy intervention is needed to overcome these stagnation points and to enable the traditional economy to achieve self-sustaining growth. Until the step is reached where the final metamorphosis from traditional to modern occurs, the colonial economy is said to be a "dual economy."

Theory of wages: The existence of dualism creates a "distortion" in the factor market. This creates a gap of 30% or more between modern sector wages and traditional sector income.

These propositions were first put forward by Lewis (1954). His theories have been modified and developed but these changes are all variations around the same central theme. For example, disputes have arisen about the size of the marginal product of a factor in the traditional sector. Is it zero, negative, or just very small? Schultz (1964: 56), for example, disputes the proposition that the marginal product of labor is zero; it is very small, he says, and this "readily misleads the casual observer who is accustomed to measuring margins in dollars. For him the difference between the penny-like margins and zero is at best difficult to discern." While these disputes are important from the perspective of economics, they are of no significance from the perspective of political economy, where the concept "marginal product" has no meaning. What is at issue is the explanatory adequacy of the general approach, thus these internal theoretical differences can be ignored.

Fisk (1962, 1964, 1971), Shand (1965), Stent and Webb (1975), and others have all used these general propositions to explain the PNG case. Consider Fisk (1964: 156):

> The subsistence group has surplus productive capacity over and above that required for the satisfaction of its subsistence requirements. This surplus capacity can be utilized for agricultural or other production

without reducing the supply of subsistence foodstuffs, housing, clothing, etc. at the traditionally acceptable level of consumption.

He dubs this "subsistence affluence" (1971: 368) and argues that it is present in many parts of Africa and the Pacific. The development problem is the one of finding ways to utilize this surplus productive capacity. Fisk's particular representation of this step-like process is in terms of a two-dimensional geometrical model that describes an income/leisure trade-off using indifference curves for different levels of the utility of money. As income rises with development, the utility of money makes a quantum leap from one step to the next. As this happens, leisure is traded for labor and the surplus-labor eventually disappears. The process is not smooth because the traditional economy may get stuck at one of the steps. Stagnation results and external nonmarket influences must be applied to produce one or more of the following effects:

1. An artificial increase in the level of cash production to lift it sufficiently above each stagnation point to reach another growth point (e.g. by persuasion or compulsion).
2. An artificial increase in the cash return per unit of labor thus effecting the jump from one C [cash] curve to the next at a lower labor input (and hence crop output) than would happen in response to market forces alone. This may be effected by temporarily subsidizing the development of marketing, transport and processing facilities, etc. or by providing government operated services for these purposes prepared to operate at a loss for some years.
3. An artificial increase in the utility of money, thus effecting the jump from one U [utility] curve to the next at an earlier point (lower total income) than would have happened in response to market forces alone. This may be effected by subsidizing temporarily the provision of goods and services for money in the area or by setting up government retail stores prepared to operate at a loss for some years. (Fisk 1964: 123)

Fisk's theory of wages, which argues that subsistence income exceeds urban wages, is at variance with the accepted orthodoxy. The justification for his theory is as follows:

Because productivity of such unskilled wage labor is so low, employers feel unable to pay more than a very small money wage. This is insufficient to sustain the worker and his family at a standard of living comparable with that available in subsistence agriculture, and involves harder and longer hours of work. As a result, workers tend to work for a certain limited "target" cash income and to return to subsistence agriculture before they have gained sufficient skill and sophistication in wage employment to be worth a substantially higher wage. (Fisk 1971: 377–78)

However, this argument (which will be critically examined below) was advanced before the sixfold increase in urban wages between 1972 and 1974 occurred. This dramatic increase in urban wages, and the widening of the urban/rural wages differential that accompanied it, changed neoclassical thinking on the wages question, swinging it into line with orthodoxy. For example, Garnaut (1973: 173) accepted that when the minimum urban wage was $A8.00 in 1972 it seemed "more likely that the village is subsidizing the plantation and the town than that the wage exceeds the value of labor in the village." But after the wage was increased to $A11.80 in early 1973, he claimed, "The new minimum would seem to exceed the opportunity cost of labor drawn from the villages by a significant margin."

A critique of these propositions must establish that their conceptualization of the distinction between the indigenous economy and the colonizing economy is inadequate, that the theory of change is ahistorical, and that the theory of wages is empirically false. To some extent the first of these tasks has been achieved in the previous chapter, where it was shown that neoclassical theorists have no means of distinguishing between different economic systems. This particular point is elaborated on in the next chapter, where additional empirical evidence on the nature of the indigenous economy, and the transformation it has undergone, will be presented.

If the traditional/modern goods distinction is inadequate it follows, as a logical consequence, that any theory of change in terms of these categories is also inadequate. However, even if this were not the case, the neoclassical theory of change does not accord with the facts of economic history because it fails to pose the correct problem. The problem they address is "economic development." This involves a description of the discontinuous steps in the transformation of a traditional sector into a modern sector, as well as a prescription to overcome stagnation points. However, the problem to be explained in PNG is not the story of the demise of the "traditional" sector and the rise of the "modern," sector but rather the simultaneous rise of both commodity production and gift production. The gift economy of PNG has not been destroyed by colonization but has effloresced. The labor-time devoted to the production and exchange of things as gifts has risen rather than fallen, a change that has occurred simultaneously with the introduction of cash crops and wage-labor. To understand this process, it is necessary to abandon the concept of dualism which classifies this part of the economy (e.g. urban sector) as "modern" and that part (e.g. rural sector) as "traditional." The fact of the matter is that the whole economy is "modern." The gift exchange practiced in PNG today is not a precolonial relic but a contemporary response to contemporary conditions. To be sure, gift exchange is an indigenous economic activity; but the gift exchange of precolonial days (of which almost nothing is known) was very different from the gift exchange of today. Economic activity is not a natural form of activity. It is a social act and its meaning must be understood with reference to the social relationships between people in historically specific settings. The essence of the PNG economy today is ambiguity. A thing is now a gift, now a commodity, depending upon the social context of the transaction. A pig may be bought as a commodity today so that it can be used in a gift exchange tomorrow. It is because of this ambiguity that the concept of dualism, with its clearly defined traditional sector, must be abandoned. The colonization of PNG has not produced a one-way transformation from "traditional goods" to "modern goods," but complicated a situation where things assume different social forms at different times and in different places.

How is this problem to be explained? The thesis advanced in this chapter is that while colonization has fathered the rise of commodity production in PNG, it has only succeeded in transforming labor and primary products into commodities, not land. Land, with the exception of the 3% that was forcibly alienated by the state and foreign companies, has not become the private property of individuals in PNG. The clan has maintained control over it and has, by and large, prevented a land market from developing. Thus the material basis for the persistence of

clan organization has not been destroyed. This fact, it is argued, explains
the efflorescence of gift exchange in PNG. This is not to say that there is
a simple monocausal link between clan land and gift exchange—indeed,
there is a sense in which clan ownership of land has persisted because
gift exchange has flourished. Clan land is merely a necessary condition—the most important—for gift exchange; it does not determine its
specific form. Other factors, such as the nature of the relationships between clans, the relations between young and old, between males and
females, and between church, state, and village, are among the important
complicating variables. The relative importance of one or other of these
cannot be assessed *a priori*. The precise determinants of the efflorescence
of gift exchange vary from time to time and place to place.

The persistence of clan organization has some implications for a theory of wages. It means that there is no landless proletariat who are forced
to work in order to survive. This is not to say that there are not some
people without land, just that this phenomenon does not exist on a large
scale. There are people willing to work but these are, for the most part,
migrant laborers who are born into a clan and return to their village to
marry and settle. Thus the reproduction cost of labor is borne by the clan.
In other words, wages are geared to single men, not married men with
dependents. The wage they get reflects the conditions of reproduction
and not the so-called inferior productivity of migrant labor. To the extent
that plantation workers' productivity is low relative to urban workers, this
is due to the lack of a replanting policy on behalf of plantation owners.

These propositions, which will be illustrated in great detail, can be
summarized as follows:

Indigenous economy: A gift economy of great complexity and diversity
where reproduction assumes either the restricted or the delayed form.

Colonizing economy: A capitalist commodity production economy.

Theory of change: An "ambiguous" economy where things are now gifts,
now commodities, depending upon the social context. Colonization has
led to the emergence of commodity production on a significant scale;
the political power of foreign governments, foreign companies, and
foreign churches has brought about this transformation of gifts into

commodities. At the same time an opposing tendency—the transformation of commodities into gifts—has proceeded apace. The material basis for this efflorescence of gift exchange is the nonemergence of land as a commodity and the subsequent failure of class organization to replace clan organization in the countryside; but the situation is conflict-ridden and unstable and varies from area to area.

Theory of wages: The gift economy subsidizes employers of wage-labor by supplying labor at less than reproduction cost.

This chapter examines the colonial PNG economy from the perspective of the commodity economy, the next from the perspective of the gift economy.

THE EMERGENCE OF COMMODITY PRODUCTION IN PNG

Background information on PNG has been given in the introductory chapter. That information, as well as the data in Table 6.1, is sufficient to enable the reader unfamiliar with the area to follow the subsequent discussion. Colonial PNG was divided up into eighteen administrative districts and these divisions—which have only undergone minor change since independence—will be used here. They can be conveniently divided up into island, coastal, and highland districts. The island districts contained 17% of the 1971 population of 2.5 million, the coastal districts 44%, and the highlands districts 39%. The island and coastal districts were colonized first from the 1880s on; the highlands districts were not effectively colonized until after the Second World War. It was the labor of the adult men of these areas, as well as the gold in the ground, that the colonizers were after.

The emergence of labor-power as a commodity

The conventional wisdom is that gift economies had unlimited supplies of labor available for the commodity market. Nothing could be further from the truth; they had none at all. Members of a gift economy had no economic need to supply their labor-power as a commodity, so the colonizers had to create this need. This was a long, drawn-out process in Melanesia,

Table 6.1
Population of Papua New Guinea by district of birth, 1971

		No		%
Island Districts				
Milne Bay	P	113,050	5	
Bougainville	NG	82,033	3	
New Britain	NG	149,796	6	
New Ireland	NG	53,866	2	
Manus	NG	25,591	1	
Total Island			424,336	17
Coastal Districts				
Western	P	72,965	3	
Gulf	P	69,072	3	
Central	P	147,836	6	
Northern	P	67,375	3	
Morobe	NG	241,441	10	
Madang	NG	169,034	7	
Sepik	NG	289,640	12	
Total Coastal			1,057,363	44
Highland Districts				
Eastern	NG	417,405	17	
Western	NG	334,255	14	
Southern	P	200,686	8	
Total Highlands			952,346	39
Grand total			2,434,045	100

Note: 'P' stands for Papua; 'NG' stands for New Guinea. *Source:* Census (1971).

as it was in Africa. It is possible to distinguish four overlapping[1] phases in this process corresponding to the degree of freedom that the workers enjoyed in the market place:

(a) forced labor (overseas indentured labor), 1863–1904;
(b) semiforced labor (domestic indentured labor), 1883–1950;
(c) semifree labor (agreement labor), 1951–1974;
(d) free labor (wage-labor), 1927 to present.

These different forms of labor will now be examined in some detail.

---

1.   Contrast these phases with Epstein's (1968) strictly chronological stages.

(a) Forced labor (overseas indentured labor), 1863–1904. In the 1860s a cane sugar industry was established in Queensland, Australia's "Deep North." The method of production was such that cheap labor inputs were required for its operation. This labor was found in Melanesia and it was recruited on conditions not unlike the system of slavery developed to supply labor for the plantations of America's "Deep South." The important legal difference in the two systems was that labor for the Queensland plantations was recruited as indentured labor. In actual practice the systems differed little, especially on the recruiting side of the operation. With the opening up of a new area of labor supply, brute force would be used to obtain recruits. This unprofitable mode of operation would quickly give way to a more orderly mode of recruitment, when a chief or head man was found who could act as agent.[2] But this method of recruitment would eventually become too costly as the recruits became more knowing and drove harder bargains. The recruiters would be forced to seek out new areas of supply, a new "labor frontier," and so it would go on. In Queensland the recruits would be given a contract to work for three years, a box,[3] and meager rations. At the end of the contract period those who did not want to sign up for a second time were sent home.[4] The system lasted until the end of the century, when the white Australian working class, and other opposition, combined with a change in the methods of production, brought the system to a close in Australia

2. Kwaisula of Ada Gege was a well-known agent. In exchange for providing recruits he was supplied with arms, kerosene, arsenic, axes, crowbars, fencing wire, and building materials (Docker 1970: 132). These agents would often deceive the recruits. For example, returned laborers interviewed on Mota Island, Sugarloaf, were told that three moons, and not three years, was the length of the contract period by Wenlolo, a native agent (Parliamentary Papers 1867–68: XLVII, 41).

3. Many recruits complained "countrymen make a row along me if I have no box" (Docker 1970: 266). This institution and its place in the gift economy will be discussed further in the following sections.

4. "Quite often it was impossible to return the laborers to their original homes: these may have been blotted out by depopulation, or more often the places were unknown to the officials responsible for repatriation . . . . Sometimes the repatriates were left stranded on shores hundreds of miles from their original home, and as a result were the prey of hostile people, or were propertyless strangers" (Belshaw 1954: 36).

(Graves 1979). All Melanesian labor still living in Queensland was forcibly repatriated. Australian plantation capital followed it and, along with German capital, it instituted the indentured labor system in Melanesia.

Table 6.2 provides a statistical overview of the system which lasted from 1863 to 1904, with a total of 62,475 men being recruited. Recruiting reached a peak in the 1880s and thereafter declined. It was in the 1880s that the new method of production—a central milling system—was introduced. This was also the time that public opposition to the system was greatest. The recruitment of the 2808 Papua New Guineans in 1883–84 was a turning point. Up until this time, the New Hebrides provided the bulk of the recruits; but by 1883 they had become familiar with the workings of the system and started bargaining for better conditions, making PNG and the Solomon Islands a more attractive field. Many of the Papua New Guineans were kidnapped and fourteen of the thirty-two voyages that went to PNG were subject to official inquiries (Corris 1968: 90). The death rate among Papua New Guineans in Queensland was very high. One man in four died due to poor feeding, bad weather, overwork, and the absence of proper care when sick (Docker 1970: 205–6). The PNG case provided the reformers with the evidence they needed and in 1885 legislation was passed which provided that no licenses to recruit Melanesians for service in Queensland were to be issued after the end of 1890 (Corris 1968: 103).

(b) Semiforced labor (domestic indentured labor), 1883–1950. Plantation and mining capital entered PNG at the beginning of the twentieth century and a system of indentured labor was instituted to provide it with cheap labor-power. This system operated in much the same way as the one that provided labor for the Queensland plantations, with the exception that the recruits did not have to travel as far and it was subject to closer government control. The growth and development of the system over the period 1890–1940 is illustrated in Table 6.3 which gives data on the number of workers engaged in the two regions. New Guinea was the focus of most activity and this received its initial impetus from an influx of German plantation capital which was expropriated by the Australians in 1914. At this time the Germans were employing 17,529 indentured laborers compared with 7,681 that the Australians were employing in Papua. Prior to the outbreak of the Second World War 49,253 Papua New Guineans were employed as indentured laborers.

Table 6.2

Origin of Melanesian labour in Queensland, 1863–1904 (Actual numbers of labourers recruited)

Area	Five year period ending									Total	
	1867	1872	1877	1882	1887	1892	1897	1904		No.	%
Loyalties	421	643	59							1,123	2
New Hebrides	1,308	2,950	7,811	9,648	7,845	4,594	2,598	3,177		39,931	64
Solomons		82	908	1,704	3,179	3,588	3,094	5,201		17,756	28
New Guinea					2,808					2,808	5
Other	34	42	74	70	205	114	318			857	1
Total	1,763	3,717	8,852	11,422	14,037	8,296	6,010	8,378		62,475	100

Source: Price and Baker (1976: 114–15).

Table 6.3

Indentured labour, Papua and New Guinea, 1890–1940

Year	Papua[a]	New Guinea[b]
1890	—	869
1909	4,266	8,311
1914	7,681	17,529
1921	7,495	27,728
1925	6,879	23,421
1930	7,274	30,062
1935	5,964	34,150
1940	9,829	39,424

[a] Figures for the years 1907–1922 give the number of workers engaged, whereas for the years 1923–1940 the average number under contract is given.
[b] This is an end of year (June 30) employment figure.
Source: Annual Reports, 1890–1940.

A colonial administrator of Papua in 1930 said,

The great advantage that the employer has under our indenture system is that it gives him a criminal remedy for a civil wrong; for by our Ordinance a native labourer who, for instance, deserts or neglects his duty, may be punished with fine or imprisonment. These "penal sanctions," which of course are not peculiar to Papuan labour legislation and which apply to employer as well as employed, put the employer in a position to exercise great control over his labour force; and they have met with disapproval in many quarters, on the ground that, in case of a breach of contract, both parties should be left to their civil remedy. Theoretically it is impossible to justify the enforcement of civil claim by criminal procedure, and the first and very natural feeling of any one [*sic*] who has a regard for justice must be one of resentment against what he would regard as a gross abuse of the criminal law. But actual experience of the administration of a Territory such as Papua will induce him to modify this feeling very considerably and to realize that, if there is to be a contract at all, there must be a remedy for its breach, and that the civil remedy is useless where the defendant has no property of any value, except the few shillings that may be due to him for wages . . . and so may break his contract with impunity. (Annual Report, Papua 1930: 10)

Of course, it was not the fact that an indentured laborer had no property that enabled him to break his contract with impunity, it was the fact that he had no economic need to sell his labor-power as a commodity, which made the penal provisions that characterized indentured labor necessary. Many free wage-laborers have no property of any value; but they cannot break their contracts with impunity because they must sell their labor-power in order to survive. This gives the employer control over his labor force without the necessity of penal provisions.

Because "unlimited supplies of labor" did not exist, recruiting was difficult and many devious methods were resorted to. For example, the Annual Report of 1922 for New Guinea notes that:

Under the German Administration a most reprehensible practice had arisen of using female natives as an inducement to recruit or to sign for a further term after the completion of an original contract. Most of the . . . wives of the planters had several native women in their employment, and these were given as wives to natives to induce them to make a new contract. No cognisance was taken of any native customs, and as the marriage code in most of the native tribes is strictly defined . . . it is easily understood that on return of the parties to their district, there was much discontent and trouble. (Annual Report, New Guinea 1922: 53)

It was also the practice of recruiters to pay a bonus to the village headman for each person who engaged to serve. This practice was sanctioned by the Australian administration. But it was recognized that "if the chief is powerful and unscrupulous, this practice is capable of abuse, for the chief, in order to obtain payments offered by the recruiter, may use force to compel unwilling natives to engage" (ibid.: 53). It was also recognized that this practice led to overrecruitment and hence depopulation in some areas. In an attempt to counteract these abuses a limit to the amount of the bonuses payable was set out in the *Native Labor Ordinance* 1922.

An indentured laborer had to work ten hours per day six days per week, was given a cash allowance of 5/- per month, a daily ration of 3.5 lb of yams, taro, or English potato together with 6 oz of canned meat or fish, 1 lb of tobacco per month, and, most important of all for the worker, a box whose specifications were stated in the *Native Labor Ordinance* 1922–28 as follows:

(a) Inside measurement	24" × 10" × 6"
(b) Lid (depth overall)	2"
(c) Sides and ends	¾"
(d) Top of lid and bottom of box	⅝"
(e) Blocks under bottom corners	2½" × 2½" × ⅝"
(f) Stops (inside of lid)	¾" × ⅜"
(g) Handles (iron, 2)	4" × 1¾"
(h) Hinges (brass, 2)	2" × ¾"
(i) Screws (brass)	¾"
(j) Hasp and staple	4"
(k) Padlock and key	

The box was the worker's link with the gift economy. In it he put various commodities acquired during his period of employment. On his return home these commodities were given away as gifts to various big-men to facilitate his reintegration into the gift economy (as will be seen in the next chapter).

Table 6.4
Gold mining statistics, Papua, 1889–1928

Period	Employment at end of period		Production of gold for the period (oz)
	Foreign miners	Indentured labourers	
1889–1899	232	988	81,109
1900–1909	102	862	206,784
1910–1919	57	511	134,443
1920–1928	27	294	129,899

Source: Annual Reports, Papua 1927–28.

The continuity of the indentured labor system is inextricably tied up with the type of capital that employs it. In this respect there is a big difference between mining capital and plantation capital. Mining capital roams the world in search of raw materials that will enable it to appropriate for itself differential rent. It is not primarily concerned to exploit cheap labor-power. Plantation capital, on the other hand, is. It requires unsophisticated, unmarried workers from the "labor frontier." It will exist for as long as the labor frontier exists. In the case of PNG the "discovery" in the 1930s that 40% of the population lived in the highlands created a new labor frontier that was not exhausted until the 1970s. Plantation capital leaves behind a legacy of old unproductive trees and an exploitative system of labor relations; the principal legacy of mining capital, on the other hand, is a hole in the ground. Table 6.4 summarizes the impact of the first wave of mining capital into Papua. It lasted forty years from 1889 to 1928 and produced 552,235 oz of gold. Sixty-five percent of this was mined in the islands of Milne Bay, 26% in Northern District, and the rest in Central District. While this capital was no doubt responsible for instituting the system of indentured labor in Papua, it was never a big employer. For example, in 1921 it employed less than 3% of all indentured labor.

Table 6.5
Gold mining statistics, Morobe District, New Guinea, 1932–1941

Year	Indentured laborers[a]	Gold (oz)[b]
1932	2,800	6,890
1933	3,875	65,355
1934	5,142	89,737
1935	6,369	127,901
1936	6,816	121,352
1937	7,394	137,325
1938	7,189	134,715
1939	7,162	158,970
1940	7,150	185,016
1941	6,438	167,462
		1,194,723

[a] Numbers of laborers employed in Morobe District.
Source: Annual Reports, NG
[b] Dredging returns for Bulolo Region, Morobe District.
Source: Healy (1967: 61).

Compare this with the second wave of mining capital, which was located in the Morobe District, the statistics for which are shown in Table 6.5. This capital was obviously much more productive. In the ten years from 1932 to 1941, 1,194,723 oz of gold was produced, twice as much as the first wave of capital produced in forty years. This employed a significant proportion (14.5%) of the indentured laborers and, as shall be seen below, transformed the Morobe District from being a net supplier of indentured labor into a net demander.

Table 6.6
Area under plantation, Papua and New Guinea, 1885–1939

	Papua		New Guinea	
Year	Area (ha)	No.	Area (ha)	No.
1885	—	—	60	n.a.
1907	594	n.a.	n.a.	n.a.
1909	3,132	130	16,024	n.a.
1914	17,370	228	31,099	n.a.
1918	23,307	244	54,213	375
1922	24,408	259	70,122	n.a.
1931	23,838	338	89,570	416
1939	23,967	n.a.	106,085	497

Source: Annual Reports, 1885–1939.

The third wave of mining capital arrived in the 1960s and situated itself in Bougainville District. This district now has one of the world's largest copper mines. Gold is only a by-product of this mine, but nevertheless in the first two years of operation, 1971–73, it produced 650,000 oz of gold. This was more than was produced in the first forty-year wave, one-half of what was produced in the second ten-year wave, and yet was only the first splash of the tidal wave to come. Another important feature of this third wave of mining capital is that it employs free wage-labor at relatively high rates of pay. Plantation capital does not have this wave-like motion. Consider Table 6.6, which shows the area under cultivation in Papua and New Guinea for the period 1885 to 1939. In Papua the initial investment was made in the eleven years from 1907 to 1917. After that, investment ceased with the area under cultivation at a plateau of 23,000 ha. Most of this investment was centered in the Milne Bay area, in the form of copra plantations, and in the Central District, where rubber was an equally important tree. These two areas accounted for 52% and 38% of the total area planted, respectively.

The area under cultivation in New Guinea has grown steadily, with a particularly sharp increase over the period 1914–22. The reason for this is to be found in the 1922 Annual Report:

> The Germans expected the properties to be taken over, but had an idea that they would be paid for at a flat rate for old and young palms, and they rushed the planting of large areas (in many cases hastily and badly planted), being under the impression that they would make a handsome profit from these plantings when receiving compensation. (Annual Report, New Guinea 1922: 124)

It should be noted that the size of the plantations in New Guinea is much larger than those in Papua. For example, in 1931 the 416 plantations of New Guinea had an average size of 215 hectares, whereas in Papua 338 plantations had an average size of 70 hectares. The significance of this fact was that conditions on the big plantations were much worse. This is partly reflected in the figures for death rates (Table 6.7). In Papua, deaths, as a percentage of indentured labor employed, averaged 1.43 compared with 1.74 for New Guinea. It was consistently less than 2% in Papua, except in 1932 and 1933, when an influenza-pneumonia epidemic swept the mainland. This difference, which was regarded by the administrator as significant, is nothing when compared with those for the Queensland plantations, where conditions were literally murderous. In 1889, 481 out of 7580 laborers died, giving a figure of 6.34%. This, it seems, was about average for in 1884 it rose to 14.75% following the recruitment of Papua New Guineans (see Parliamentary Papers 1892: LVI, 255; Docker 1970: 216).

The impact of mining and plantation capital on the various districts of New Guinea is shown in Table 6.8. Plantation capital was first located in the New Britain District. By 1925 the labor frontier in this district had disappeared and labor from other districts had to be sought. Plantations were later developed in the other island districts—New Ireland and Manus—and they too became net demanders of labor. This demand was met from the mainland of New Guinea and in particular from the swamplands of the Sepik District. The impact of the second wave of

Table 6.7
Deaths and desertions among indentured laborers, PNG, 1926–1940

Year	Papua Deaths		New Guinea Deaths		Desertions	
	No.	% of Papua labor	No.	% of N.G. labor	No.	% of N.G. labor
1926	118	1.22	525	2.22	494	2.09
1927	131	1.57	589	2.18	631	2.33
1928	94	1.12	488	1.72	378	1.33
1929	57	0.84	622	2.07	1,110	3.69
1930	95	1.31	557	1.84	601	1.99
1931	51	0.83	457	1.64	892	3.21
1932	144	2.74	665	2.55	849	3.19
1933	110	2.17	450	1.59	917	3.24
1934	67	1.29	489	1.58	1,041	3.37
1935	63	1.05	519	1.52	898	2.62
1936	91	1.31	604	1.63	936	2.53
1937	87	1.09	501	1.24	1,051	2.61
1938	177	1.83	616	1.47	1,116	2.67
1939	132	1.35	646	1.55	1,218	2.92
1940	181	1.84	595	1.51	877	2.22

Source: Annual Reports, 1926–1940.

mining capital on the Morobe District is striking. From being a net supplier of labor, this area became a net demander recruiting 6688 workers from outside the district in 1936.

A similar situation existed in Papua. The capital was concentrated in two districts—Milne Bay and Central—and labor was supplied from those districts where there was no capital invested, such as Gulf and Western District. Without this uneven spatial distribution of capital the indentured labor system could not have persisted.

(c) Semi-free labor (agreement labor), 1951–1974. During the Second World War the Japanese occupied New Guinea, and the battles that ensued extracted a heavy toll both in terms of capital and labor. The war also meant that the exploitation of the last labor frontier—the highlands—was delayed. In the immediate postwar period the Australian Labor Party abolished the penal provisions of the indentured labor system, thus transforming it into what was known as an "agreement labor" system. All the highlanders were recruited under this system. Meanwhile, in

Table 6.8

Supply and demand of indentured labor by district, New Guinea, 1925–1940

Year	Net demanders				Net suppliers			Net flow of labour
	New Britain	New Ireland	Manus	Morobe	Sepik	Madang	Bougainville	
1925	4,492	75	675	-1,202	3,254	75	711	5,242
1926	4,654	543	903	-1,338	3,414	639	709	6,100
1927	4,819	181	747	-489	3,305	1,114	809	5,747
1928	4,657	1,237	896	-373	4,571	941	905	6,790
1929	4,642	1,648	705	0	4,449	1,712	834	6,995
1930	4,633	1,405	706	7	5,156	961	634	6,751
1931	3,892	1,413	793	534	5,291	773	568	6,632
1932	3,014	1,299	750	1,254	5,010	632	675	6,317
1933	2,841	1,200	597	2,066	5,535	660	509	6,704
1934	2,325	1,778	518	3,910	6,840	1,182	509	8,531
1935	2,418	1,466	475	5,667	7,691	1,846	489	10,026
1936	2,854	1,544	463	6,688	9,022	1,993	534	11,549
1937	4,205	1,813	576	5,305	9,117	2,073	709	11,899
1938	5,012	2,200	394	4,536	9,674	1,750	718	12,142
1939	4,996	2,191	295	4,935	9,516	2,100	801	12,417
1940	4,554	2,028	177	4,663	8,388	2,239	795	11,422

Source: Annual Reports, New Guinea, 1925–1940.

Table 6.9
Transition from indentured labor to agreement and free wage-labor,
Papua New Guinea, 1948–1952

Year	Indentured labor	Agreement labor	Free wage-labor		Total
			Private	Gov't	
1948	13,378	—	12,614	11,399	37,391
1949	15,593	—	15,355	12,536	43,484
1950	16,890	—	17,532	13,763	48,185
1951	9,192	11,001	18,572	12,748	51,513
1952	—	24,488	18,719	13,705	56,912

Source: Annual Reports, 1948–1952.

the old labor frontiers the transformation of the gift economy was such that free wage-labor was forthcoming. In the postwar period this came to be the dominant mode of employment—evidence of the successful transformation of labor-power into a commodity. Table 6.9 illustrates the employment trends in the immediate postwar period. In 1948 total employment stood at 37,391, of whom 13,378 were employed as indentured laborers. By 1952 total employment was 56,912, 43% of whom were employed as agreement laborers and none as indentured laborers. The agreement labor system still existed in 1972 but accounted for only 26% of total employment of 120,014 (see Table 6.10). In 1974 the system was abolished. However, the conditions of plantation labor have barely changed as a result.

Table 6.10
Workforce and population, Papua New Guinea, 1971–1972

	Workforce (1972)		Population (1971)		Workforce / Population
	No.	%	No.	%	%
Rural					
Agreement labor	32,071	(26)			
Wage-labor	39,369	(33)			
Total rural	71,440	(59)	2,203,636	(91)	(3)
Urban wage-labor	48,574	(41)	231,873	(9)	(21)
Total	120,014	(100)	2,435,509	(100)	(5)

Source: Maro Board Report (1974: 15, 24); 1971 Census.

In terms of the real cost to the employer there was little difference between the forced labor system that operated in Queensland and the agreement labor system. Consider Table 6.11. This compares the daily ration prescribed by regulation for a laborer recruited for Queensland in 1867 with that for PNG in 1951. A greater variety of food was prescribed in 1951 but there were corresponding reductions in the quantities of the major staples prescribed: 4 lb yams and 1 lb meat per day were prescribed in 1867, compared with 3½ lb yams and 6⅔ oz meat in 1951. The other major expense that the employer faced was recruitment cost and, if this is taken into consideration, agreement labor is cheaper. Plantation capital operating in Queensland had to face rising costs of recruitment. In 1867 it was £7 per man; by 1882 it had risen to £22 (Docker 1970: 45, 164). Agreement labor, however, is recruited by the state rather than private enterprise and a flat fee of £7 was charged in postwar PNG (Cochrane Report 1970: 28). These figures are current prices; in real terms the recruitment cost of agreement labor would be much less.

Table 6.11
Daily ration scale prescribed by regulation in 1867 and 1951

Item	Indentured laborer 1867	Agreement laborer 1951
1 Yams	4 lb[a]	3½ lb[b]
2 Peanuts	—	4 oz[c]
3 Barley	—	4 oz
4 Meat	1 lb	6⅔ oz
5 Fat	—	2 oz
6 Sugar	2 oz	2²⁄₇ oz
7 Tea	½ oz	²⁄₇ oz
8 Salt	—	⅓ oz
9 Fruit	—	1 lb
10 Water	6 pints	6 pints

[a] Options were 1½ lb rice, or 1½ lb maizemeal.
[b] Options were 1 lb rice, or 1½ lb bread, or 3½ lb kau kau, or 3½ lb taro, or 3½ lb English potato, or 1 lb sago.
[c] Options existed for items 2, 3, 4, 5, 6, 7 and 9.
Source: Parliamentary Papers, 1867–1868 (XLVII); Annual Report, New Guinea (1951: 134–135).

The last labor frontier. The moving labor frontier is illustrated clearly in
Table 6.12. In 1949 all agreement and free wage-labor was supplied from
the coastal districts, with most of it coming from the Sepik District. Over
the next twenty years Sepik supply dropped from 9145 to 6437 in absolute
terms and from 87% to 22% in relative terms. The importance of the highlands districts as a source of labor rose correspondingly. They supplied no
labor in 1949, but by 1968 they supplied 13,267 men or 45% of the total
net supply. The movement of the frontier within the highlands districts is
also apparent. The Eastern Highlands District was the first area opened up;
this was followed by the opening up of the Western Highlands District.
The Southern Highlands, which was opened up in the 1960s, was the last
frontier. In 1969 a Department of Labour report noted that "the Southern
Highlands, the last 'frontier,' is thought to have reached or be approaching
a peak level of supply; certainly there are limits to any further substantial
increase over the present" (Highlands Labour Report 1969: 10). Most of
this labor was sent to either New Britain District, where it was employed
on copra plantations, or Central District, where it was employed by the
administrative headquarters or on copra and rubber plantations.

Table 6.12
Supply and demand of agreement labor by district, PNG, 1949–1968

	1949	1960	1968
District of Net Demand			
Central	4,586	7,620	13,487
Island	5,875	15,128	16,225
Total	10,461	22,748	29,712
District of Net Supply			
Coastal			
Sepik	9,145	9,964	6,437
Other coastal	1,316	5,164	10,008
Highlands			
Eastern	—	6,772	10,084
Western	—	796	(-2,213)
Southern	—	52	5,396
Total	10,461	22,748	29,712

Source: Cochrane Report (1970: 31).

Table 6.13
Agreement labor as a component of the total workforce, 1953–1968

Year	Highland agreement labor		Total agreement labor		Total workforce
	No.	% total agreement labor	No.	% total workforce	No.
1953	2,101	7	29,390	49	59,459
1960	6,979	22	31,192	42	72,938
1965	14,481	55	26,215	29	91,753
1967	14,718	60	24,569	23	109,000
1968	14,178	62	22,746	20	115,517

Source: Cochrane Report (1970: 33).

The crisis that plantation capital began to face toward the end of the 1960s is illustrated in Table 6.13. The supply of agreement labor fell from 29,390 in 1953 to 22,746 in 1968. The percentage of highland labor in this total rose from 7% to 62%, but this was not enough to offset the decline in the overall supply. Government control over recruiting, through the application of the "25% rule," further restricted supply. This rule was learned by cruel experience. In times gone by, a labor shortage brought about by the exhaustion of a labor frontier was met by overrecruiting. But this invariably led to depopulation. To overcome this problem a District Officer would check that the departure of the agreement laborers did not deplete the village manpower by more than 25%.

The actual operation of this rule can be seen by examining Tables 6.14 and 6.15. In Table 6.14 the figures for employed adult males as a percentage of total adult males is shown by highlands district and subdistrict. The Eastern Highlands District labor frontier was clearly exhausted by 1967 as 21% of adult males had been recruited. The Western Highlands District labor frontier, with 4% of adult males recruited, and the Southern Highlands District labor frontier with 13% of adult males recruited, still had exploitable potential.

Table 6.15 breaks down the figures for two subdistricts into their respective census divisions. Kundiawa subdistrict of the Eastern Highlands District and Lagaip subdistrict of the Western Highlands District have been chosen because they are the areas of highest and lowest recruitment, respectively. Kundiawa subdistrict, a major center in the

Table 6.14
Males, 16–45 years, working outside district, highlands, PNG, 1967

District Sub-district	Total males[a] 16–45	Working[b] outside district	%
Eastern			
Henganofi	7,995	988	12
Wonenara	3,328	707	21
Okapa	10,297	1,392	14
Kainantu	9,288	1,513	16
Goroka	19,111	2,643	14
Kundiawa	20,430	6,202	30
Gumine	9,188	2,265	25
Chauve	6,972	1,744	25
Kerowagi	7,173	2,019	28
Total	93,782	19,473	21
Western			
Hagen	29,839	962	3
Wabag	19,795	1,557	8
Minj	8,086	315	4
Lagaip	11,782	234	2
Lake Kopiago	1,986	46	2
Total	71,488	3,114	4
Southern			
Mendi	7,769	666	9
Kagua	7,122	905	13
Ialibu	8,647	1,363	16
Nipa	7,249	600	8
Tari	8,167	1,384	17
Koroba	4,835	647	13
Total	43,789	5,565	13
Grand total	209,059	28,152	13

[a] The majority of the censuses were carried out between August 1966 and August 1968.
[b] Includes agreement workers and others.
Source: Highlands Labour Report (1969: App. F).

highlands, was overrecruited in two areas—Mitnande (47%) and Niglkande (49%)—but was at or below the legal limit in other areas. Lagaip, a remote part of the highlands, was underrecruited in 1967. No census division in this subdistrict had more than 5% of its adult manpower recruited.

The pattern of recruitment seems to be that when an area is first opened up it is the young men who are sent off. In subsequent recruitment more

Table 6.15

Males, 16–45 years, working outside district, Kundiawa and
Lagaip sub-districts, PNG, 1967

Sub-district Census division	Total males 16–45	Working outside district	%
Kundiawa			
Waiye	2,742	684	25
Dom	1,792	409	23
Sinasina	6,000	1,561	26
Yonggamugl	2,593	704	27
Mitnande	3,549	1,663	47
Niglkande	1,963	963	49
Karimui	704	145	21
Daribi	765	40	5
Bomai	184	19	10
Tura	52	8	15
Pio	86	6	7
Total	20,430	6,202	30
Lagaip			
N.E. Lagaip	1,209	9	1
S.E. Lagaip	902	1	—
W. Lagaip	1,222	66	5
S.W. Lagaip	2,089	40	2
Wage	1,781	27	2
Lai Mariant	2,370	33	2
N.W. Mariant	796	32	4
Porgera	788	1	—
Paiela	625	25	4
Total	11,782	234	2

Notes and source: See previous table.

old men tend to volunteer. In the Koroba subdistrict of the Southern Highlands, for example, Harris found that in 1966, 80% of recruits were aged between 16 and 24 years, while in 1970 only 51% of recruits were in this age group. He also found that there was a significant increase in the percentage of recruits who were married: 11% in 1966, 25% in 1970 (see G. Harris 1972: 129). Of course, most wives were left behind in the village. However, the law did allow men to take their wives if the employer consented. In such cases the employer was bound to provide accom-modation and rations for the wife and children. In a survey conducted by the Department of Labour it was found that some 48.9% of workers were married. However, only 27.6% of workers were accompanied by their families (Maro Board Report 1974: 6).

The exit of plantation capital. Capital that relies on the exploitation of la-bor by paying it a single man's wage cannot reproduce itself, because the labor cannot reproduce itself. It can only last as long as the labor frontier lasts. When the frontier is exhausted the capital must be invested in other ways. When it is foreign capital it usually leaves the host country. This was the case in PNG in 1972.

Approximately one-half of the plantation capital was owned by the "Big Three" trading companies that operate in PNG: W. R. Carpenter (PNG) Ltd.; Steamships Trading Co.; Burns Philp (NG) Ltd. In the two years ended 30 June 1968 they employed 49% of agreement labor recruits. Another company, The British New Guinea Development Co., employed 13% of the recruits; the remaining 38% were employed by plantations owned by private individuals. (See Table 6.16.)

Table 6.16
Major employers of highlands agreement labor, 1968

Company	No. of recruits 2 years ended 30 June 1968	%
W. R. Carpenter Group	3,250	21
Steamships Trading	2,398	15
Burns Philp (NG) Ltd.	2,038	13
The British New Guinea Development Co.	1,954	13
Other	5,857	38
	15,497	100

Source: Highlands Labour Report (1969: 11).

Burns Philp (NG) Ltd. is a subsidiary of Burns Philp and Co. Ltd., an Australian-based multinational. This group has had a long contact with PNG and it made quite substantial profits from recruiting Melanesi-ans for the Queensland canefields in its formative years (Bolton 1967: 119–20). The geographical origin of the group's 1973 profits is shown in

Table 6.17
Burns Philp and Co. Ltd.—geographical origins of net profit, 1973

Region	Profit $A (000s)	%
Austalia	4,433	59.2
P.N.G.	1,963	26.2
South Seas[a]	695	9.3
New Hebrides	390	5.3
Total	7,481	100

[a] Includes Fiji, Western Samoa, American Samoa, Tonga, Niue Island.
Source: Chairman's address, BPNG (1973).

Table 6.18
Dividends paid by Burns Philp PNG group, 1965–1973

Year	Dividend $A
1965	237,500
1966	2,118,750[a]
1967	550,000
1968	550,000
1969	550,000
1970	550,000
1971	2,750,000[b]
1972	9,625,000[c]
1973	1,500,000

[a] Bonus share dividend of $1,500,000 included.
[b] Bonus share dividend of $2,000,000 included.
[c] Bonus share dividend of $4,500,000 included.
Source: Registrar General's Office, Pt Moresby.

Table 6.17. $A4,433,000 or 59% of the total profit of $A7,481,000 came from its Australian operations, 26% came from PNG, and the remaining 15% from other Pacific islands. In 1972 the company introduced a policy of "making the group less dependent on its Island Operations" (Chairman's address, BPNG 1973). This meant, in effect, the withdrawal of its plantation capital.

Table 6.19
Burns Philp and Co. Ltd.—profits from subsidiary and associated companies in PNG, 1970–1973

Company	Average profit ($A p.a.)	Average dividend ($A p.a.)	Div / profit %
Primary Industry			
Kulon Plantations Ltd.	148,295	206,006	138
New Ireland Plantations Ltd.	64,879	127,000	195
New Hanover Plantations Ltd.	113,202	151,425	133
New Guinea Plantations Ltd.	10,366	10,750	103
New Britain Plantations Ltd.	136,583	170,000	124
Robinson River Plantations Ltd.	30,585	47,812	156
Total Primary	503,910	712,993	141
Tertiary Industry			
Burns Philp (NG) Ltd.	2,059,632	1,981,250	96
BNG Trading Co. Ltd.	425,473	229,120	53
Hotel Moresby Ltd.	13,613	14,375	105
Moresby Hire Services	374	—	
Warirata Estates Ltd.	(-5,072)	—	
Local Laundries	15,297	18,000	117
Papua Hotel Ltd.	11,435	11,250	98
Bunting Stevedores	116,400	120,000	103
Total Tertiaty	2,637,152	2,373,995	90
Grand total	3,141,062	3,086,988	98

Source: Registrar General's Office, Pt Moresby.

Tables 6.18 and 6.19 demonstrate this. In Table 6.18 the annual dividends paid by the PNG-based company to its parent are shown. In 1972 an abnormally high dividend of $A9,625,000, which included a bonus dividend of $4,500,000, was paid. To grasp the nature of this transfer we must further disaggregate the data. Table 6.19 does this and it shows the dividend/profit ratios for the subsidiaries of the PNG subsidiary for the four years ended June 1973. It is clear that the origin of the transfer comes from running down the reserves in the plantation-based companies. In all cases the dividend/profit rate exceeds 100% and is 141% in the aggregate. For companies engaged in commercial operations, on the other hand, the equivalent figure is only 90%.

A similar exit of plantation capital can be detected in the accounts of W. R. Carpenter (PNG) Ltd. Table 6.20 shows the annual dividends paid by this company to its parent company in Australia. Again one is struck by the payment of an abnormally high dividend in 1972 of $A5,525,700. The origin of this was once more "plantation redevelopment reserve no longer required." Table 6.21 illustrates this clearly. The ratio of dividends to profits in the plantation-based companies was 171% compared with 92% for the tertiary industry companies.

The other big trading company, Steamships Trading Co. Ltd., was the exception, as Table 6.22 shows. No abnormally high dividends were paid in 1972.

Table 6.20
Dividends paid by W. R. Carpenter (PNG) Ltd., 1970–1973

Year	Dividend ($A)
1970	937,000
1971	950,000
1972	5,525,700
1973	876,000

Source: Registrar General's Office, Pt Moresby.

The year 1972 is, of course, significant. Not only was the last labor frontier exhausted by this time but it was also the year of self-government for PNG; in addition, a dividend withholding tax of 15% was mooted. (It was introduced in 1973.) The combination of these circumstances was sufficient incentive for two of the "Big Three" to export their plantation capital to Australia and to instigate a process wherein ownership of the plantations will eventually pass to Papua New Guinean hands. It is now Papua New Guinean Government policy to transfer expatriate-owned plantations to Papua New Guinean groups, and a special fund to purchase plantations has been set up. The primary motive of this was to enable Papua New Guineans to regain control of the land alienated by plantation capital. However, what they are acquiring are worn-out industries that require very low-paid labor to keep them going. As a recent government report said, in the copra and rubber industries, "a large proportion of trees are either senile or rapidly becoming senile and what little replanting has been carried out has not made use of new improved planting material that has been available for many years" (Maro Board Report 1974: 10).

Table 6.21
W. R. Carpenter (PNG) Ltd.—profits from subsidiary
companies in PNG, 1970–1973

Company	Average profit ($A p.a.)	Average dividend ($A p.a.)	Div / profit %
Primary Industry			
Coconut Products Ltd.	1,349,268	2,503,900	185
Island Estates Ltd.	209,620	286,660	136
Garua Plantations Ltd.	40,272	41,701	103
Tovarur Plantations Ltd.	54,840	54,952	100
Dylup Plantations Ltd.	67,015	61,654	92
Total Primary	1,721,015	2,948,867	171
Tertiary Industry			
New Guinea Co. Ltd.	128,131	73,750	57
Boroko Motors Ltd.	71,443	34,750	49
W. R. Carpenter (Properties) Ltd.	46,646	27,250	58
Southern Cross Marine Insurance Co. Ltd.[a]	43,331	175,000	403
Taubmans (PNG) Pty Ltd.	41,427	22,500	54
Gas Suppy (NG) Pty Ltd.	77,743	45,000	57
Total Tertiaty	408,721	378,250	92
Grand total	2,129,736	3,327,117	156

[a] For the years 1971–73 only.
Source: Registrar General's Office, Pt Moresby.

Table 6.22
Dividends paid by Steamships Trading Co. Ltd., 1970–1973

Year	Dividend ($A)
1970	815,314
1971	815,314
1972	815,314
1973	592,955

Source: Registrar General's Office, Pt Moresby.

The role of neoclassical economists. Table 6.23 shows the value of an agreement laborer's rations over the period 1945 to 1976. Until 1972 the bulk
of this wage was paid in kind. This included food, clothing, shelter, and
tobacco, and was estimated to be to the value of $A3.86. In addition to
the wages paid in kind, a small cash allowance was also made. This was

35 cents per week in 1945 and rose to $A1.13 per week by 1971. In 1972 an all-cash wage was introduced and the wage rose from $A5.90 per week to $A9.43 per week by July 1976. The wage movements reflected not the growth of trade unionism among the agreement workers—they are still weak and disorganized—but rather the practical application of neoclassical economic theories. A number of Australian economists were called upon to prepare reports, and the movements in wages reflect the implementation of their recommendations.

The first major report was the "Isaac Report," prepared in 1970 by Professor J. E. Isaac of Monash University (later to become Deputy President of the Commonwealth Conciliation and Arbitration Commission).

Isaac described the Agreement Labor System as "a practical and economical way of drawing labor from the surplus labor areas with low incomes to areas of higher incomes with a smaller labor surplus" (Isaac Report 1970: 24). He noted that a labor shortage was emerging and that this provided "a *prima facie* case for a rise in the rural wage and/or an improvement in the conditions of work" (ibid.: 14). A description of the system in Lewis-type labor-surplus terms inevitably led to a Lewis-type prescription. Isaac obtained "a figure of roughly $A200 per annum as the *income per worker* in subsistence production" (ibid.: 15, emphasis added), and argued that "if we regard $A200 as the current opportunity cost of the recruit for rural employment, following Professor Arthur Lewis' formula for a loading of something like 50% on top of this, the 'appropriate' rural wage comes out at $A300 per annum" (ibid.: 15). He recommended the introduction of an all-cash wage and in gross terms his recommendations amounted to an increase of $A0.90 per week for a single man. However, for married men the impact of his recommendation was a *decrease* in their wages by amounts ranging from $A1.67 upward per week depending upon the number of dependents. The ordinance existing in 1910, Isaac argued, discouraged

the employment of workers with accompanying dependants because of the substantially greater immediate cost of employing such workers as compared with single workers or those without accompanying dependants. . . . A more positive policy towards securing a more stable labour force would require an amendment of this section of the Ordinance, at least to remove the obligation of the employer in respect of rations and other issues for accompanying dependants. (Isaac Report 1970: 27)

Table 6.23
Value of agreement labor rations, 1945–1976 (weekly in $A)

	Cash component	Kind component[a]	Total
1945	0.35	3.86	4.21
1956	0.58	3.86	4.44
1960	0.63	3.86	4.49
1961	0.75	3.86	4.61
1962	0.75	3.86	4.61
1963	0.75	3.86	4.61
1964	0.75	3.86	4.61
1965	0.75	3.86	4.61
1966	0.75	3.86	4.61
1967	1.00	3.86	4.86
1968	1.00	3.86	4.86
1969	1.00	3.86	4.86
1970	1.00	3.86	4.86
1971	1.13	3.86	4.99
1972	5.90[b]	—	5.90
June 1974	6.40[c]	—	6.40
Aug 1974	8.00	—	8.00
Mar 1975	8.50	—	8.50
Sept 1975	8.90	—	8.90
July 1976	9.47	—	9.43

[a] The kind component consisted of the following allowances: $0.87 for accommodation, $2.50 for food, $0.36 for clothing, and $0.13 for tobacco, thus totalling $3.86. A married man received extra rations for his wife and family valued at between $1.31 and $2.59 per dependant.
[b] This "all-cash" wage was subject to the following deductions: $0.87 for accomodation, $2.50 for food, $0.36 for clothing, $0.25 for repatriation, and $0.50 for deferred wages, thus totalling $4.48. The repatriation and deferred wage deduction was refundable if the contract was completed.
[c] The deductions were adjusted as follows: $3.00 for food, $0.43 for clothing, and $1.00 for deferred wages, thus totalling $4.43.
Source: Fleay Report (1974: 12); Cochrane Report (1970: 14-15, 161-64); Waka Board Report (1974: 3); Maro Board Report (1974: 16); PNGLIB9 1972.

Such was the logic of the argument that recommended a wage reduction for approximately one-quarter of the agreement labor workforce.

The belief that wages should be related to "subsistence sector income" is widespread among neoclassical economists who operate in the Third World.[5] However, aside from the fact that the "subsistence sector" is a misconception and that it makes no sense to price the quantities of gifts

---

5.   See Jorgenson (1961), Johnson (1965), Turner (1965), Berg (1969), and Bhagwati (1971).

produced and exchanged, the notion of "subsistence sector income" is faulty even in its own terms. The minimum size of a "subsistence" unit is a man, his wife, and their two children. This means that it consists of two workers at the very minimum. Using Isaac's estimates, this implies a figure of $A400 per annum. By recommending a figure of $A300 p.a. for agreement labor wages, he was in fact prescribing that the "subsistence sector" *subsidize* the "monetary" sector. In our terms, he was prescribing that the gift economy bear the bulk of the reproduction cost of agreement labor. But this was precisely what had been going on since 1883. Labor at less than reproduction cost is only available from a labor frontier, and it was because this no longer existed that a crisis emerged.

Isaac's report was considered by a Board of Inquiry established to investigate rural minimum wages. This Board was chaired by Professor Donald Cochrane, a Professor of Economics at Monash University, and included Dr. Richard Shand, a "primitive affluence" theorist (see Shand 1965). Their policy recommendations, which were eventually put into practice in 1972, were identical to those advanced by Isaac. Their impact is shown in Table 6.24. Only the wage for a single man increased, and this was by $A2.91. The wage of a married man decreased by $A1.54, the wage of a married man with one child decreased by amounts ranging from $A2.85 to $A4.13, depending on the sex and age of the child, and the wage of a man with more than one child decreased by amounts ranging from $A4.16 upward. This wage was described as "somewhat akin though not identical to the concept of a family wage" (Cochrane Report 1970: 60).

Table 6.24
The impact of the Cochrane report recommendations

Family unit	Value of rations 1971 $A		All cash wage 1972	Increase (+) or decrease (-)	
	min	max		min	max
M	4.99		5.90	+0.91	
M + W	7.44		5.90	-1.54	
M + W + 1	8.75	10.03	5.90	-2.85	-4.13
M + W + 2	10.06	12.62	5.90	-4.16	-6.72

Note: The dependants' allowance varies according to the age and sex of the children and does not take into account accomodation expenses.
Source: Cochrane Report (1970: 115).

While the practical outcome of the Cochrane Report recommendations was identical to that of the Isaac Report, the theoretical justification was slightly different. Less emphasis was placed on "subsistence sector income" as a criterion for wage setting and more placed on profits. It was argued that "although the notion behind the Lewis concept provides a useful guide to the direction in which wage policy should move, we do not believe the concept itself is sufficiently refined to use for wage determination purposes" (ibid.: 49). The Cochrane Report recommended that the wage be set "at the highest level which the capacity of rural industry and the economy can sustain" (ibid.: 116), and explicitly argued that wives living on plantations should subsidize the wages of their husbands by preparing gardens to compensate for the loss of the marriage allowance (ibid.: 116).

The $A0.50 increase in wages in June 1974 was the recommendation of another Board of Inquiry. The membership of this board included two employer representatives, two employee representatives, Professor Anthony Clunies-Ross (former Professor of Economics at the University of PNG), and a chairman. One of the employee representatives on the Board resigned because he felt that the recommendations were biased in favor of employers.

The most significant feature of this Board's report was what the unions called the "increasing misery clause." This was a clause that provided for an automatic adjustment mechanism for wages over time. The essence of it was that when profits were rising, real wages were to remain constant; when profits were falling, real wages were to fall. Thus, if profits fluctuated over time, real wages would steadily fall in a step-like fashion. Only in the unlikely event of a fall in the consumer price index was it possible for real wages to rise. The clause read:

> If in the year concerned a is less algebraically than b the minimum wage per week shall be fixed as (100 plus a) per cent of $6.40 calculated to the nearest multiple of $0.10; and if in the year concerned a is greater algebraically than b, the minimum wage per week shall be fixed as (100 plus c) per cent of $6.40, calculated to the nearest multiple of $0.10. (Waka Board Report 1974: App. 7)

where a is the percentage change in the consumer price index, b the percentage change in the export price index, and c the arithmetic mean of a and b.

Thus, if $a < b$ then

$$w_t = (100 + a)\, 6.40 = \text{constant real wage}$$

If $a > b$ then

$$w_t = (100 + c)\, 6.40 = \text{falling real wage because } a > c$$

A negative a was to be treated as a rise, and in this way real wages could rise.

Another significant feature of this Board's report was the decision to increase the deduction for deferred pay from \$A0.50 to \$A1.00. Thus, at the end of his contract, an agreement worker was to get \$A104 instead of \$A52, with corresponding reductions in his weekly pay. The deferred pay system meant, in effect, that the employer acted as the employee's banker. But in aggregate, it also meant that the employees were giving the employers an interest-free loan every year of around \$A2 million.

When the Board made its recommendations the Minister for National Development immediately set up a new board to look into the question of agreement labor wages because he "was not entirely satisfied that the interests of rural workers had been safeguarded" (Maro Board Report 1974: 2). It was significant that he appointed as a member of the Board P. G. Williamson, an economist in the "development of underdevelopment" school of A. Gunder Frank.

In this report we are given a rather different view of the agreement labor system. The report argued that,

Development is not likely to occur, either spontaneously or through government action, in these areas when a large proportion of able-bodied men are absent. The system of migrant labour itself (combined with a low wage policy) may in fact be contributing to the "development of under development" in those areas it is supposed to be assisting. (Maro Board Report 1974: 45)

It argued that the low productivity of plantation labor was largely the result of bad management rather than the lack of skill and sophistication of the workers, citing evidence that "about 43% of coconut palms were planted at least 50 years ago and thus are senile or near senile. Replantings in the last eight years were sufficient to replace only about one fifth of the old palms" (ibid.: 11). So far as this Board was concerned, the fact that the worker was not getting paid a family wage was evidence that "the village sector has been subsidizing the plantation sector for many years" (ibid.: 6), an argument previously put forward by Belshaw (1957: 244) and Rowley ([1965] 1972: 110–11). The Maro Board recommended the abolition of this subsidy and proposed a wage of $A8.00 as a first step toward this end. This wage included a 12.5% loading on a single man's wage. This was to be adjusted every six months to maintain real wages in the face of inflation. The "increasing misery" clause of the Waka Board was abandoned.

Reviewing this period of PNG's wages history, a union advocate argued that wage theorizing of the "gloomy professors of the dismal science" (i.e. the neoclassicals) was "based on tendentious or false assumptions, and justified by colored and dubious logic" (PSA 1974: 2). It is difficult to disagree with this assessment.

(d) Free labor (wage-labor), 1927 to present. In 1927 a bill was passed to allow for the employment of free wage-labor. The aim of the bill was "to make ready for the time when the indenture system may be abolished." It was argued in 1927 that "when the time does come, the less will be the upheaval and the inconvenience that would follow the substitution of free labor for the indenture system" (Annual Report, Papua 1927: 2).

Indentured labor and agreement labor prepares the way for that time. It introduces the worker to capitalist commodity production and exchange and in so doing widens his horizons. He quickly becomes aware of the subordinate status of labor *vis-à-vis* capital. Ex-agreement workers "nowadays speak of having been tricked by Europeans who 'ate' the profits of their labors, putting aside a minute proportion for wages. . . . [They] reiterate the point that however much they as wage-earners benefit, the owners of the business (employers) benefit more" (M. Strathern 1975: 33, 38). They, therefore, do not reengage as agreement workers but instead return home to the gift economy and engage in sideline commodity production to acquire the cash they need to pay taxes and to buy commodities. Those who cannot engage in sideline commodity production for whatever reason (e.g. remoteness of village) engage in sideline free wage-labor to acquire the cash they need. Thus there emerges a group of people willing to offer their labor-power for sale for a limited period of time.

Even as early as 1928 we find this process evolving. For example, in the Papuan Annual Report of that year we read that there were "thousands of experienced native workers in the villages willing to work under contract for twelve-month periods" (Annual Report, Papua 1928: 65). However, employers were unwilling to employ this free labor. They feared that they would have no control over it and preferred indentured labor under a two- to three-year contract.

In the post-Second World War period we find a continuation of this willingness to work as free wage-labor for a short period of time; and, what is more, capital willing to employ it. The intention of the worker only to stay for a short period of time is important. The gift economy is the reference point and the commodity economy is seen to be a parallel road upon which one travels for a short while before hopping off (M. Strathern 1975: 313). A short sojourn as a free wage-laborer on the commodity road appeals to the adventurous young, for whom it is often regarded as a form of initiation. But the reality is that the commodity economy is the high road and the gift economy the low road, in that the former dominates the latter.

The commodity economy transforms the gift economy and for a variety of reasons a short stay tends to become a long stay and the date of return becomes more indefinite. Wage-labor frees one from the web of gift-debt but traps one in a wage-labor contract where all money earned must be spent on food and housing. As they say, "We just eat up our money! All our money goes on food and we are fed up!" (ibid.: 110). This makes it take just that much longer to accumulate the money that they are expected to take home as gifts. Eventually wives are brought to the towns to accompany their husbands. They become completely dependent on their husbands because of the unavailability of jobs, and whatever status and power they had in the gift economy is lost. They become subordinate to men, who are in turn subordinate to employers. Their indirect subordination to employers acquires a new dimension when they begin to produce children in the urban areas, for these children are the future free wage-laborers. They make short trips to the gift economy but these short stays tend to become shorter rather than longer. Their education, which is usually not more than six years, prepares them for a different life. They have been raised to reproduce labor-power as a commodity.

Among migrant workers the clan, and the relations of domination
and control associated with it, loses all significance. Everybody is an
equal in this context. "There is strong pressure . . . against anyone who
publicly tries to behave like a big-man in the town context" (ibid.: 372).

Table 6.25
Trade union membership, Papua New Guinea, 1963–1974

	1958	1963	1965	1966	1967	1974
P.S.A.	nil	2,064	3,879	6,432	8,030	15,885
Other	nil	2,556	5,504	7,043	19,284	24,335
Total	nil	4,620	9,383	13,475	27,314	40,220

Source: R. M. Martin (169: 16); PNGLIB9 (1972).

The growth and development of the unions of free wage-labor is shown
in Table 6.25. The first unions were formed in 1959 and the union movement grew rapidly over the next fifteen years: in 1966 membership of
unions totaled 13,475 persons; by 1974, 40,220 people were members of
unions, representing approximately 33% of the total workforce and 45%
of the free wage-labor workforce. The Public Service Association is by
far the biggest union. Of the total 1974 membership of 40,220 people,
15,885 or 39% belonged to the Public Service Association. However, it
must be remembered that 43% of the urban workforce are employed by
the state.

The impact of the unions on the wage structure of the economy is
shown in Table 6.26. It is clear that since 1972 a dramatic widening in
the rural/urban wage differential has occurred. This reflects the relative
success the different unions have had in fighting for a wage that reflects
the reproduction cost of supplying labor-power as a commodity. The urban unions have almost succeeded in eliminating the subsidy from the
gift economy, but the rural unions have barely begun to do so. We have
already seen in the case of agreement labor, for example, that the August
1974 wage increase was only a step in the direction of a family wage: it
represented a single man's wage plus a loading of 12.5%.

In 1974, a detailed investigation into urban wages was made. A Board
was formed, chaired by Charles Lepani, that included no economists. It
considered a large body of evidence given by community development
workers, employees, housewives, teachers, and economists (including

Table 6.26
Rural and urban minimum wages, PNG, 1961–1976 ($A weekly)

	Rural (plantation) minimum wage	Urban (Pt. Moresby) minimum wage	Urban rural ratio (%)
1961	4.61	6.00	130
1962	4.61	6.00	130
1963	4.61	6.00	130
1964	4.61	6.00	130
1965	4.61	6.50	141
1966	4.61	6.50	141
1967	4.86	6.50	134
1968	4.86	6.50	134
1969	4.86	6.50	134
1970	4.86	7.00	144
1971	4.99	8.00	160
1972	5.90	13.80	234
1973	5.90	13.80	234
1974	8.00	20.00	250
1975	8.50	25.80	303
1976	9.43	27.18	288

Source: PNG Department of Labour

myself). The evidence showed among other things that primary school children were suffering from malnutrition. The Board recommended a wage of $A25.00. This figure, it was argued, was a conservative estimate of the cost to maintain a man, his wife, and one child. In other words, in the opinion of this Board the gift economy was still subsidizing the production of labor-power as a commodity at a wage of $A25.00.

The propensity for neoclassical economists to analyze wage differentials such as these in terms of marginal cost instead of reproduction cost produces many naïve theories of the transformation process. The Harris–Todaro model of migration (J. Harris and Todaro 1970) is one, and this model has been applied to the analysis of PNG by the World Bank (1978). It has argued that the widening urban/rural wage ratio "has contributed to excessive migration from rural to urban areas and to high urban unemployment rates" (ibid.: 36). Doubtless a high correlation could be found between the wage differential and migration but this would explain nothing.

The "rural/urban" distinction for wage purposes is based on politics and not geography. This is brought out clearly in Table 6.27, which shows the population of the principal towns and the classification of these towns for wage purposes. All towns above 2500 in population are classified as urban, but below that figure a number of anomalies occur. For example, Mendi, with a population of 2493, is "rural" whereas Vanimo, with a population of 1877, is "urban." The greatest anomaly of all is Bwagaoia. This place has a population of around 200 and yet it is classified as "urban." However, it just so happens that it is the home of a prominent trade union leader! It should also be noted that within the category "urban," there are two divisions and that these divisions bear little relation to the actual population of the towns.

Table 6.27
Urban populations and wage divisions, 1974

Urban area	Population[a]	Wage division
Port Moresby	76,507	Urban I
Lae	38,707	Urban I
Rabaul	26,619	Urban I
Madang	16,865	Urban I
Wewak	15,015	Urban I
Arawa-Kieta-Panguna	14,431	Urban I
Goroka	12,065	Urban I
Mt. Hagen	10,621	Urban I
Daru	5,744	Urban II
Popondetta	4,494	Urban I
Lorengau	4,323	Urban II
Bulolo	4,001	Urban II
Kavieng	3,301	Urban I
Kerema	2,653	Urban II
Alotau	2,499	Urban I
Mendi	2,493	Rural
Kundiawa	2,380	Rural
Angoram	2,159	Rural
Sohana	2,158	Rural
Kaimantu	2,124	Urban II
Kokopo	2,062	Rural
Samarai	1,948	Urban II
Wau	1,914	Urban II
Vanimo	1,877	Urban II

Table 6.27 continued

Urban area	Population[a]	Wage division
Kimbe	1,172	Rural
Kwikila	1,154	Rural
Kiunga	1,114	Rural
Maprik	1,081	Rural
Wabag	1,077	Rural
Aitape	1,035	Rural
Kerowagi	1,030	Rural
Sogeri	1,013	Rural
Banz	998	Rural
Ambunti	989	Rural
Balimo	765	Rural
Minj	744	Rural
Buin	727	Rural
Kagamuga	710	Rural
Laiagam	691	Rural
Bogia	678	Rural
Bereina	670	Rural
Kikori	670	Rural
Baimuru	666	Rural
Tapini	660	Rural
Losuia	625	Rural
Tari	604	Rural
Miak	586	Rural
.	.	.
.	.	.
.	.	.
Bwagaoia	200[b]	Urban II

[a] Includes expatriates.
[b] An estimate. This town is not classified 'urban' by the Statistics Dept.
Source: Census, 1971.

Secondly, the reference point for understanding migration is not "rural" employment but the gift economy. In fact, because many plantations are situated near the big towns many people used to sign up for agreement labor so that they could move to the towns. In a study of migration from one highlands tribe it was revealed that of 41 agreement workers recruited for work on plantations, only 21 returned to the village. The rest deserted the plantation and went to live in the town. It is also interesting to note that these workers were recruited over the period 1956 to 1971, and that of the 18 recruited between 1967 and 1971, *all* deserted the plantation. This tendency for second-generation workers to desert is widespread (M. Strathern 1975: 46–47). This pattern of migration cannot be explained in terms of the wage differential because it emerged before 1971, the year the differential started to widen.

Table 6.28
Government employees in urban workforce in Papua New Guinea at June 30, 1972

	Indigenes		Non-indigenes		Total	
	No.	(%)	No.	(%)	No.	(%)
Government	20,908	(33)	8,134	(13)	29,042	(46)
Non-government	27,666	(44)	6,827	(11)	34,493	(54)
	48,574	(77)	14,961	(24)	63,535	(100)

Source: PNGLIB9 (1972).

Table 6.29
Wages and salaries of urban workforce in PNG for the financial year to June 30, 1972

	Indigenes		Non-indigenes		Total	
	($A'00 000)	%	($A'00 000)	%	($A'00 000)	%
Government	713	(32)	881	(39)	1,594	(71)
Non-government	271	(12)	380	(17)	651	(29)
	984	(44)	1,261	(56)	2,245	(100)

Source: PNGLIB9 (1972).

The role of the state. The emergence of free wage-labor cannot be understood independently of the role of the state. Since the war it has become a major employer of labor. This can be seen by examining Table 6.28. Of the total urban workforce of 63,535 in 1972, government employees numbered 29,042 or 46% of the total. Of these, 20,908 were indigenes and 8134 non-indigenes, mainly Australians. The latter were the most highly paid members of the workforce. They accounted for 13% of the urban workforce yet appropriated 39% of the urban wages bill (see Table 6.29). The average earnings of these public servants is three times that of Papua New Guinean public servants and eleven times that of Papua New Guineans employed by private capital. The latter group were clearly the most exploited of all workers. They comprised 44% of the total urban workforce, yet their share of the wage bill was only 12%.

The state, then, has emerged as an employer of relatively highly paid workers. But what has been the origin of the capital to employ these

Table 6.30
Government budget receipts, 1955–1973

	1955 ($A'000)	(%)	1960 ($A'000)	(%)	1965 ($A'000)	(%)	1970 ($A'000)	(%)	1972 ($A'000)	(%)	1973 ($A'000)	(%)
Internal revenue	6,308	(31)	13,188	(34)	27,929	(31)	72,442	(37)	95,253	(45)	93,068	(43)
Australian Govt. grant	14,257	(69)	25,617	(66)	55,999	(62)	97,271	(50)	69,875	(33)	78,180	(36)
Australian Govt. loans	—	—	—	—	—	—	5000	(2)	11,700	(6)	9,450	(4)
General loans	—	—	—	—	6,318	(7)	19,236[a]	(10)	25,541	(12)	27,600	(13)
International loans	—	—	—	—	—	—	1,384	(1)	8,131	(4)	7,869	(4)
Other	—	—	—	—	—	—	344	—	—	—	—	—
Total	20,565	(100)	38,805	(100)	90,246	(100)	195,677	(100)	210,500	(100)	216,167	(100)

[a] Includes $A12.5 million raised for purchase of equity in Bougainville Copper Pty Ltd. Of this, $A3.6m was borrowed from the Commonwealth Loans Consolidation and Investment Reserve by Private Treaty Loans.
Source: Compendium (1973: 85).

workers? The answer is supplied in Table 6.30. Since 1960 there has been a massive injection of Australian aid into the country. In current price terms, it rose from $A25m in 1960 to $A97m in 1970 and accounted for 50% of budget receipts for that year. This can be explained. Until the 1960s, Australian policies in PNG were based on the assumption that Australia would remain in administrative control for a long time to come. Its main function was to ensure a cessation of warfare between antagonistic tribes and clans, and to keep plantation capital supplied with agreement labor. This policy was criticized by a visiting UN Mission in 1962 and the Australian government began serious moves to prepare PNG for self-government. But the new policies differed little from those of old. They encouraged mining capital to reenter by offering it a generous tax holiday. When it entered the government helped it become established by literally bulldozing villagers off the land that was needed. The mine that was subsequently established in the Bougainville District began operations in 1972 and had a dramatic effect on the economy in Gross Domestic Product terms. In 1970 the GDP was $A531m but had doubled by 1974, when it was estimated to be $A1.003bn. However, the massive $A158m that the company earned in the first year of its operation went untaxed because of the provisions in the original agreement (it was subsequently renegotiated); furthermore, it had a marginal effect on employment as the capital-intensive methods of production used needed only 3000 men to operate them.

The main impact of Australia's aid, then, has been the development of a massive bureaucracy based on the Australian model, and staffed by bureaucrats fed on Australian food. Consider Table 6.31, which shows the value of commodities imported into the country in 1972–73. Commodities valued at $A121,340,000 were imported from Australia. This represented 54% of the total value of imports. But with food, one of the most important imports apart from machinery, 84% of all imports came from Australia. Thus it is obvious that whatever capital entered PNG as aid from Australia soon found its way back to Australia to pay for food and other imports.

Table 6.32 disaggregates the food imports by commodity and contrasts the consumption patterns of the well-paid expatriates with the poorly paid Papua New Guineans. The typical diet of an urban Papua New Guinean consists of rice, canned meat, and white bread. All of these come from Australia; very little of what he eats is produced in PNG. Canned fish is becoming popular and most of this comes from Japan. For example, 90% of the $A4,574,000 worth of canned fish was Japanese.

Table 6.31
Value of commodities imported from Australia and elsewhere, 1972–1973

Commodity	From Australia ($A'000)	Total value of imports	Aust. as % total
Food	40,129	47,734	84
Beverages and tobacco	3,154	5,025	63
Fuels	2,103	11,851	18
Animal and vegetable oils	314	357	88
Chemicals	8,558	12,435	69
Manufactured goods	23,352	39,214	59
Machinery	27,503	73,533	37
Miscellaneous	16,227	35,347	46
	121,340	225,496	54

Source: International Trade Statistics, 1972/73, Bureau of Statistics, Pt Moresby.

The expatriate has a much more wholesome diet. He consumes fresh meat, dairy products, and fresh fruit and vegetables. Hardly any of these commodities are produced in PNG; they have to be imported and most of them come from Australia, as Table 6.32 shows.

These statistics illustrate how plantation capital, in partnership with the state, develops underdevelopment. Plantation agriculture is not geared to supplying food demand within the plantation economy. Instead, it is geared to overseas consumption requirements. Essential food inputs have to be imported and foreign aid raises the effective demand for such food.

The emergence of primary commodity production

In the previous section it has been shown how the entry of plantation and mining capital into PNG, aided and abetted by the state, transformed labor-power into a commodity. A second phase in this process was the transformation of indentured and agreement laborers into smallholder commodity producers and the emergence of primary commodity production.

The state played an active part in this transformation process too. It supplied negative encouragement in the form of taxes and positive encouragement in the form of advice and the supply of infrastructure.

Table 6.32

Value of food, beverages, and tobacco imported from Australia and elsewhere, 1972–1973

	From Australia ($A'000)	Total value of imports	Aust. as % total
Mostly indigenous consumption			
Canned meat	6,270	6,681	94
Canned fish	164	4,574	3
White rice	6,767	6,778	99
Flour	2,164	2,234	97
Sugar	3,380	3,499	96
Flavoured water	699	700	99
Beer	565	588	96
Rough tobacco	557	1,443	39
Total	20,566	26,497	78
Mostly expatriate consumption			
Fresh meat	6,071	6,385	95
Dairy products and eggs	2,849	3,119	92
Frozen fish	241	589	41
Brown rice	1,031	1,031	100
Cakes, biscuits, etc.	2,846	3,151	90
Fruit and vegetables	3,435	3,899	88
Sugar preparations and honey	668	88	75
Coffee, tea, cocoa, spices	921	1,349	68
Wines and spirits	881	1,733	51
Cigars and cigarettes	449	1,003	44
Total	19,392	23,147	84

Source: International Trade Statistics, 1972/73, Bureau of Statistics, Pt Moresby.

The use of the tax weapon was a common device in the colonial world for forcing people into primary commodity production. It also had the effect of forcing returned laborers to resell their labor-power in those areas where marketing facilities did not develop. This was particularly so in those areas with unfavorable natural endowments, for example the swamplands of Sepik, Gulf, and Western Districts. The natural endowment of a district also governs the type of commodity that could be produced there.

Consider Table 6.33, which shows indigenous primary commodity production by district and crop in 1971. The island and coastal districts specialize in the production of copra and cocoa, whilst the highland districts have tended to specialize in the production of coffee because of natural comparative advantage.

Table 6.33

Indigenous primary commodity production by district, PNG, 1971

| | Area bearing (hectares) | | | | | |
	Copra	Cocoa	Coffee	Other[a]	Total	%
Island Districts						
Milne Bay	9,896	15	261	—	10,172	8
Bougainville	12,023	4,091	149	9	16,272	13
New Britain	26,952	6,379	42	—	33,373	27
New Ireland	12,990	376	23	2	13,391	11
Manus	1,673	65	2	—	1,740	1
Total Island	63,534	10,926	477	11	74,948	60
Coastal Districts						
Western	480	—	4	—	484	1
Gulf	5,425	—	68	180	5,673	4
Central	7,036	4	101	64	7,205	6
Northern	1,178	1,032	925	99	3,234	3
Morobe	3,007	214	2,232	—	5,453	4
Madang	6,232	891	377	—	7,500	6
Sepik	5,700	129	1,812	—	7,641	6
Total Coastal	29,058	2,270	5,519	343	37,190	30
Highland Districts						
Eastern (inc. Chimbu)	—	—	7,755	279	8,034	6
Western	—	—	4,476	710	5,186	4
Southern	—	—	117	105	222	—
Total Highlands	—	—	12,348	1,094	13,442	10
Total PNG	92,592	13,196	18,344	1,448	125,580	100

[a] Rubber in the lowlands; tea and pyrethrum in the highlands.
Source: PNG Summary of Statistics, 1973–73 (Table 60).

The natural endowment of an area does not determine the choice of a crop, it only provides the constraints. The demands of private capital and the policies of the state are the critical determinants of what is grown. In this respect it should be noted that the crops introduced—copra, coffee, cocoa, and so on—are all export crops produced to satisfy foreign consumption demands and not local demands. Of course, the only local demand would come from wage-laborers and other workers; but these were fed imported rice, canned fish, and tinned meat, as we have seen from Table 6.32 above.

From Table 6.33 it can be seen that 60% of the total area bearing cash crops was located in the island districts, with New Britain

District accounting for almost half of this. These were the areas of first recruitment for plantation capital as indentured laborers. In other words they constituted the first labor frontier. The second labor frontier was the coastal districts of the mainland; they have the second largest area under crop, 30%. The highlands districts constituted the last labor frontier and they have the lowest area under crop, 10%. These figures illustrate in aggregate the process of transformation of agreement laborers into smallholder commodity producers and the accompanying process of the transformation of the products of the land into commodities. When an agreement laborer returns home and finds that he needs money to pay taxes and also to satisfy his new-found needs for commodities such as clothing, steel axes, and tobacco, he satisfies these needs by planting a coconut tree here or a coffee tree there and in so doing begins sideline commodity production within the context of a gift economy. In some cases it becomes mainline production and this introduces stresses and strains into the gift economy that threaten its very existence.

Table 6.34 illustrates some of the conflicts that emerge. These data were collected by Epstein (1965) from one village in the New Britain District of New Guinea that was part of the area first colonized by the Germans in 1883. The men from this village supplied their labor up until the beginning of the Second World War, because the lack of infrastructural development gave them few options. However, as this situation changed, the returned laborers began to plant coconut and copra trees. Other households followed suit owing to the demonstration effect; but the time lag involved created a division between the ex-laborer households and the others. By 1960 the ex-laborers had planted 668 coconut trees and 1824 cocoa trees compared to the 445 coconut trees and 925 cocoa trees planted by the others.

However, cutting across this schism is the elder/junior division that is so important for the gift economy. Within the ex-laborer group the elders planted many more trees than the juniors. The same is true within the "other households" group. However, it is the ex-laborers who first took the initiative to go into commodity production, and the trees planted by the elder non-laborers must be seen as an attempt to maintain control in a changing situation.

Table 6.34
The process of differentiation among households, Rapitok, New Britain, PNG, 1960

| | Ex–laborer households | | | Other households | | | |
| | Elders | Juniors | Total | Elders | Juniors | | Total |
					Married	Single	
Area under food crops (acres/household)	1.52	1.37	2.89	1.10	1.02	1.40	3.52
Area under tree crops (acres/household)	8.73	4.67	13.40	6.62	3.92	0.98	11.52
No. of coconut trees (per household)	476	192	668	260	123	62	445
No. of cocoa trees (per household)	1261	563	1824	527	398	—	925

Source: Epstein (1965: 179).

Similar processes were going on in other areas. Consider Table 6.35, for example. This shows the pattern of coffee planting in the highland districts. The first area of the highlands opened up for labor recruiting was the Eastern Highlands in the late 1940s. As the laborers returned from their spell as agreement workers they went into commodity production and the number of trees planted rose accordingly: 408 in 1955, 3979 in 1960, and 13,914 in 1965, by which time the income from coffee was estimated to be $A3,635,000. When this area was exhausted of recruits the Western Highlands was moved into. A similar process was set in motion there: 19 trees were planted in 1955, 451 in 1960, and 4900 in 1965, yielding an estimated income of $A1,266,000 for that year. By the late 1950s the last frontier, the Southern Highlands, was opened to recruiters. The planting of coffee trees only began in 1960 when it was recorded that five trees were planted. By 1964 the number of trees planted had risen to 80.

The ex-agreement laborer become primary commodity producing farmer does not restrict his activities to the sphere of production. He moves into the sphere of exchange and sets up business as a small shopkeeper. There has been a phenomenal growth in the number of indigenous-owned trade stores in PNG in recent years and, of course, this

Table 6.35
Indigenous coffee production, highlands, PNG, 1955–1965

Year	Eastern Highlands		Western Highlands		Southern Highlands	
	Trees planted	Income ($A'000s)	Trees planted	Income ($A'000s)	Trees planted	Income ($A'000s)
1955	408	n.a.	19	n.a.	—	—
1956	425	n.a.	30	n.a.	—	—
1957	700	n.a.	35	n.a.	—	—
1958	1,100	n.a.	140	n.a.	—	—
1959	3,122	290	202	30	—	—
1960	3,979	n.a.	451	n.a.	5	n.a.
1961	4,610	n.a.	886	n.a.	30	n.a.
1962	6,155	n.a.	1,107	n.a.	39	n.a.
1963	7,391	n.a.	2,257	n.a.	51	n.a.
1964	10,498	n.a.	2,648	n.a.	80	n.a.
1965	13,914	3,635	4,900	1,266	n.a.	2

Source: Highlands Labour Report (1969: 15-16).

growth and development process has mirrored the growth and development of primary commodity production.

This can be seen by examining Table 6.36, which summarizes the results of a trade store survey in 1968–69. Consider the data for the highlands districts. This shows the familiar pattern of development. In the Eastern Highlands, the first area of labor recruitment and primary commodity development, 2190 trade stores had been developed by 1968–69. This compares with a figure of 218 for the Southern Highlands, the last labor frontier. As we might expect, these stores have a high failure rate in the early stages of their development. There is a contradiction between the gift-credit system of exchange and the money-credit system of exchange. Many storekeepers are obligated to extend money-credit—often unlimited—to their kinspeople and this brings financial ruin in a very short time. On the other hand, unpaid labor can be found to run the shop (Trade Store Survey 1968–1969: 10). In the latter stages of their development the stores become more profitable as they move from being a sideline activity to being a mainline one. Compare the average annual sales per store per district. In the island and coastal districts, which have had a much longer contact with the commodity economy, the figures are much higher: $A487 for the island districts and $A715 for the coastal districts, compared to $A269 for the highland districts.

Table 6.36
Indigenous retail trading—private trade stores, 1968–1969

	Number of stores	Total annual sales $A	Av. sales per store $A
Island Districts			
Milne Bay	118	79,400	672
Bougainville	299	117,800	393
New Britain	565	272,300	482
New Ireland	155	86,800	560
Manus	92	42,000	456
Total Island	1,229	598,300	487
Coastal Districts			
Western	56	37,700	673
Gulf	348	309,500	889
Central	463	553,600	1,195
Northern	225	96,000	426
Morobe	596	261,900	439
Madang	356	209,600	588
Sepik	212	144,300	681
Total Coastal	2,256	1,612,600	715
Highland Districts			
Eastern	2,190	465,100	212
Western	593	304,800	514
Southern	218	37,500	172
Total Highlands	3,001	807,400	269
Total PNG	6,486	3,018,300	465

Source: Trade Store Survey, 1968–1969 (5-6).

These stores, apart from providing their owners with profits, provide the villagers with their new diet: rice, canned fish, flour, and sugar. As the Trade Store Survey reported, "Examination of stock holdings shows an almost total import content, with canned fish, flour, rice and sugar predominating" (ibid.: 4)

Private trade stores are not the only form of retail outlet established by the people. Cooperative stores also figure prominently and in many areas they were the first store to be established. As the Trade Store Survey reports,

[C]o-operative stores usually operated in conjunction with co-operative marketing of produce such as cocoa and copra. These consumer/producer co-operative societies operate successfully in many parts of the Territory. In other areas, e.g. in the vicinity of Port Moresby, the societies only operate a store. In some villages, competition from group and individual trade stores has forced the liquidation of the co-operative trade store. Co-operative stores do not normally develop where private trade stores provide an adequate service. (Trade Store Survey 1968–1969: 17)

Data on the cooperative stores are given in Table 6.37. Comparing this table with the previous one, the striking fact that is revealed is the size of the cooperative. In 1968–69 the annual sales per cooperative were $A9310. This compares with $A465 for the private trade store. It is also interesting to note that by 1969 only one cooperative was established in the highlands, whereas 3001 private trade stores had been established.

The integration of this local merchant capital with foreign merchant capital provides the means by which a rise in export prices is translated into a rise in imports of beer, canned fish, canned meat, and rice rather than in the expanded reproduction of local primary commodity production. In other words, it is the means by which the economy becomes an integral part of the global system of commodity production and reproduction. The high coffee prices that followed the destruction of the Brazilian trees in 1976 illustrate this point. As a highlands politician reported in 1976,

> From my own recent fact-finding in the Eastern Highlands, I think I could claim that the people in most Highland areas have more than doubled their purchases of such items as beer, tinned fish, rice and frozen meats in the past three months. Heads of families in Highland rural areas are in some cases spending on average more than $A20 a day on these goods. Men making new gardens are even being scorned by the community. (Holloway 1976: 4)

The emergence of land as a commodity

Only 3.3% of the total land area of PNG has been alienated. The bulk of this was appropriated by the state (see Table 6.38). Foreign companies

Table 6.37

Indigenous retail trading—co-operative stores, 1968–1969

	Number of societies	Annual sales $A	Average sales per society $A
Island Districts			
Milne Bay	36	245,700	6,825
Bougainville	12	203,400	16,950
New Britain	23	244,600	10,635
New Ireland	26	75,200	2,892
Manus	11	119,000	10,818
Total Island	108	887,900	8,221
Coastal Districts			
Western	3	138,600	46,200
Gulf	33	288,300	8,736
Central	50	317,500	6,350
Northern	8	51,000	6,375
Morobe	7	86,100	12,300
Madang	14	54,100	3,864
Sepik	12	109,100	9,092
Total Coastal	127	1,044,700	8,225
Highland Districts			
Eastern	1	264,700	264,700
Western	—	—	
Southern	—	—	
Total Highlands	1	264,700	264,700
Total PNG	236	2,197,300	9,310

Source: Trade Store Survey, 1968–1969 (6).

Table 6.38

Alienated land in Papua New Guinea, 1968

Owner	Hectares	%
Foreign	218,919	0.47
Administration	1,308,676	2.83
Indigenes: under land tenure		
conversion	1,999	0.03
Total in commodity-form	1,529,594	3.33
Total in gift-form	44,637,962	96.67
Total land area	46,167,557	100.00

Source: Compendium of Statistics for PNG (1973).

alienated 0.47% to establish plantations, while only 0.03% has emerged as a commodity without the use of external force. This was done under the Land (Tenure Conversion) Act of 1963. This Act was developed because it was generally considered that the most efficacious method of promoting the agricultural development of the country lay in the provision of a method which guaranteed individual titles to land (see Fitzpatrick 1980: 114). A conversion order was not made unless all persons with interests in the land agreed to the conversion. An example of this is the case of Sinake Giregire, a leading highland district coffee grower and politician. He now owns approximately 60 acres of land. Formerly this belonged to three clan segments but he was able to gain exclusive control of the land by getting the clan elders to sign land tenure conversion statements like the one below:

> I am a close kinsman of the applicant and I have land interest, according to native custom, in Yanowa. I am clear in my mind that if this application is successful I will lose my rights. But I am happy to renounce these rights of mine in favor of Sinake who has worked to develop the land. (Quoted in Finney 1973: 112)

It is not difficult to understand why such a small amount of land has been alienated in this way. It requires people to choose to be landless or to simply give away some of their rights to land without compensation. Illiterate villagers, who have different perceptions of the nature of the transaction, can be tricked into signing such statements; but tenure secured in this way is not very secure. Land is the ultimate inalienable gift and, because of the complex hierarchy of rights over it, it is not easily converted into the simple private property right of an individual. Some recent research by Fingleton (1980) on tenure conversion contains many fascinating case studies which illustrate this point. He shows that the apprehension of the people concerned of what was involved in tenure conversion differed significantly from the actual legal situation. The ownership of land under tenure conversion was not seen as excluding clan obligations. For example, Fingleton found that one of the blocks appropriated by Sinake Giregire under tenure conversion was occupied by his "uncles," who were not paying any rent. It seems that the "uncles" agreed to sign the tenure conversion in the first place on the expectation of a share of the profits in a business venture Giregire planned to build on the site. When the business venture did not materialize they repudiated their consent and recovered their occupation of the land. At the time of the research (1978), Giregire had taken no action to recover the land; if and when he does, a serious confrontation will ensue (ibid.: 288–90). In any case, Giregire did not perceive of the transfer as giving him private property rights over the land. As he said: "I can't sell the land. Under our custom if I sold the land I would ruin the clan and ruin my own name" (ibid.: 295).

The strength of the inalienable rights clans have over their lands is particularly well illustrated by the Tolai case of New Britain District. This area is one of the most extreme cases of population pressure in New Guinea. It is also an area with the longest history of cash cropping. Furthermore, a higher proportion of Tolai land has been alienated by foreign companies for plantation purposes than anywhere else. Yet these pressures have had relatively little effect on the internal distribution of land control between clans. Indeed, there has been a trend toward a more equitable distribution of land through the "persistence of indigenous attitudes towards land tenure" (Salisbury 1970: 91).

> In more recent times, as uncleared land has become scarce, "family land" has commonly been created by the purchase of cleared land . . . though such purchases, despite the payments of large sums of *tabu*, or shell money, do not make the land into "family land" into perpetuity. During the buyer's lifetime, if the original owners return the payment in full, the land is supposed to revert to the original clan. If the owner has not designated an heir before his death, the land is transferred according to the normal matrilineal rules and becomes clan land. (Salisbury 1970: 70)

This preference for clan ownership of land is a PNG-wide phenomenon. In 1973 a Commission of Inquiry was set up to investigate the land question. The Commission's report, which reflects popular opinion gathered at hundreds of meetings and interviews all over the country, proposed a legal regime that builds on a "customary base." The basic social structure of the people was to be maintained and the Commission was concerned not to recommend either collective or individualistic extremes. They were particularly concerned to avoid the creation of a landless proletariat which the forces of colonization had set in motion. Another matter to which the Commission gave particular emphasis was the return of alienated plantation land. As a result the government enacted the Lands Acquisition Act of 1974, under which the government buys up foreign-owned land for redistribution to the customary land-owning groups. This is being put into effect, albeit slowly, and some plantation land has returned to clan ownership.

It can be seen, then, that there are many legal and social forces working against the emergence of land as a commodity in PNG. These forces have created a contradictory situation, whereby cash crops are being produced on clan land. In terms of the analytical categories developed in this book, commodities (cash crops) are being produced by a gift (land). This gives land an implicit exchange-value and leads to conflict as different people struggle to gain from this. Not only does it set the individual against the clan, it also sets clan against clan as neighboring groups argue about the location of clan boundaries. Colonization had the effect of freezing boundaries at the time of contact. Boundaries were traditionally in a state of flux and, with the freezing of these boundaries at an arbitrary point in time, some clans found themselves in possession of land to which they held few rights, while others found themselves dispossessed of land they held strong claims to. Subsequent transfers of land have been made to overcome some of these problems, but where the land in question was producing commodities new problems have arisen (Hide 1971: 48). This has created endless disputes, some of which have sparked off interclan warfare.

Another effect of the nonemergence of land as a commodity has been to create the necessary conditions for gift exchange to flourish and develop under the impact of capitalism. This is examined in the next chapter.

CHAPTER VII

The transformation of commodities into gifts in colonial Papua New Guinea

This chapter has a threefold purpose. The first is to develop the analysis of the previous chapter. In this respect it attempts to demonstrate the following proposition.

Proposition I. *The gift economy of PNG has not been destroyed by colonization, but has effloresced. This is reflected in a tendency for European commodities to be transformed into gifts.*

The second purpose of the chapter is to show that gift reproduction in PNG is either the restricted or delayed type and, in so doing, to provide further illustration of two propositions advanced in Chapter IV, namely:

Proposition II. *Moiety and phratry clan organization is associated with the restricted exchange of women-gifts, the balanced exchange of thing-gifts, and the leadership of elders.*

Proposition III. *The incremental exchange of thing-gifts presupposes tribe and nation clan organization, and is associated with the delayed exchange of women-gifts and big-manship.*

The third purpose of the chapter is to demonstrate the inadequacy of the neoclassical conception of the "traditional" goods economy by illustrating, once again, Mauss' proposition "that there has never existed, either in the past or in modern primitive societies, anything like a 'natural' economy" ([1925] 1974: 3).

Selected cases from the Sepik District, highlands districts, Milne Bay District, and Central District are considered. These have been chosen to illustrate not only the great diversity to be found in the indigenous economic systems but also the uneven effects of colonization. Particular attention is given to the so-called aberrant cases (e.g. Mundugumor) and to other cases which appear to contradict the propositions.

RESTRICTED REPRODUCTION IN THE SEPIK DISTRICT

While there is a tremendous variety of different forms of kinship organization in this district, the predominant form is restricted reproduction. The cases from this area provide a good illustration of Proposition II because neither incremental gift-exchange nor big-manship is prevalent here.

Case 1. Banaro

The Banaro tribe of the Keram River was studied by Thurnwald in 1912–15. He published his findings in 1916 and no follow-up work has been done since. At the time of Thurnwald's visit the Banaro had a relatively simple system of reproduction. In the ideal case it was identical to one of the models considered in Chapter IV.

Clan organization was of the phratry type and these groups were named as shown in Figure 7.1.

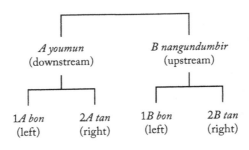

Figure 7.1.

An additional division was between males and females. Using upper case letters for males and lower case for females, these four groups become eight: 1*A*, 1*a*, 2*A*, 2*a*, and so on. These were reproduced as shown in Figure 7.2. On land *A* the males of group 1*A* and their "wives," 1*b*, produce "children" who belong to groups 2*A* and 2*a*. At the same time, on land *B*, the males of group 1*B* and their "wives," 1*a*, produce "children," 2*B* and 2*b*. To enable the process to be continued, 2*A* and 2*B* exchange "sisters." In the next generation the males of group 2*A* and their "wives," 2*b*, reproduce 1*A* and 1*a* on land *A*. On land *B* the males of group 2*B* and their "wives," 2*a*, reproduce 1*B* and 1*b*. 1*A* and 1*B* exchange "sisters," and so the process goes on.

Land	Father	Mother	Son	Daughter
A	1*A*	1*b*	2*A*	2*a*
A	2*A*	2*b*	1*A*	1*a*
B	1*B*	1*a*	2*B*	2*b*
B	2*B*	2*a*	1*B*	1*b*

Figure 7.2. Restricted gift reproduction in Banaro.

Of course this was an ideal and unfortunately Thurnwald does not give us any data on actual exchanges. However, he does mention that when there was a shortage of females, exchanges were made with neighboring tribes (1916: 274). These were not exchanges of women for women, but of women for things and were commodity exchanges according to Thurnwald. If there were no relations of reciprocal dependence established with neighboring tribes, the argument seems reasonable. If correct, it means, then, that when women circulated within the Banaro they assumed the gift-form and when they circulated on the boundaries they assumed the commodity form, or at least were closer to the commodity exchange end of the gift–commodity continuum. This evidence should be seen in the light of Marx's argument that the "exchange of commodities . . . first begins on the boundaries of [clan-based] communities" ([1867] 1965: 91). Marx was referring to things but the argument applies equally to people.

Thurnwald notes that a "gerontocracy derive their power from real or asserted knowledge they possess" (1916: 282). In other words seniority,

rather than competitive gift-giving, was the source of political power in
this society. This accords with the hypothesis advanced.

Case 2. Umeda

The Umeda were studied by Gell (1975) in 1969–70. They too practice
a form of restricted reproduction. But it is much more complicated than
the Banaro system. The Umeda have the familiar phratry-type of clan
organization (see Figure 7.3).

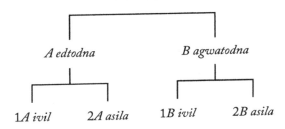

Figure 7.3.

However, to understand the working of the system in the ideal case it
must be assumed, says Gell, that the subgroups 1*A*, 1*B*, 2*A*, and 2*B* are
further subdivided into three groups. It is convenient, for the purposes
of exposition, to relabel the groups as in Figure 7.4. It is these sub-sub-
groups which are exogamous, not the moieties.

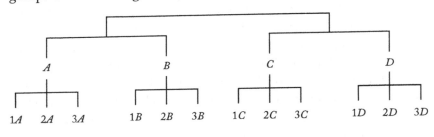

Figure 7.4.

In this system, which is patrilineal and patrilocal, the ideal marriage
is one where a man marries his "father's father's father's sister's son's
son's daughter (*fffzssd*)" (Gell 1975: 67). These facts imply a model of

Land	Father	Mother	Son	Daughter
A	1A	1d	2A	2a
A	2A	2b	3A	3a
A	3A	3c	1A	1a
B	1B	1c	2B	2b
B	2B	2a	3B	3b
B	3B	3d	1B	1b
C	1C	1b	2C	2a
C	2C	2d	3C	3a
C	3C	3a	1C	1a
D	1D	1a	2D	2d
D	2D	2c	3D	3d
D	3D	3b	1D	1d

Figure 7.5. Restricted gift reproduction in Umeda.

gift-reproduction of the form of Figure 7.5. By tracing out the genealogy of a male group it is possible to verify that a male marries his *fffzssd*.
Take 3A, for example. His *f* is 2A, his *ff* is 1A, his *fff* is 3A, his *fffz* is 3a,
his *fffzs* is 1C, his *fffzss* is 2C, and his *fffzssd* is 3c, who is his "wife." The
procedure employed in tracing out a genealogy is analogous to Sraffa's
(1960: Chap. VI) "reduction to dated quantities of labor" method. The
genealogy traces out a logical time sequence rather than a historical time
sequence.

This model is a form of restricted reproduction because it generates
the rather complicated set of restricted exchanges between the twelve
groups seen in Figure 7.6.

These exchanges of women-gifts create gift-debt relations between
the transactors, of the form shown in Figure 7.7. 1A gives to 1D, making 1A dominant over 1D, but 1D simultaneously gives to 1A, creating
mutual indebtedness, thereby balancing, but not cancelling, the relations
of domination. 1C and 1B form the other exchanging pair in this group.
In the next group 2A and 2B form one exchanging pair, 2C and 2D the
other. In the last group, 3A and 3C form one exchanging pair and 3B and
3D the other.

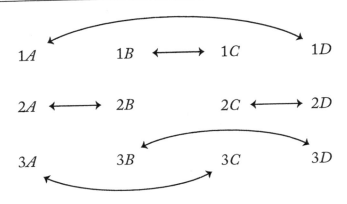

Figure 7.6. Restricted exchange in Umeda.

		Receivers (debtors)												
		1A	1B	1C	1D	2A	2B	2C	2D	3A	3B	3C	3D
Givers	1A	0	0	0	1	0	0	0	0	0	0	0	0
(creditors)	1B	0	0	1	0	0	0	0	0	0	0	0	0
	1C	0	1	0	0	0	0	0	0	0	0	0	0
	1D	1	0	0	0	0	0	0	0	0	0	0	0
	2A	0	0	0	0	0	1	0	0	0	0	0	0
	2B	0	0	0	0	1	0	0	0	0	0	0	0
	2C	0	0	0	0	0	0	0	1	0	0	0	0
	2D	0	0	0	0	0	0	1	0	0	0	0	0
	3A	0	0	0	0	0	0	0	0	0	0	1	0
	3B	0	0	0	0	0	0	0	0	0	0	0	1
	3C	0	0	0	0	0	0	0	0	1	0	0	0
	3D	0	0	0	0	0	0	0	0	0	1	0	0

Figure 7.7. Umeda gift-debt matrix.

Compare with the matrix shown in Figure 7.8, which shows the classificatory kinship terms for Umeda males. The relation between exchanging pairs is called *awk*. This shows that the restricted exchange of women-gifts creates relations of equal order between the transactors. But compare the relation of producer to produced (*aiya*), 1A to 2A, for example.

		1A	1B	1C	1D	2A	2B	2C	2D	3A	3B	3C	3D
Givers	1A	–	3	2	1	5	4	6	7	4	–	–	–
(creditors)	1B	3	–	1	2	4	5	7	6	–	4	–	–
	1C	2	1	–	3	6	7	5	4	–	–	4	–
	1D	1	2	3	–	7	6	4	5	–	–	–	4
	2A	8	–	–	–	–	1	3	2	5	7	4	6
	2B	–	8	–	–	1	–	2	3	7	5	6	4
	2C	–	–	8	–	3	2	–	1	4	6	5	7
	2D	–	–	—	8	2	3	1	–	6	4	7	5
	3A	4	–	–	–	8	–	–	–	–	2	1	3
	3B	–	4	–	–	–	8	–	–	2	–	3	1
	3C	–	–	4	–	–	–	8	–	1	3	–	2
	3D	–	–	–	4	–	–	—	8	3	1	2	–

Receivers (debtors)

Figure 7.8. Umeda kinship terms. *Read:* 1A (row 1) is the *ate* (3) of 1B (col. 2). *Key:* 1 *awk*, 2 *mag*, 3 *ate*, 4 *asi*, 5 *aiya*, 6 *hmun*, 7 *na*, 8 *afse*.

This is a relation of domination and the reciprocal term, *afse*, is one of subordination. However, the relation of producer to reproduced (*asi*), 3A to 1A, for example, is one of equality: the reciprocal of *asi* is *asi*.

It should be obvious that in an interdependent model of reproduction, where inalienable labor is being produced, one group must bear some relation to another; these terms merely show how the Umeda labeled these relations. So whereas the exchange of labor in a commodity economy gives rise to the phenomena of wages, prices, and profits, the exchange of women-gifts in a gift economy gives rise to the phenomenon of classificatory kinship terms. The former are to be explained with reference to the methods of production whereas the latter must be explained with reference to the methods of consumption.

Now this model is clearly an ideal one; it is too complicated to work out in practice. But what we would expect to find is a tendency for the actual groups that make up the society to engage in restricted exchange. Furthermore, because of the nature of the debt established between exchanging partners, incremental gift-giving and big-manship should be absent according to Proposition II. This is in accord with Gell's account of the Umeda. Gell does not give empirical evidence on the forms of exchange but he does note that "the proportion of actual sister-exchanges

is very high" (1975: 27) and that there was no "primitive money" and
no "brideprice" (ibid.: 17–18). Gell also notes (ibid.: 36) that when one
group is threatened with collapse, either through demographic imbal-
ances or other reasons, wholesale reclassifications take place to prevent
collapse. For example, if no members of *2B* group were born then the
system would collapse because of the interdependencies; but if, say, half
the members of *2A* were reclassified as *2B* then the system could continue to exist. Such strategies, while not part of a prescriptive logical
time model, are a necessary condition for self-replacement of the system
in historical time.

Case 3. Ilahita Arapesh

The Ilahita Arapesh were studied by Tuzin (1976) in 1969–70. Whereas
the two cases above were studied in the early stages of *de facto* colonization, the Ilahita Arapesh had a long history of colonization by the time
Tuzin arrived. The people were missionized and labor migration had become an established way of life. The latter posed a threat to the authority
of the elders. As Tuzin (ibid.: 36) notes,

> [T]he change of greatest significance was the growing universality of
> labor out-migration. Young men now had horizons of experience un-
> dreamt-of by their fathers, and in a culture where knowledge and experi-
> ence of arcane things matter so critically, this edge . . . was potentially
> subversive of the old men's exclusive authority. Moreover, each new wave
> that returned contrived some grounds for asserting that their achieve-
> ment outshone that of the men who had gone before. In the beginning
> men contracted for two years and journeyed by boat through the stormy
> Vitiaz Strait separating New Guinea and New Britain. Later, it was still
> contractual, but the way was a comfortable ride on an inter-island air-
> liner. Finally, it became undignified to sign a contract and travel at the
> employer's expense. Today's friends or kinsmen already there look after
> him and help him get a job.

Coffee and dry rice were introduced as cash crops in the 1960s and already
the people were "awakening to a self-inflicted land shortage" (ibid.: 36).
However, as yet, land has not emerged as a commodity and the concept

of ground-rent is unfamiliar. As a consequence, restricted reproduction has flourished and the transformation of commodities into gifts has proceeded apace. The elders have an interest in seeing that this tendency exerts itself because this maintains their authority in a changing situation.

Clan organization in this society is extremely complicated but the phratry principle is the basis of it, as Figure 7.9 shows.

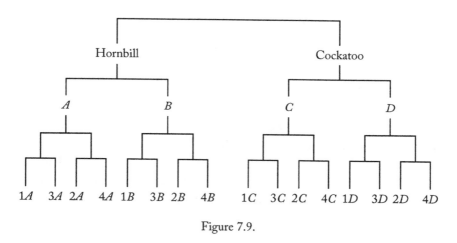

Figure 7.9.

For the system to work there should be at least 16 clans. In fact there are 21 clans and 42 subclans (the latter are the units that exchange women). However, there is no ideal marriage rule and no ideal system of reproduction. But Tuzin does provide some quantitative data on the exchanges of women.

Consider Table 7.1 This shows some aggregative data for the exchange of women between the two moieties, hornbill ($A + B$) and cockatoo ($C + D$). Most of the exchanges were internal to these groups, 50 in the case of hornbill and 103 in the case of cockatoo. But a tendency for restricted exchange between these groups is to be observed: hornbill gave cockatoo 20 women and received 18 in return. It would be interesting to know the pattern of exchanging within these groups, but unfortunately Tuzin's data cannot be disaggregated. However, he does tell us that more than 30%, and possibly as many as 50%, were restricted exchanges between subclans. Thus it can be concluded that there is a tendency for restricted reproduction.

Table 7.1
Exchange of women-gifts among the Ilahita Arapesh,
Sepik District, PNG

		Receivers		
		Hornbill (A + B)	Cockatoo (C + D)	Total
Givers	Hornbill (A + B)	50	20	70
	Cockatoo (C + D)	18	103	121
	Total	68	123	191

Source: Tuzin (1976: 92-98)

The spatial dimension of these exchanges is shown in Table 7.2. Most of the exchanges are intravillage, as evidenced by the fact that in 55% of all cases neither the husband nor the wife moved. But of those exchanges that involve a spatial dimension there is a tendency for patrilocal residence: in 37% of all cases the wife moved while in only 4% of all cases the husband moved.

Table 7.2
Spatial dimension of exchange of women-gifts among the
Ilahita Arapesh, Sepik District, PNG

	No.	%
Female moved	121	37
Male moved	15	4
Neither moved	179	55
Both moved	12	4
Total	327	100

Note: Includes data for the six residential wards plus 25 women received from other villages.
Source: Tuzin (1976: 98).

In this society yams are produced and these are exchanged between different people and groups as gifts. Some of these exchanges involve incremental gift-giving. Thus "big-men" exist in this tribe. Incremental gift-giving is, however, a subordinate activity, and it is the elders, rather than the big-men, who have power and influence in this tribe (ibid.: 232).

In summary, it seems that this society has elements of both restricted and generalized reproduction. But the former dominates and, as predicted by Proposition II, this is associated with the restricted exchange of women, the dominance of elders, and the relative unimportance of incremental gift-giving.

Case 4. Mundugumor

This society was studied by Mead in 1931–33. It has been described as "teratological" and "aberrant" (Heusch 1958: 240–41) and it appears, at first sight, that this case provides evidence against the hypothesis advanced. However, it can be shown that this case is a variation on the simple model in Case I, and that the peculiarities of this system arise because of the *superabundance of land* that exists in this area. According to Mead ([1935] 1963: 176–77), the society is not organized into clans.

> Instead Mundugumor social organization is based upon a theory of natural hostility that exists between all members of the same sex, and the assumption that the only possible ties between members of the same sex are through members of the opposite sex. Instead therefore of organizing people into patrilineal groups or matrilineal groups, in either one of which brothers are bound together in the same group as either their father or their mother's brother, the Mundugumor have a form of organization that they call a rope. A rope is composed of a man, his daughters, his daughters' sons, his daughters' sons' daughters; or if the count is begun from a woman, of a woman, her sons, her sons' daughters, her sons' daughters' sons, and so on. All property, *with the exception of land, which is plentiful and not highly valued*, passes down the rope; even weapons descend from father to daughter. A man and his son do not belong to the same rope. . . . A man leaves no property to his son, except a share in the *patrilineally descended land*; every other valuable goes to his daughter. (emphasis added)

Mead also notes that in the ideal case, there is a restricted exchange of women-gifts between the ropes every four generations (ibid.: 178, 183). As Lévi-Strauss ([1973] 1977: 131) has pointed out, this means that a man marries his *ffffzsssd*. This rule is equivalent to marriage with the *ffzsd* (Paul Jorion, personal communication).

For this system to satisfy the conditions of self-replacement, there must be at least eight ropes and marriage between these ropes must be organized as shown in Figure 7.10.

By following the line of descent of X (a male) it can be verified that his daughter (x), his daughter's son (X), and so on, all belong to the same rope.

Figure 7.10 only shows the alliance and descent relations between ropes. It does not describe the kinship system as a method of consumption, that is, it does not relate the people to land and hence food. Clan organization usually performs this function. But where land is superabundant, the question of land tenure ceases to be a pressing one and the relations of reproduction need not express the relation of people to land explicitly. This is what the Mundugumor do. It is obvious, however, that people must live off the land; it follows, therefore, that a system of clan organization must be implicit in the Mundugumor ropes. This implicit clan structure has been superimposed on Fig. 7.10 as the letters 1*A*11, 1*A*21, 1*B*11, and so on. The structure behind this lettering convention is shown in Figure 7.11. Thus, behind the Mundugumor ropes there is a complicated clan structure, the basis of which is a simple exogamous moiety system. To see this it is necessary to reexamine Mundugumor reproduction from the perspective of the clans. This is done in Figure 7.12. This model generates restricted exchange of the type shown in Figure 7.13. It is clear from this that a person from moiety A always marries a person from moiety B. At the moiety level, then, reproduction has the form as shown in Figure 7.14. This is identical to the Banaro (Case 1).

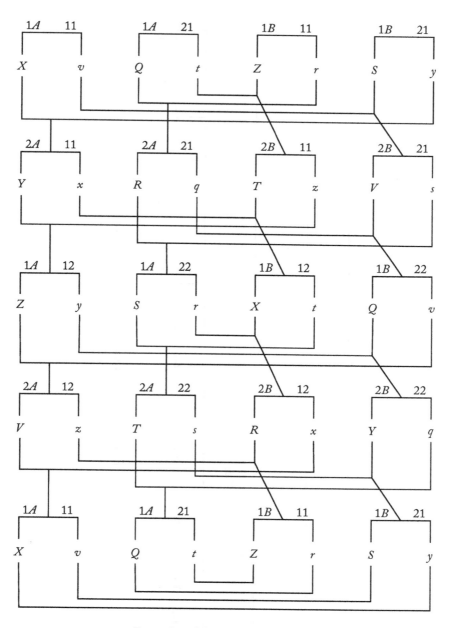

Figure 7.10. Mundugumor marriage.

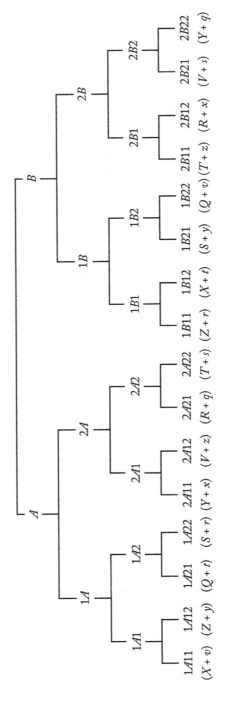

Figure 7.11. Mundugumor implicit clan structure.

Clan land	Father	Mother	Children
1*A*1/2*A*1	1*A*11	1*B*21	2*A*11
	2*A*11	2*B*11	1*A*12
	1*A*12	1*B*22	2*A*12
	2*A*12	2*B*12	1*A*11
1*A*2/2*A*2	1*A*21	1*B*11	2*A*21
	2*A*21	2*B*21	1*A*22
	1*A*22	1*B*12	2*A*22
	2*A*22	2*B*22	1*A*21
1*B*1/2*B*1	1*B*11	1*A*21	2*B*11
	2*B*11	2*A*11	1*B*12
	1*B*12	1*A*22	2*B*12
	2*B*12	2*A*12	1*B*11
1*B*2/2*B*2	1*B*21	1*A*11	2*B*21
	2*B*21	2*A*21	1*B*22
	1*B*22	1*A*12	2*B*22
	2*B*22	2*A*22	1*B*21

Figure 7.12. Mundugumor implicit clan reproduction.

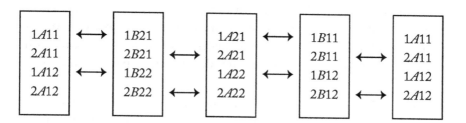

Figure 7.13. Restricted exchange in Mundugumor.

Moiety land	Father	Mother	Children
A	1A	1B	2A
A	2A	2B	1A
B	1B	1A	2B
B	2B	2A	1B

Figure 7.14.

DELAYED REPRODUCTION IN THE HIGHLANDS

Both restricted[1] and delayed reproduction exists in the highlands, but the predominant mode is a patrilineal/patrilocal[2] variety of the latter. Cases from this area illustrate Proposition III because delayed reproduction in the highlands is associated with bridewealth, the incremental exchange of thing-gifts, and big-manship. However, it must be noted that delayed reproduction does not assume the form of *ex-ante* rules that can be described in terms of ideal models. Rather, it emerges *ex-post* in the statistics on marriage exchanges. The cases from this area also illustrate Proposition I because both incremental gift exchange and bridewealth have effloresced in the highlands. The material basis of this has been the persistence of clan ownership of land. However, this is only a necessary condition. The efflorescence of gift exchange must be analyzed in terms of relations between competing big-men, relations between young men and old men, relations between males and females, and the relation of people to land. These relations are all different aspects of the same

1. Manga, Maring, Daribi are examples (see Meggitt and Glasse 1969).
2. "[I]t seems prudent to think twice before cataloguing the New Guinea Highlands as characterized by patrilineal descent. Clearly, genealogical connection of some sort is one criterion for membership of many social groups. But it may not be the only criterion; birth, or residence, or a parent's former residence, or utilization of garden land, or participation in exchange and feasting activities, or in house-building or raiding, may be other relevant criteria for group membership," says Barnes (1962: 6). He suggests "cumulative patrifiliation" as the alternative. Compare La Fontaine (1973).

totality and the relative importance of them varies from place to place and from time to time.

Case 5. Siane

The Siane were studied by Salisbury in 1952–53 and the results of his study published in his now famous monograph, *From stone to steel* (1962).

The Siane, according to Salisbury (ibid.: 103), have a rule of preferential patrilateral crosscousin marriage. All this rule does, other anthropologists have pointed out (Meggitt 1969: 13, fn. 13), "is to say 'we have delayed exchanges of women.' So that in effect it is a *post hoc* evaluation of all marriages already made—an interpretation nicely compatible with evidence from other highland societies." In other words, they have a system (patrilineal/patrilocal) of delayed reproduction that manifests itself after the event rather than as a prescriptive norm. Associated with this is bridewealth, a competitive gift exchange system and big-manship as predicted by Proposition III. The restricted exchange of women-gifts is taboo among the Siane.

The delayed exchange of women-gifts occurs simultaneously with the delayed exchange of thing-gifts, that is, "bridewealth" occurs. The number of valuables given in these bridewealth payments has "greatly increased," Salisbury (1962: 100) reports.

Nexus	Types of goods and services	Social relationships	Property
subsistence (*umaiye*)	vegetable foods help in garden work	intra-clan	clan
ceremonial (*gimaiye*)	pigs, shells	inter-clan group relationships	clan
luxury	pandanus oil trinkets	intra-clan individual relationships	private

Figure 7.15. Nexus of exchange, Siane.

Other forms of gift exchange have flourished too. The Siane distinguish three nexus, which Salisbury (ibid.) has translated as "subsistence," "luxury," and "ceremonial." Each nexus is characterized by the type of goods

Table 7.3
Impact of technological change on the allocation of time,
Siane, highlands district, PNG, 1933–1953

Activity	Time spent (%)		
	Females	Males	
	1933 and 1953	Stone technology 1933	Steel technology 1953
At home, sick, etc.	10	10	10
Visiting	5	3	6
Ceremonials	3	7	18
Subsistence work	82	80	50
Introduced activities	—	—	17
	100	100	100

Source: Salisbury (1962: 108).

used in it, the type of property, and the social relationships to which it applies (see Figure 7.15). According to the categories used in this book, the subsistence and ceremonial nexus are forms of gift exchange, and the luxury nexus is a form of indigenous commodity exchange (barter). The luxury nexus formed part of an intertribal trading network that has been destroyed by colonization (see Hughes 1973). However, before they were destroyed these trading routes played an important role in bringing about the transformation and development of the gift exchange nexus. In the early stages of colonization these trade routes served to carry European commodities to highland villages not yet directly colonized. The most popular item on these trade routes was the steel axe. As a result, the highlands ceased to be a "Stone-Age" economy long before they were directly colonized. The transition from stone to steel had a significant effect on the gift economy, and Salisbury has attempted to quantify these effects for the Siane case. His results, reproduced in Table 7.3, show the impact of steel axes on the allocation of male and female labor-time. It can be seen that the effect has been to lighten the work load of men in the "subsistence" sphere while leaving women's work unchanged. This is because men specialize in the primary stage of the sweet potato production process, a process which involves axe work felling trees and clearing underbrush. Women specialize in the secondary and tertiary stages which involve activities such as planting, weeding, harvesting. Women's work, then, did not (and still does not) involve the use of axes. Thus steel axes increased the productivity of male labor but had no effect on the work of women. The labor-time saved was allocated to "ceremonial" activities (gift exchange) and "introduced" activities such as wage-labor and government work.

Not only did gift exchange flourish as a result of the introduction of steel axes, direct colonization changed the rank-order of the objects of the gift exchange. In precolonial times, pearl shells had the top rank and these came from the coast via the trade routes. When the Europeans colonized the area they observed that the shells were "valuable" and they brought them in by the plane load to buy food, labor, and other favors. The oversupply of shells rendered them useless as gifts because a debt could too easily be repaid. Pigs then became relatively more important. However, pigs have to be produced and this involves hand feeding them from garden produce. This was women's work. Thus while steel axes gave the men more time to engage in gift exchange, it also meant that the women had to spend more time in the production of sweet potatoes and pigs. The conclusion to be reached, then, is that steel axes have enabled the production of things for gift exchange to flourish.[3] This conclusion is supported by the evidence from Goodenough Island. Here, notes Young, "steel axes stimulated the production of subsistence crops" (1971: 255). (Young's use of the term "subsistence" is a misnomer. On this island yams are produced and they, unlike sweet potatoes, double as food and instruments of gift exchange because of their durability.) Steel axes also stimulated the production of salt among the Baruya. But this case is slightly different because salt was produced for commodity exchange by the Baruya (Godelier and Garanger 1973; Clarke and Hughes 1974).

Competitive gift exchange (*gimaiye*) involves transactions in pigs on a delayed exchange basis. For example, if *A* gives *B* a sow, then *B* will give *A* one of the sow's offspring when it is born. A gift-debt of one sow

---

3.   Compare Belshaw's interpretation: "[U]nlike our own agricultural revolution, [the introduction of steel] did not involve the increase in material production that might have been expected: instead of producing more with the same time, Melanesians preferred to produce the same in less time. The saving in time was not used to produce further material goods so much as to produce utility in non-material forms such as leisure, gossip, and social activity" (1954: 89). See also Sharp (1952).

is repaid when one sow of any size is returned, although the borrower
may return more if he chooses. Any increment given reverses the debtor/
creditor relationship. Gift-giving of this type is common between a man
and his wife's brother. This gives a husband an acknowledged claim over
the brother's pigs and, Salisbury (1962: 92) notes, "if the wife deserts her
husband, her brother may prefer to make her return rather than surrender his pigs. In this way the lending and borrowing of pigs and the indebtedness involved serve to maintain the existing relationship between
the husband, his wife, and her brothers." Thus *gimaiye* serves to give men
greater control over women.

Pigs circulate with a high velocity, which means that claims to pigs
exceed the number of pigs in circulation. The ultimate aim of these
transactions is the Pig Feast.

> The largest ceremonial, and the ultimate aim of all "financial" manipula-
> tion of pigs, is the Pig Feast, which each group holds every three years.
> Piglets that are too small to kill at one feast are kept to form a basis for
> future pig raising and to be in their prime for the next feast. Large pigs
> are jealously hoarded by using piglets from later litters to repay debts, to
> provide for unexpected rites of passage, or to create new indebtedness.
> The announcement ceremony, performed about ten months before a Pig
> Feast, in effect creates a moratorium on pig dealing. If another group
> asks for the repayment of a pig, the claim can then be refused by say-
> ing "The pig belongs to the ancestors" and cannot leave the village. A
> feast giver tries to obtain more pigs by claiming repayments from other
> clans, but may be frustrated if another clan announces it is giving a feast.
> Thus there is much competition about announcing future Pig Feasts.
> Sometimes it is advantageous to be the first to celebrate in an area and
> to forestall other clans; it may be best to be last, for then no other clan
> can refuse to repay debts; sometimes a year's delay may put a clan in the
> position of being the only celebrants. But although the production and
> accumulation of pigs is directed towards having the maximum number at
> one moment in time, the ultimate aim is not to eat them but to distrib-
> ute all, except a nucleus for future production, to other clans. (Salisbury
> 1962: 93)

The killing of pigs, and their presentation as pork, by reducing the stock of pigs in circulation, decreases the ratio of the number of pigs to pig-claims and hence makes it harder to repay debts. This "destruction strategy" (see Chapter III) is to be contrasted with the "finance strategy" used in the Western Highlands (see Melpa and Enga examples below) and the "production strategy" (see Wiru example below) used in the Southern Highlands.

Another aspect of the colonization process was the recruitment of male labor for work on the coastal plantations. This did not destroy the gift economy. Instead, agreement labor became a form of *rite de passage*[4] for young men. Upon recruitment they would be sent away to the coast to work on a plantation. This would effect a transformation in their labor from gift-form to commodity-form. Whilst on the coast they would accumulate commodities in their box so as to have something to take home at the expiration of their contract. Upon return to their village their labor and the commodities they brought with them had to be transformed back into gift-form. Special rituals were developed for this process. Salisbury gives the following account for the case of the Siane:

> As the laborers enter their village the women scream and wail literally as though the youths had returned from the dead. They are now "hot," and go straight to the men's houses where they are secluded and not allowed to touch food which women's cooking has made "cold." For three months they must have no sexual contact with women. On the day of their return they cook their own food, using cooking pots or tin cans which they used on the coast. When the other villagers have assembled in the men's house clearing, they open their valuables boxes, amidst screams of amazement and delight. They then distribute about half of their goods, giving one or more valuables to the lineage heads of their own men's house, a little more to the village *luluai* [Government-appointed official], and something to the big-men of other men's houses. They do this using the *gimaiye* [gift exchange] ritual, as if these were presents being made to members of foreign clans. (Salisbury 1962: 127–28)

---

4.   This is a widespread phenomenon. See Young (1971) for another Melanesian example and Watson ([1958] 1964) for an East African example.

Table 7.4

Distribution of gifts brought back by an agreement laborer,
Siane, highlands district, PNG, 1952

Status of recipient (No.)	Article	Cost (est.) $ Aust.	% total cost
Govt. appointed officials (3)	2 laplaps	1.20	
	1 feather headdress	0.30	
	1 tin ointment	0.20	
		1.70	7
Big-men (5)	3 laplaps	1.80	
	1 shell	0.80	
	1 handkerchief	0.15	
		2.75	11
Lineage heads (5)	2 laplaps	1.20	
	2 axes	1.60	
	2 handkerchiefs	0.30	
	1 gold-lip shell	3.00	
		6.10	25
Close relatives (4)	3 laplaps	1.80	
	1 axe	0.80	
	1 handkerchief	0.15	
		2.75	11
Retained for himself	2 laplaps	1.20	
	1 handkerchief	0.15	
	some white buttons	0.20	
	2 leather belts	0.60	
	1 pair shorts	0.75	
	1 pair scissors	0.50	
	1 machete	0.75	
	1 football	1.50	
	1 gold-lip shell	3.00	
	1 pound note	2.00	
	4 shilling pieces	0.40	
		11.05	45
Total cost of gifts		24.35	100
Cash received		27.00	

Source: Salisbury (1962: 129).

Table 7.4 shows the commodities brought back by one agreement laborer of the Siane tribe. Of the total cash received by the laborer of
$A27.00, only $A2.65 was spent on the coast, the rest was brought home

in either commodity or money form. Forty-three percent was given away as gifts to Government-appointed officials, big-men, or lineage heads to re-establish his position in the gift economy; 11% was given away to close relatives (his mother, his mother's brother, and his brother's wife's brother); and 45% was kept for himself.

Case 6. Chimbu

The Chimbu, a neighboring tribe of the Siane with a very similar social structure, provides an illustration of the proposition that gift exchange has effloresced (Proposition I), insofar as it relates to the secondary impact of colonization in the highlands. This involved the establishment of primary commodity production, mainly coffee, and with it pressures on land.

Table 7.5
Changes in land-use patterns, Chimbu, highlands district, PNG, 1958–1967

	1958		1967	
	ha	*%*	*ha*	*%*
Central area				
sweet potato	84	18	109	23
mixed garden	55	12	13	3
coffee	7	1	63	13
fallow	328	69	289	61
Total	474	100	474	100
Peripheral area				
sweet potato	15	4	58	17
mixed garden	3	1	1	0
coffee	0	0	2	1
uncultivated	321	95	278	82
Total	339	100	339	100

Source: H. Brookfield (1973: 140, Table 6.1).

Consider Table 7.5. This shows the changes in land-use patterns in the Chimbu District of the highlands over the period 1958 to 1967. In 1958 coffee trees accounted for 1% of the central land area under cultivation.

By 1967 they accounted for 13%. This was met by a reduction in the area producing mixed produce of the type that adds variety to the diet—taro, sugar cane, green vegetables, and so on—and in a reduction of the area under fallow. The extra sweet potato needed to feed the growing human and pig population had to be met by moving the cultivation of this crop to the peripheral areas. Coffee production traps its producer in the world commodity economy. Whereas sweet potatoes tie up the land for six months or so and provide food for local consumption, coffee trees tie up land for upward of twenty years and provide food for foreign consumers. It means that a producer is no longer free to change the technique of production. It also means that as more coffee is planted the producer is forced to spend more of the money earned from the sale of coffee on the purchase of imported food. However, notwithstanding these forces, the introduction of cash into the economy has not led to the demise of Pig Feasts: to the contrary. Consider the following:

> Chimbu *mogena biri* [vegetable heaps] have reached very complex and large dimensions, with purchased foods dominating local produce, and an extensive set of preparatory gifts preceding the main event. I witnessed such a series in April and May 1976 when each of several nearby and neighboring tribes made separate gifts, with dance and large distribution, consisting of thousands of bundles or parcels of foods, to the Siambuga-Wauga tribe. All of these were received by kinsmen, affines, and friends on more than five separate occasions on different days in a three week period. Each time, some food was consumed and distributed to neighbors, kinsmen and friends. The culminating gift, from the Siambuga-Wauga to the Nogar subtribe of Gena, was bigger than any of the contributing gifts. It was said to be a repayment for pandanus nuts, which the Gena, who live in the high altitude zones, presented to Siambuga-Wauga some years ago. Oil pandanus and peanuts, both lower altitude crops, were the most important elements in the gift. The total heap was about fifty meters in diameter, including cartons of beer, fish cans, meat cans, cooked pork and other meats purchased for the occasion, along with bananas, sugarcane, taro, yams, and corn. Decorative features were split bamboo bound around tins of fish, and bamboo poles and boards to which flowers and paper money in two *kina* notes (about $US5.00) were attached, and long sticks holding beer cartons,

peanuts, and red pandanus fruits. Live cows and pigs were also given at such feasts. The crowd of spectators, donors, and recipients must have numbered thousands, and with many men calling the recipients, the distribution lasted five or six hours. (P. Brown 1978: 221)

Brown's observations were made on the eve of the coffee price boom. For the fifteen years prior to 1975 the New York price of coffee averaged $US0.43 per pound. In 1976, following the Brazilian crop failure, it rose to $US1.42. In 1977 it reached $US2.29, which was a peak. For the next three years it averaged $US1.51. This price boom gave coffee producers huge surpluses and injected large amounts of money into the highlands. These surpluses, it seems, were not ploughed into productive capitalist investment, but into the purchase of imported consumption goods and gift exchange, as the next example shows.

Case 7. Hagen

Since colonization, the amount of pigs, shells, and money involved in bridewealth transfers in this area has tended to increase. Local government councilors have attempted to curb this inflation by fixing the number of pigs and shells at ten and twenty, respectively (A. J. Strathern and M. Strathern 1969: 146). They have had limited success. In a study based on thirty marriages prior to 1970 it was found that the average bridewealth consisted of 17.3 pigs, 20.2 shells, and $A51 (M. Strathern 1972: 336). The giver of a bridewealth is motivated to be generous because "a generous bridewealth allays desire on the part of the girl's kin to entice her away from the husband, and helps (as Hageners say) to stabilize the marriage" (ibid.: 114). In any case, the principle of delay that governs these exchanges means that a generous bridewealth will return to the giving clan sometime in the future. The balance that delayed exchange achieves over time is illustrated in Table 7.6, which shows the patterns of giving and receiving of women-gifts between the twelve subclans and four clans of two highland tribes. Tipuka tribe gave twenty-seven women and received twenty-one in return. Balance such as this is not arranged beforehand, it is evaluated after the act (A. J. Strathern and M. Strathern 1969: 157).

Table 7.6

Exchange of women-gifts among two highland tribes, PNG, 1965

GIVER ↓ / RECEIVER →			Kawelka Tribe				Tipuka Tribe								Totals		
			clan *j*		clan *k*		clan *p*			clan *q*					sub-clan	clan	tribe
Tribe	Clan	Sub-clan	1	2	3	4	5	6	7	8	9	10	11	12			
Kawelka Tribe	clan *j*	1								1	4				5	11	27
		2						2				3		1	6		
	clan *k*	3					2	1		2	1	1	1	1	9	16	
		4					2		1	1	1	1		1	7		
Tipuka Tribe	clan *p*	5	1			1									2	10	21
		6	3	2	1	2									8		
		7													–		
	clan *q*	8	2			1									3	11	
		9		1											1		
		10	1		1	1									3		
		11													–		
		12	2	1		1									4.		
Totals	sub-clan		9	4	2	6	4	3	1	4	6	5	1	3			
	clan		13		8		8			19							
	tribe		21				27										

Notes: Refer to Figure 2.2 for fuller details of clan structure.
Source: A. J. Strathern (1971: 156).

The majority of marriages made by these men are with women living within a radius of about two hours' walk. But the effect of colonization has been to lengthen this radius. As M. Strathern (1972: 66) notes, "[A] more extensive network of government roads and the existence of Hagen market, a center of communication, have resulted in a wide spread of marriages."

These roads of debt are the basis of the *moka* incremental gift exchange system that these people have. Bridewealth consists of two parts: "items which are exchanged and those for which no direct return is expected" (ibid.: 101), that is, those which create debt and those which do not. The former sets off a flow of gifts which should develop into *moka*. "Ideally, as the marriage matures, the flow of gifts between affines should develop into *moka*, although engagement in it always remains optional. . . . Most men, however, by no means restrict their *moka* partnerships to affines" (ibid.: 97).

Moka creates roads of debt in much the same way that the exchange of women creates roads of debt. The only difference is that the roads are of a different order, a different rank. Women have low rank in this area because wife-takers are regarded as superior to wife-givers (ibid.: 75). Thus, from the Hageners' perspective, women are not the supreme gift.

What distinguishes the *moka* system from the examples above is that pigs are not killed at the major festivals. This gives the system its "finance strategy" bias. As a result long chains of gift-debt are created between clans. The "chains," which are also called "roads" or "ropes," bind groups together in an incredibly complex way (see Figures 3.4, 3.5, and 3.6 in Chapter III).

The impact of colonization on the traditional shell trade routes and on the allocation of productive labor-time was the same as for Siane: shells were deranked, male productive labor-time fell, female productive labor-time rose, and men used the extra time to engage in gift exchange and contract labor. The introduction of cash cropping did not alter the "woman the producer"/"man the transactor" division. It simply meant that women became involved in the production of coffee for sale along with their other normal food production and child-rearing duties.

Moka is a sphere of exchange in which men compete for prestige. But as a form of exchange it is critically dependent on production and in particular female labor. The reversal of the shells/pig ranking posed a

Table 7.7
Kundmbo clan's money Moka, 12 December 1977 (in PNG kina)

A. Money pary of gift		
Intra-clan contributions	4,870	
Inter-clan contributions	300	
		5,170
B. Commodity purchases		
7 pigs	3,210	
1 cassowary	290	
		3,500
C. Home reared pigs		
cash equivalent		2,500
D. Items not properly accounted for		1,330
E. Total.		12,500

Note: These figures give the main outline of the gift. Not all the relevant details could be recorded by the anthropologist.
Source: A. J. Strathern (1979: 543).

serious threat to male superiority. Shells, because they were obtained by commodity exchange, represented alienated labor. Men, therefore, had complete control over them, unlike pigs, which were the product of in-alienable female labor. The inalienable right women have over pigs enables them to intervene indirectly in the exchange process. This potential threat to male dominance which would have come about if pigs became the top-ranking gift was met by replacing shells by money as the top-ranking gift. This replacement process took place at a very rapid rate. In February 1965 a transaction involving 1100 pearl shells was recorded in Hagen; in 1974 shells were out and a money *moka* involving a brand new Toyota Land Cruiser (value c. $A4000) and c. $A10 000 in bundles of notes was made (A. J. Strathern 1979: 537). Table 7.7 records the details of a money *moka* made by Kundmbo clan on December 12, 1977. Most of this money came from the coffee flush. Of particular interest is the K3210 used to purchase pigs as commodities from neighboring tribes. Consider A. J. Strathern:

[M]en were engaged in a remarkable feat of appropriation and mystification symbolized by the quest for exotic pigs. For home pigs they would be directly dependent on wives; even for ones obtained by financial methods from supporters and partners, dependence on women is indirectly implied. But in taking money and seeking out pigs reared by totally unrelated persons, indeed commercial firms, they assert that even the process of obtaining pigs can now be done independently of women! And on top of this they claim that obtaining them is done specially to please women on the recipient side. Indeed women did come to admire the huge pigs as they also praised the money. (A. J. Strathern 1979: 544)

As Strathern (ibid.: fn.13) also notes, the use of purchased pigs relieves pressure on the productive work of women to produce home-reared animals, but only in a context where they are already working rather harder to grow and sell coffee.

Pork used to be given as initiatory gifts to *moka* partners. This has been replaced by beer, which is consumed, by and large, only by adult men. This has further distorted male/female relations and introduced new conflicts because the pork it replaced was consumed by women and children.

The male/female opposition, and the ideology that surrounds it, explains, in part, why even village capitalists engage in *moka*. This is because "if a businessman made money but did not engage in exchanges, he could in some ways be seen as a 'rubbish-man' rather than a big-man, and a rubbish-man in turn may be categorized with women" (ibid.: 531).

Case 8. Enga

A variation on the themes presented in the Hagen case can be found in the Enga case (see Meggitt 1971 and 1974; Feil 1978). Here the competitive gift exchange system is called *te* and, like the Hagen *moka*, it has greatly expanded since colonization. Meggitt (1974: 171) stresses the importance of the people/land relationship for explaining this resurgence in the Enga case:

[T]he Mae do not compete for prestige just for its own sake. Prestige achieved through presentations helps a clan to maintain its territorial boundaries, by attracting both present military allies and wives who produce future warriors. The basic preoccupation of the Mae is, it seems to me, with the possession and defense of clan land. Participation in the *te*, as in other prestations, is but a means to this end.

Thus the persistence of clan ownership of land is not only a necessary condition for gift exchange to flourish, gift exchange must flourish in order for clan ownership of land to persist. The greater the penetration of commodity exchange through cash cropping, the greater must be the efflorescence of gift exchange to neutralize the corrosive effects of commodity production on indigenous land tenure.

Case 9. Wiru and Kewa

In these two cases gift exchange has been dampened as a result of colonization (A. J. Strathern 1978: 78; LeRoy 1979: 182). Before this is taken as evidence against Proposition I, a closer examination of the nature of exchange in this area, as well as its particular history of colonization, must be made.

Table 7.8
Origin of pigs killed at Wiru festivals, highland PNG, 1967–1974

		No.	%
Exchange		50	11
Given by close kin	21		
Given by affines	20		
Other	9		
Production		399	89
Total		449	100

Source: A. J. Strathern (1978: 95).

In the *moka* and *te* exchange systems considered above, the incremental exchange of live pigs along a line of groups is the predominant form of exchange. In this area, by way of contrast, the nonincremental exchange of dead pigs (pork) between individuals is the predominant form of exchange. These exchanges are usually between transactors related by marriage and can be seen as installments of bridewealth, of child-payments, or extensions of death payments (A. J. Strathern 1978: 80). Elaborate pig-kill ceremonies are held on the occasion of these exchanges. The killing of the pigs is highly significant. It renders them virtually useless as instruments of exchange and means that transactors have to resort to production strategies in order to acquire them. Thus the complicated exchange networks of pig-debt that characterize the *moka* and *te* systems are not to be found here. The emphasis on production in these ceremonies has been stressed by A. J. Strathern (1978) and is demonstrated clearly in the statistics he has collected from Wiru. These have been produced as Table 7.8, which shows that almost 90% of all pigs used were produced by the transactor himself. Given that big-men acquire some of their status from their skill in manipulating exchange networks, it is not surprising that the big-man complex is somewhat attenuated in these areas (ibid.: 78; LeRoy 1979: 183).

Table 7.9

South Kewa shell exchanges between affines, highlands PNG, 1971 (in percentages)

Category of other	Received from other	Given to other	Total
Wife-giver	7.1	52.2	59.3
Wife-taker	21.0	3.3	24.3
Other	9.2	7.2	16.4
Total	37.3	62.7	100.0

Source: LeRoy (1979: 199).

Another important instrument of exchange in these areas is the pearl shell. These move in opposition to pork. However, these shell–pork exchanges must be seen as gift exchanges that symbolize marriage exchanges. Men are expected to give pearl shells to their immediate wife-givers on behalf of their children (A. J. Strathern 1978: 89). In Kewa, most of the shell-gifts actually corresponded to this ideal. Table 7.9 shows that 73% of shell transactions between affines were to wife-givers. These affinal shell transactions, LeRoy notes (1979: 199), accounted for 50% of all shell transactions, with intraclan transactions accounting for 44%, and other 7%. Thus most of the interclan shell transactions were to wife-givers. Given that an exchange of pearl shells controls that of pork (LeRoy 1979: 189), most pork-gifts must have gone to wife-takers. Shells are said "to eat pork" (ibid.: 189) when exchanged for them. Thus, given that eating is often used as a metaphor for copulation, the exchange can be seen as a symbolic marriage between men (shells) and women (pork). The purpose of such exchanges is regularly to reproduce marriage alliances. They do not create new alliances between groups, as do *moka* and *te*, because they are part of the marriage-gift, not separated from it as *moka* and *te* are. These shell exchanges, then, can be seen as a prototype of *moka*-type exchanges (A. J. Strathern 1978: 88).

The effect of colonization has been to dampen pig production and, as a result, pig-kills and pork-exchanges. The number of shells per pork transaction has increased as in other areas of the highlands, but this could not lead to an efflorescence in exchange because of the productive nature of the exchange system.

The dampening of exchange in Wiru can be explained, as A. J. Strathern (1978) has done, in terms of the particular colonial history of this area. Wiru is part of the Southern Highlands, which was one of the last areas of PNG to be colonized. Wiru only became "derestricted," that is, declared free of warfare and open to European travelers, in 1962. The Wiru, along with other Southern Highlands people, were faced with an all-out government attempt to "modernize" them. This meant an abandonment of traditional inputs of work into gardening and ceremonies. Twenty-five percent of the adult male population were dispatched to coastal plantations and the remainder forced to pay taxes in the form of labor for local infrastructural development. Thus in the 1960s a problem of the allocation of work between ceremonies and business or government work emerged and the power of the colonizers meant that the latter predominated. What of the future? A. J. Strathern (1978: 100–1) has the following view:

> In prospect, it is possible to suggest for the Wiru that a different pattern is emerging, which bears a resemblance to processes the Melpa are already experiencing. Government patrolling has been reduced since Independence and the people have a little more time to themselves. "Village courts," to be run by the people themselves, have been or shortly will be introduced as they have been in Hagen. Agricultural officers are more aware of the needs of subsistence farming; at the same time coffee, and

some (though certainly not all) of the cattle schemes are beginning to prove worthwhile. It would be in line with my hypothesis if these developments gave scope to an interrelated further redevelopment of disputes over land and more elaborate ceremonies as an assertion of individual and group strength. Tunda men, at any rate, told me in 1974 that next time they killed pigs—perhaps as soon as December 1977—they would once more wear the *alipo* "top hat," which was in the past a sign of men's confidence in their pig-rearing capacities and an assertion of their ability to stand against enemies and rivals. In other words—though such predictions are hazardous—a phase of "revival" may begin. In Hagen such a revival, including the resurgence of actual intergroup warfare, had already begun in the late 1960s, and Melpa leaders continue to struggle with its implications for the future.

The Kewa data contain little information on the effects of colonization. LeRoy (1979: 180–81) does note that Kewa was colonized in the early 1950s, that money is beginning to replace pearl-shells, and that about 20% of adult males were away from the village in some kind of work. Given the productive nature of the exchange system, it is possible that the system will never flourish in the ways others have done while so much labor is absent.

THE *KULA* GIFT EXCHANGE SYSTEM OF THE MILNE BAY DISTRICT[5]

Kula is perhaps the best known gift exchange system in the world and this is due, among other things, to Malinowski's classic description of it in his *Argonauts of the Western Pacific* ([1922] 1961). However, as recent fieldwork evidence shows (Leach and Leach 1983), Malinowski's account, while not incorrect, has been found to be incomplete in many important respects. *Kula* is not the unique system that many people think it is. It differs little from the systems of incremental gift exchange found in the highlands of PNG and like them has effloresced since colonization.

---

5.   This section owes much to the many hours of discussion I have had with colleagues at the 1978 and 1981 *kula* conferences.

Its material basis is, as predicted by Proposition III, delayed reproduction. What distinguishes this area from the highlands is that Milne Bay systems of reproduction tend to be matrilineal rather than patrilineal, that yams rather than sweet potatoes are the staple food, and that the area has been colonized for much longer (ninety years compared to forty years or less). There is also more emphasis on the gift exchange of things at death rather than marriage here.

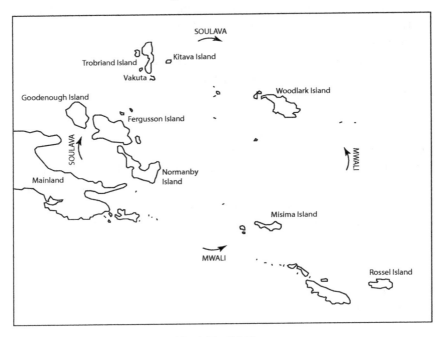

Map 3. The *Kula* Ring.

The popular image of *kula* gift exchange has been formed from the following summary account given by Malinowski:

> The *kula* is a form of exchange, of extensive, intertribal character; it is carried on by communities inhabiting a wide ring of islands, which form a closed circuit. This circuit can be seen on . . . [Map 3], where it is represented by the lines joining a number of islands to the North and East end of New Guinea. Along this route, articles of two kinds, and these two kinds only, are constantly travelling in opposite directions. In the

direction of the hands of a clock moves constantly one of these kinds—long necklaces of red shell, called *soulava*. . . . In the opposite direction moves the other kind—bracelets of white shell called *mwali*. . . . Each of these articles as it travels in its own direction on the closed circuit, meets on its way articles of the other class, and is constantly being exchanged for them. (Malinowski [1922] 1961: 81)

From the perspective of the physical movement of things around the islands this description is accurate. However, from the perspective of the social movement of gifts (inalienable things) between people it is inaccurate, because from this perspective the *kula* is linear rather than circular. This contradiction, which is one between the social and the natural, must be seen in the light of two very important concepts, *kitoum* and *keda*, neither of which was discussed by Malinowski.

The concept *kitoum* epitomizes all that has been said about the distinction between commodities and gifts in this book. It refers to the right that a person has over an object, a right that is inalienable when the thing is circulated as a gift, and alienable when the thing is circulated as a commodity. For example, if *A* possesses an armshell and it is his *kitoum*, then he can do what he likes with it. He can sell it to a tourist for money, or he can give it away to *B* as a gift in *kula*. Now when *A* sells it to the tourist the object acquires a market-price and *A* loses all rights over it; but when *A* gives it to *B* as a *kula* gift he does not lose his rights over it. In the latter case, then, gift-debt is created. Suppose now that *B* gave *A*'s *kitoum* to *C*, that *C* gave it to *D*, and *D* gave it to *E*. As the *kitoum* is still *A*'s shell, this series of transactions creates a road of debt as follows:

$$A \rightarrow B \rightarrow C \rightarrow D \rightarrow E$$

E owes *D*, *D* owes *C*, *C* owes *B*, and *B* owes *A*. This road of debt is called a *keda*. Now *E* can cancel this debt if he has a *kitoum* of the same rank as *A*'s. As this passes along the road toward *A* the debt is canceled. But as the fundamental aim of gift transactors is to maximize debt, *E* is more likely to send two or more gifts along the road toward *A*. If he did this the road would have a new direction as follows:

$$A \leftarrow B \leftarrow C \leftarrow D \leftarrow E$$

A owes *B*, *B* owes *C*, *C* owes *D*, and *D* owes *E*.

Just as gift exchange in the highlands creates minor and major roads of debt, so too does *kula* gift exchange. These roads link up in a complicated fashion and the type of road is related to the exchange of the gifts involved. Shells are not the only objects exchanged: yams, pigs, and other less durable items are an integral part. The precise exchange-order of the things varies from place to place. On Woodlark Island it is as follows (Damon 1978: 93):

top rank:	big armshells and necklaces
	small armshells and necklaces
middle rank:	pigs
	clay pots/sleeping mats
	yam seeds/taro seeds
bottom rank:	betel nut/betel pepper

The armshells and necklaces have a number of subdivisions and these rankings are roughly similar on all the islands. Where the interisland variation lies is in the ranking of the lower-ranking, less important, gifts.

What gives *kula* its special features is the rule that certain things must move in a certain direction. For example, armshells must move in an anticlockwise direction and necklaces in a clockwise direction. The effect of this rule is that it has a tendency to make the roads of debt longer. In the limiting case, for example, it means that a minimum of three people are required to "play" *kula*; in other types of gift exchange, by way of contrast, only two people are required to "play." This rule also has the effect of linking up the *islands* to form a ring of giving. But it does not necessarily link up the *transactors* to form a ring. Consider the example above. Suppose *A* lived on island *a*, *B* on island *b*, *C* on island *c*, *D* on island *d*, and *E* on island *a*. This road can be written as follows:

$$A_a \rightarrow B_b \rightarrow C_c \rightarrow D_d \rightarrow E_a$$

where the subscript represents the island of the transactor. This road is circular from the perspective of the islands but linear from the perspective of the transactors. *A* and *E* live on the same island, but this is of little significance insofar as understanding *kula* is concerned.

Another special feature of the *kula* is the spectacular overseas journeys made for the purpose of exchanging shells. These trips were, and still are, undertaken in specially constructed canoes built with local materials. Gawa Island specializes in the production of *kula* canoes and it is interesting to note that the canoes are traded as gifts not commodities. As Munn (1977: 45) notes, "[T]he canoe's irreversible journey as an exchange valuable does not alienate it from its producers." *Kula* journeys are governed by the delayed exchange principle too. One year men from island *A* will go to island *B* to transact, the next year men from island *B* will go to island *A*. The aim of these journeys is to bring back opening gifts (*vaga*). The big-men from the visiting island compete with one another to acquire the best of these so that they may gain prestige by giving them away to other islanders.

The sexual symbolism of *kula* is explicit. Consider Malinowski ([1922] 1961: 356):

> The equivalence of two gifts, *vaga* and *yotile*, is expressed by the word *kudu* (tooth) and *bigeba* (it will bite). Another figure of speech describing the equivalence is contained in the word *va'i*, to marry. When two of the opposite valuables meet in the *kula* and are exchanged, it is said that these two have married. The armshells are conceived as the female principle, and the necklaces as the male.

There could be no better linguistic evidence for the proposition that the gift exchange of things is to be explained with reference to marriage, and marriage with reference to the methods of consumption.

Case 10. The Trobriand Islands

The matrilineal/avunlocal version of this system has already been discussed in Chapter IV. But it has also been described as "patrilocal" (Malinowski [1935] 1966: 36) and it is useful to consider that version here. The Trobrianders have four clans, *A* iguana, *B* dog, *C* pig, and *D* snake. They also have a prescriptive marriage rule (*fzd*) and from these facts it is possible to construct an ideal model of self-replacement of the form of Figure 7.16.

Land	Father	Mother	Son	Daughter
A	IGUANA	dog	DOG	dog
A	DOG	iguana	IGUANA	iguana
B	DOG	pig	PIG	pig
B	PIG	dog	DOG	dog
C	PIG	snake	SNAKE	snake
C	SNAKE	pig	PIG	pig
D	SNAKE	iguana	IGUANA	iguana
D	IGUANA	snake	SNAKE	snake

Figure 7.16. Delayed reproduction in the Trobriands.

This generates delayed exchange of women-gifts as follows:

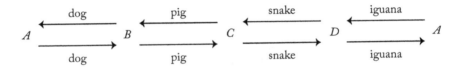

Thus like is exchanged for like over time. This is a classic example of gift exchange in its purest form.

This is clearly the ideal, and the question that is posed is the correspondence of practice to this ideal. It would be impossible for the system to work properly because of the demographic imbalance of the clans. Iguana clan, for example, is much smaller than the rest. Data for one village, Omarakana, show that it had a population of 317 in 1950 (Powell 1956: Table 3). Only 5% belong to iguana clan. For the other clans the figures were 25%, 47%, and 22%, for dog, pig, and snake clan, respectively. Notwithstanding these facts, the data on the exchange of women-gifts between clans does seem to reveal a tendency for delayed exchange and how a system of delayed exchange balances out over time (Table 7.10). For example, pig gave dog thirteen females, and dog gave pig thirteen females in return. Between snake and dog a similar equality was established with four females being given and received. However, the latter exchanges are "irregular" according to the ideal model. Other "irregular" transactions are the intraclan exchanges for the pig and snake clans. However, most of these were marriages of chiefs. It is a common practice of chiefs to marry within their own clan.[6] It is a strategy they use to consolidate their positions of power and influence.

Table 7.10
Exchange of women-gifts over four generations, Omarakana village, Trobriand Islands, PNG

Giver	Iguana (A)	Dog (B)	Pig (C)	Snake (D)
Iguana (A)	n.a.	n.a.	n.a.	n.a.
Dog (B)	0	0	13	4
Pig (C)	0	13	4	16
Snake (D)	0	4	10	2

Note: Only the data on the major sub-clans are shown: Lobwaita (pop. 53) of Dog clan (pop. 81), Tabula (pop. 23) of Pig clan (pop. 148), and Bwaydaga (pop. 25) of Snake clan (pop. 71). No data on Iguana clan (pop. 17) were available.
Source: Powell (1956, Appendix).

The Trobriand Islands is one of the few places in PNG that has a chieftainship system. It is also one of the few places that has a system of gift-giving that takes the form of a "tribute." On the Trobriands, yams are produced and every year, after the annual harvest, about half of these (Malinowski [1935] 1966: 8) are circulated according to a set rule, the essence of which is that yams must flow in the same direction as women-gifts.[7] So, in terms of the model above, dog gives yams to pig clan this generation, and pig gives to dog in the next generation. At the level of the clan, such a system of giving establishes equality in the ideal case. However, at the level of the subclan there is no necessity for equality to be established either in theory or in practice. Subclans have a rank order and the chief belongs to the top subclan. It is his subclan that

6. This is especially so among the African systems, where chieftainship systems are much more common. Consider Kuper's account of the Swazi, for example: "Only in the case of the royal clan—the Nkosi—is intermarriage between sub-clans permitted" (1950: 86).
7. "Fathers and brothers give yams; husbands receive yams" (Weiner 1976: 197).

appropriates a disproportionate share of the yams that are given to his clan (see Table 3.2, Chapter III). This mode of exchange reverses the usual order: the receiver is dominant and not the giver. These yams were, and still are, ostentatiously displayed in yam houses and in many cases left to rot. Yams, it will be recalled, are unlike sweet potatoes in that they are durable and storable; as such, they can be used as instruments of gift exchange and symbols of a chief's power and authority.

This case would seem to provide evidence against Proposition III because it was argued that the absence of chieftainship and the presence of bridewealth gift exchanges were the conditions of existence of incremental gift exchange.[8] But *kula* does not exist in many parts of the Trobriands; it flourishes in those areas where the chieftainship system is weakest. On Vakuta Island, for example, the chieftainship system is almost nonexistent and *kula* flourishes here (Campbell 1983). In other words, *kula* flourishes in those parts of the Trobriands that are relatively "egalitarian," which is what the theory predicts. *Kula* is an interisland form of exchange but it facilitates intraisland competition for rank and status (Campbell 1983). This is because a number of roads of debt pass through each island. On any island, then, big-men do not compete directly because they are not on the same road. But they do compete indirectly. When they visit other islands they compete to get the highest-ranking shells to pass along their own road. This is because the higher the rank of the shells that pass along a road, the higher the status of the road, and the higher the status of the transactor.

Case 11. Woodlark Island

This island, which was studied by Damon in 1973–75, plays a very important role in the *kula* gift exchange system. A system of delayed reproduction exists here that is very similar to the Trobriand system. But there are a number of significant differences. First, the island has eight clans. Four of these are the same four that exist on the Trobriands. These clans are called the "old" clans. The other four clans are called the "new" clans. As Damon notes, "[T]he 'new' clans constitute some embarrassment for the Muyuw [Woodlark] people. They believe there should be only four clans, and the fact that they have eight is taken by them to be indicative of a slight disorder

---

8.   This case provides additional evidence for Proposition I. Weiner (1976) describes how the extremely complicated Trobriand mortuary ritual has flourished. She gives particular attention to the analysis of women's wealth.

in their culture" (1978: 207). Secondly, the exchange of women-gifts is not governed by an ideal rule as it is for the Trobriands. Thirdly, there is no chieftainship system on Woodlark, a difference which the Woodlark Islanders explain in terms of different food taboos. Fourthly, and this is related to the last point, the system of yam giving by the brothers of one subclan to the husbands of another subclan is relatively unimportant on Woodlark.

These facts make it impossible to construct an ideal model of the system of reproduction on Woodlark; but a tendency for delayed reproduction to assert itself is present. *Kitoums* are involved in marriage transactions and they give rise to a complicated series of gift exchanges, which sometimes culminate in *kula* gift exchange (ibid.: Chap. 8).

The thesis that gift exchange is to be explained with reference to the methods of consumption is also illustrated by the linguistic data from Woodlark. The term used to describe the transaction that produces a gift debt is *vag*. The same term is used in connection with the birth of children. Furthermore, there is a homology between the terms used to describe people of different ages and the exchange-order of things as gifts. For example, the highest ranked armshells are likened to old men, armshells of intermediate rank are likened to mature men, and so on. The necklaces that move in the opposite direction also have rank: the highest is likened to an old woman, the next to a mature woman, and so on. The exchange of things as gifts is likened to a marriage.

Further illustrations of Proposition III are provided by the data from other islands in the *kula* region such as Dobu (Fortune [1932] 1963), Gawa (Munn 1977), and Normanby (Thune 1983). These systems are by no means identical, however. Dobu, for example, has an alternative pattern of residence whereby a man lives in his wife's village for part of the year and the wife lives in the husband's village for the other part of the year. These different places are only alike in the sense that restricted exchange of women-gifts does not occur at marriage.

GIFT EXCHANGE AND CAPITAL ACCUMULATION IN CENTRAL DISTRICT

Case 12. Poreporena village

This village lies in the heart of Port Moresby, the national capital. The British colonizers raised their flag in Poreporena in 1884 and the city has

grown up around the village. There is, therefore, no village that has been
more affected by colonization in PNG than this, and as such it provides
a crucial test for the proposition that gift exchange has effloresced under
the impact of colonization.

From the perspective of the commodity economy, Poreporena appears to be a working-class ghetto. Compared to the neighboring colonial residences, the village is overcrowded and the houses are of inferior
quality. The economic basis of the village is wage-labor. In 1950, 82% of
all men from the village were employed, almost all of these in skilled or
semiskilled jobs. Since 1950 there has been an increase in the number
of women employed as typists and secretaries, as well as an increase in
the proportion of men unemployed. The village is one of the largest
in PNG and the population has grown from 3600 to 5600 in the past
twenty years.

In spite of the tremendous changes that have occurred in the village,
the clan structure has been fortified. This has been largely due to the
influence of the United Church (formerly London Missionary Society).
They suppressed the traditional gift exchange system and usurped the
power of the traditional big-men. Nowadays big-men are no longer. They
have been replaced by church deacons, the "neo-big-men" of the new gift
exchange system that has been established by the church in order to raise
money. It was the rise of these men that saved the clan (*iduhu*) system
from collapsing. As Groves (1954: 13) reported, "[T]he *iduhu* structure
. . . has persisted most effectively . . . in the election of church deacons,
whose power in the village draws much of its force from the *iduhu* structure." The deacons are subclan leaders and are elected by the members
of their sub-clan. In 1979 there were fifty-four subclans and twenty-
five clans, the structure of which is shown in Figure 7.17. The deacons
compete with each other for status in a system called *boubou*, established
in 1948. After the war a locally trained pastor was appointed to replace
an expatriate as head of Poreporena church. Faced with the problem of
raising money for his church, he designed a flag called *Boubou Kwalim
Toana* (collection-winner-sign) and arranged for the deacons to compete
for it in an annual gift-giving competition. A competition between clans
crosscuts the deacons' competition and each year a ranking of clans and
deacons is produced. The success of the system can be judged by comparing Tables 7.11 and 7.12. The first shows the money raised in 1950, the

Table 7.11
Gifts to Poreporena church, Central District, PNG, 1950

		$A
Hohodae clans		49.05
Tupa	—	
Dubara	22.40	
Taurama	14.50	
Geakone	12.15	
Poreporena clans		495.91
Kahanomona Mavara }	55.35	
Kwaradubuna	51.25	
Tubumaga	61.21	
Apau	32.30	
Vahoi	28.20	
Botai	140.88	
Gunina	122.20	
Geavana	4.52	
Elevala village		191.49
Total clan		736.45
Other sources		1,173.70
Grand total		1,910.15
Allocation		
LMS general funds	400.00	
Pastor's pocket money	30.00	
Hanuabada mission teachers	56.00	
Church building fund	1,354.22	
Unknown	69.93	
Total		1,910.15

Source: Belshaw (1957: 184).

latter the amount raised in 1974. The system has been a colossal success. In 1974, $A45,137 was raised, compared to $A736 in 1950. Since 1974, the money raised has increased at an almost geometric rate. In 1979, K70,090 was raised, in 1980 K116,050.[9] The crosscutting ranking of clan and deacon that the competition achieves is also shown in Table 7.12. In 1974, deacon number 34 of clan *k* was first but clan *h*, Gunina of Hanuabada, won the clan competition.

9. The kina was introduced in 1975 on a par with the Australian dollar. It was subsequently revalued.

Table 7.12
Gifts to Poreporena Church, Central District, PNG, 1974

Iduhu	Deacon	Amount (K)		Ranking	
				Iduhu	Deacon
a. Hohodae	1	1,507.64			
	2	650.50			
	3	939.50			
	4	1,118.11	4,215.75		
b. Kahanomona	5		476.60		
c. Mavara	6–9		2,786.73		
d. Kwaradubuna	10	969.00			
	11	1,111.00	2,080.00		
e. Tubumaga	12–15		1,455.56		
f. Vahoi/Apau	16	1,293.89			
	17	662.50			
	18	668.20			
	19	527.60	3,152.19		
g. Botai	20	816.95			
	21	606.00			
	22	502.20			
	23	1,280.00			
	24	1,255.90	4,461.05	third	
h. Gunina	25	2,113.00			third
	26	1,523.03			
	27	2,211.20			second
	28	1,820.00			
	29	577.60			
	30	438.00	8,682.83	first	
i. Kuriu	31	37.20			
	32	68.00	105.20		
j. Gunina	33		552.50		
k. Botai Idibana	34		4,317.47		first
l. Abisiri	35		1,137.85		
m. Botai Laurina	36		354.39		
n. Gunina Pore Idibana	37		752.64		
o. Gunina Pore Laurina	38–39		1,021.89		
p. Gunina Hagwaipi	40	454.36			
	41	256.00			
	42	506.00	1,216.36		
q. Hoboimo	43–45		5,509.75	second	
r. Botai Idibana	46		805.00		
s. Botai Laurina	47		142.59		
t. Vahoi	48		1,910.56		
	Total		45,136.91		
	Other		995.58		
	Grand Total		46,132.49		

Source: Poreporena church handout.

VILLAGE   VILLAGE DISTRICTS   IDUHU   CODE

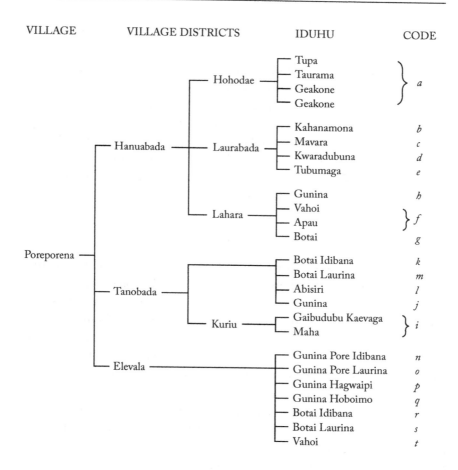

Figure 7.17. Clan structure of Poreporena village, 1979. *Note:* This is constructed from a 1979 Poreporena church hand-out and therefore excludes the few non-Christian *iduhu* in the village.

The size of bridewealth in Poreporena has also risen dramatically since colonization. For example, in 1975 one bridewealth was recorded consisting of $A3245, 67 bags of rice, 14 hands of bananas, 836 armshells, and 31 bags of sugar. Some indication of the relative size of the monetary component of the marriage-gift can be gauged from the fact it was two and a half times the annual income of a minimum wage earner. High bridewealth payments such as this effectively prevent outsiders marrying into the village. Unlike many other areas of PNG, it is not possible to speak of delayed exchange of women between clans, because the clan is not the relevant group for purposes of marriage. In Poreporena a man must not marry his *taihuna*, an ego-centered group that includes third cousins. The composition of such a marriage group varies from person to person, and it may or may not coincide with that person's *iduhu* group.

This competitive gift exchange system is not restricted to Poreporena village. The United Church has colonized a large number of villages up and down the coast where similar competitions are operating. Large sums of money are raised in these villages too. Boera, for example, is a small village consisting of about 700 people and 13 *iduhu*. In November 1979 they managed to raise K11,487.

Case 13. Hiri Development Corporation

Impressed by the success of the United Church at raising money by the gift exchange system, a young university-educated Papuan set up a Village Development Corporation and tried to raise money in the same way. Every fortnight the fourteen villages of the Hiri Local Government Council would get together for a *moale hebou, gaukara hebou, anihebou* (fun-work-food gathering). The villages would take it in turns to host the occasion, the primary aim of which was to raise money by competitive gift-giving between them.

At the ceremony I attended on September 15, 1974, in Roku village, $A1427.50 was raised. Ten of the fourteen villages were in attendance. The meeting was chaired by the village pastor, who opened it with prayers and a hymn. The fun then started. A blackboard with the names of all the villages was placed on a table in the center of the gathering. As the name of each village was called out the members of this village would move forward and place their contribution on the table. This was duly counted and recorded on the blackboard. The presentation of the money was done with great ceremony: the donors would congregate together and slowly move toward the table singing traditional songs and waving their paper money contributions in the air. At the end of the first round the host village, Roku, had raised the greatest amount, $A447. Second was Boera with $A165.50 and third Papa with $A155.10. Papa then decided to try to beat Boera to second place by making another contribution. This raised $A27.52 to bring their total to $A182.62. Boera responded to this challenge by giving another $A31.71, raising their total to $A197.21 and thereby consolidating their second position. Roku, whose position of supremacy was never in doubt, then decided to show off by making a second contribution too. This added another $A60.80 to their contribution, bringing their total to $A507.80 and the combined total to $A1427.50.

All the money collected belonged to the host village. They decided how it should be distributed. In this case most went to the Village Development Corporation in the form of share capital. Roku became indebted to the other villages to the extent of their contribution less what Roku contributed to the other villages when it attended their *hebou*.

This system never "took off." It had a very short life and was nonexistent in 1979 when I returned for a visit. The Development Corporation was still going, but only just. Some of its businesses had closed down and others were floundering.

The failure of the Development Corporation is due, in part, to the nature of the Hiri system. In the Poreporena case, no gift-debt is created, whereas in the Hiri case gift-debt is created that has to be repaid. So that, while the Roku leaders had $A1427.50 cash assets in September 1974, they also had an intervillage debt of $A919,70 and an intravillage debt of $A507.80. Of the two systems, the Poreporena system is obviously more conducive to capital accumulation in the context of a commodity economy. This is because it involves the *alienation* of things (money in this case) from people, which means that when clansmen give money to the church no debt is created. But with the Hiri system there is no alienation, debt is created. In other words the Poreporena system leads to the accumulation of assets *without* the accumulation of liabilities, whereas the Hiri system leads to the accumulation of assets *with* the accumulation of liabilities.

The alienation of gifts from their owners is, as has been seen in Chapter III, a feature of gift exchange systems that employ the destruction strategy. The potlatch system of the North West Cape of America, where large quantities of blankets and other things are thrown into a fire, is the classic example of this type of gift exchange. Paradoxically, therefore, it is this destruction element inherent in some gift exchange systems that provides scope for capital accumulation.[10] Destructive gift-giving can, as

---

10. See Gregory (1980) for an elaboration of this argument.

Mauss noted ([1925] 1974: 12–15), be interpreted as a "gift to god." If such gifts take the form of money or valuable commodities, and if they are given to an intermediary rather than sacrificed, it is obvious that the intermediary will be able to accumulate wealth. The Poreporena church, by modifying the indigenous gift exchange system and by establishing itself as an intermediary in a new system, has been able to do precisely this. The Hiri Development Corporation, because it was unable to establish a gift-to-god system, failed.

Conclusion

In 1871 Jevons ([1871] 1970: Preface) complained that Ricardo shunted the car of economic science onto a wrong line. However, the conclusion that emerges from this book is that it was not Ricardo but Jevons who misdirected things. By developing the economics approach in opposition to the political economy approach, Jevons has led a generation of scholars into a cul-de-sac. He developed a closed system of thought, where subjectivist concepts, such as "modern" goods or "traditional" goods, derived from axiomatic premises, are mechanically applied to whatever new data emerge. These categories fail to describe even the basic features of a gift or commodity economy, let alone explain their interaction; they cannot even establish the elementary distinction between gifts and commodities, let alone a framework for classifying the many different types of gift and commodity economies. Indeed, as has been seen in Chapter V, they may even positively hinder the perception of reality by blinding their user to what is really happening. Jevons' misdirection of economic analysis has had major social and political consequences because, being the dominant orthodoxy in university economics departments, it has had a major impact on economic policy making both in Europe and in the non-European parts of the world.

The way out of the cul-de-sac, it has been argued here, is the political economy approach. The system of analysis developed by Quesnay, Smith, Marx, and others offers an open system of thought, free from the dangers of academic specialization, capable of expansion and modification in the light of new historical and anthropological data. It does not provide a list of mechanical rules for applying to the data but rather a framework within which relevant questions can be posed concerning the social relations of reproduction: How are the means of production distributed between various groups that make up the society? What social form does the surplus-product take? How is this produced, exchanged, redistributed, consumed, and reproduced? And so on. The early political economists have not by any means provided all the theoretical answers to these questions. The state of the world is such that these questions can never be answered once and for all: new historical epochs and new anthropological data render old theories obsolete or, at best, limited in their applicability. The political economy approach must, therefore, be constantly changing and evolving to keep pace with the changing historical circumstances. The twentieth-century anthropological approach to the economy founded by Morgan, Mauss, and Lévi-Strauss, I have argued, expands and develops the historical and comparative tradition of nineteenth-century political economy. The theory of commodities developed by the latter is compatible with the theory of gifts developed by the former, and a synthesis of the two in the light of evidence from PNG provides a constructive alternative to the theory of goods presented by the economics approach. This alternative is superior on all counts: it provides better concepts for describing the indigenous economy, and classifying its various types; as a consequence, it is able to provide a better explanation of the historical changes that have occurred in colonial PNG.

The modified political economy approach developed here has a relevance that extends beyond PNG. This is not so much in the theories developed—some are relevant only to particular areas of PNG—but to the direction it gives to research and the questions it poses. Enough anthropological evidence from Asia, Africa, and America has been presented in the first section of this book to illustrate the importance of the gift in the indigenous economies of these countries. There are, however, a multitude of different types of gift reproduction, and the threefold classification into restricted, delayed, and generalized is only a starting point. A subclassification of types in the restricted/delayed range has been attempted with the PNG data but data from elsewhere are needed to complete this. For example, it would be interesting to investigate Lévi-Strauss' ([1949] 1969: 46) claim that an "axis of generalized exchange" runs from Western Burma to Eastern Siberia in the light of the contemporary anthropological and historical evidence. It would also be interesting to assess the relationship between leadership and gift exchange by contrasting the African chieftainship systems with Melanesian big-men systems. The analysis of the uneven impact of colonization poses further interesting questions. Foreign mining companies, plantation companies, governments, and missionaries have affected different countries in different ways. The impact of these institutions cannot be analyzed, as the economics approach would have it, by reasoning from *a priori* principles; a concrete analysis of each situation is needed before generalizations can be developed, but there is some evidence[1] to suggest that the efflorescence of gift exchange argument and wages subsidy argument developed here has some generality beyond PNG.

The propositions developed to explain the particular case of PNG—that restricted reproduction is associated with eldership and balanced gift exchange, while delayed reproduction is associated with big-man-ship and incremental gift exchange—were developed from an examination of the data from just three of the eighteen districts of PNG. The complexity of PNG societies is legendary and the relevance of these propositions for understanding other areas in PNG is another question. Many Melanesian-wide generalizations have been shown to be invalid with the production of new ethnographic data or the rediscovery of old data. Indeed, the "Melanesian big-man" concept is one such overgeneralization that this book has attempted to call into question. The typology of gift exchanges developed here makes no claim to completeness. The analysis has concentrated on marriage-gifts and interclan gift-giving. Intraclan gift-giving has barely been analyzed; birth-gifts and death-gifts have not been considered at all. From the perspective of a model of self-replacement, birth, marriage, and death are different aspects of the same thing and it is interesting to note that certain areas tend to stress one of these events at the expense of the others. For example, in the highland districts marriage-gifts seem to predominate, in Milne Bay it is death-gifts, while in some areas of New Britain (see, e.g., Chowning 1978a, 1978b) birth seems to be the event that gift exchange is centered on. If this is indeed the case then the causes and consequences of these

---

1.   See Watson ([1958] 1964); Weeks 1971; Wolpe (1972); Meillassoux (1972, 1973, 1975).

phenomena pose a number of interesting questions. The further analysis of intraclan gift-giving poses the question of the meaning of the category "clan." This raises questions more narrowly focused on extremely complicated issues of anthropological theory. For the purposes of this book a clan was defined as an exogamous land-owning group. This was a simplification adopted in Chapter II in order to contrast it with the category "class." However, as the analysis approached a more empirical level in Chapter VII, it was seen that the land relation is sometimes only implicit (the Mundugumor case), while in other cases (Poreporena) the marriage group and the named clan group did not coincide. While these complications can be passed over at a highly abstract level of analysis, concerned with the contrast between capitalist and noncapitalist economies, they are the essence of a more concrete analysis of PNG and they have important consequences for the analysis of intraclan gift-giving.

While this book has addressed itself primarily to a critique of economic theory, it contains a number of propositions that have a bearing on anthropological theory, the significance of which has not been brought out explicitly. Apart from placing the "formalist/substantivism" debate in its correct theoretical context, the argument in this book has implications for the theory of kinship. By freely appropriating aspects of the theories of anthropologists such as Morgan, Mauss, and Lévi-Strauss, and developing these in the light of the theories of Smith, Ricardo, Marx, and Sraffa, it has been possible to present an interpretation of classificatory kinship terms as exchange relations analogous to prices. Furthermore, just as the classical political economists have been able to explain prices in a self-replacing class-based society with reference to the methods of production and productive consumption, it has been possible here to explain kin terms in a self-replacing clan-based society with reference to the methods of consumption and consumptive production, a demonstration which involves the conceptualization of kinship as a method of consumption. There can be no doubt that this approach differs significantly from other approaches,[2] but whether it is superior or not is an altogether different question whose investigation is left to the reader.

---

2. For example, contrast the different attempts to explain Trobriand kinship terms: Malinowski ([1929] 1968); Leach (1962); Lounsbury (1965); Powell (1969a, 1969b); Weiner (1979).

Mathematical Appendix
A matrix approach to the calculus of kinship relations[1]

CLASSIFYING KINSHIP SYSTEMS USING MATRICES

The basic exchange structure of many gift reproduction systems can be described by means of five elementary matrices.

Suppose there are four marriage groups numbered 1, 2, 3, and 4. There are three possible ways for these groups to engage in the restricted exchange of women-gifts. The first is where groups 1 and 2 form one exchanging pair, and groups 3 and 4 the other. This can be represented in graph form as

$$1 \longleftrightarrow 2$$
$$4 \longleftrightarrow 3$$

or in matrix form as

$$R_1 = \begin{pmatrix} 0 & 1 & 0 & 0 \\ 1 & 0 & 0 & 0 \\ 0 & 0 & 0 & 1 \\ 0 & 0 & 1 & 0 \end{pmatrix}$$

1. See Gregory (1986) for an elaboration of some of the points developed here. See Tarski ([1941] 1965), Copilowish (1948), Sierpinski (1958), and Lange (1962) for a general discussion of the logic of relations.

where the rows represent the givers and the columns the receivers.

The second possible way to arrange restricted exchange is where groups 1 and 4 form one exchanging pair, and groups 2 and 3 the other. The graph form of this is

$$
\begin{array}{cc}
1 & 2 \\
\updownarrow & \updownarrow \\
4 & 3
\end{array}
$$

and the matrix form is

$$
R_2 = \begin{pmatrix}
0 & 0 & 0 & 1 \\
0 & 0 & 1 & 0 \\
0 & 1 & 0 & 0 \\
1 & 0 & 0 & 0
\end{pmatrix}
$$

The third case is where groups 1 and 3 form one exchanging pair and groups 2 and 4 the other. This has the graph form

and the matrix form

$$
R_3 = \begin{pmatrix}
0 & 0 & 1 & 0 \\
0 & 0 & 0 & 1 \\
1 & 0 & 0 & 0 \\
0 & 1 & 0 & 0
\end{pmatrix}
$$

If generalized exchange is allowed, two possibilities emerge. In the first case group 4 gives to group 3, who gives to group 2, who gives to group 1, who completes the circle by giving to group 4. This has the graph form

and the matrix form

$$G = \begin{pmatrix} 0 & 0 & 0 & 1 \\ 1 & 0 & 0 & 0 \\ 0 & 1 & 0 & 0 \\ 0 & 0 & 1 & 0 \end{pmatrix}$$

The second generalized case is where the direction of giving in the above case is reversed. This has the graph form

```
1  ————→  2
↑            |
|            ↓
4  ←————  3
```

and the matrix form

$$G' = \begin{pmatrix} 0 & 1 & 0 & 0 \\ 0 & 0 & 1 & 0 \\ 0 & 0 & 0 & 1 \\ 1 & 0 & 0 & 0 \end{pmatrix}$$

Where G' is the transpose of G.

In matrix terms, then, an exchange matrix E is of the restricted exchange type if $E = E'$ and of the generalized exchange type if $E \neq E'$.

Given these five matrices, the exchange structure of the models discussed in Chapter IV can be described as follows:

Restricted exchange (e.g. Kariara): $E_1 = R_1$
Generalized exchange (e.g. Kachin): $E_2 = G$
Delayed exchange (e.g. Trobriands):
$$E_3 = \begin{bmatrix} G & 0 \\ 0 & G' \end{bmatrix}$$

The latter matrix is an 8×8 matrix and can be written out in full as follows:

$$\begin{bmatrix} G & 0 \\ 0 & G' \end{bmatrix} = \begin{pmatrix} 0 & 0 & 0 & 1 & 0 & 0 & 0 & 0 \\ 1 & 0 & 0 & 0 & 0 & 0 & 0 & 0 \\ 0 & 1 & 0 & 0 & 0 & 0 & 0 & 0 \\ 0 & 0 & 1 & 0 & 0 & 0 & 0 & 0 \\ 0 & 0 & 0 & 0 & 0 & 1 & 0 & 0 \\ 0 & 0 & 0 & 0 & 0 & 0 & 1 & 0 \\ 0 & 0 & 0 & 0 & 0 & 0 & 0 & 1 \\ 0 & 0 & 0 & 0 & 1 & 0 & 0 & 0 \end{pmatrix}$$

If Figure 4.30 (p. 94) is examined in the light of this, it can be verified that the *tama* (wife-giver) relation has this structure. If the rows are considered to be women and the columns men, then this matrix also describes the *tabu* (wife-of) relation.

The rather complicated versions of restricted reproduction discussed in Chapter VII can also be described using these matrices.

Umeda exchange matrix:
$$E_4 = \begin{bmatrix} R_2 & 0 & 0 \\ 0 & R_1 & 0 \\ 0 & 0 & R_3 \end{bmatrix}$$

This is a 12 × 12 matrix and it can be seen that Figure 7.7 (p. 182) has this structure.

Mundugumor exchange matrix: $E_5 = \begin{pmatrix} R_2 & 0 & 0 & 0 \\ 0 & R_3 & 0 & 0 \\ 0 & 0 & R_2 & 0 \\ 0 & 0 & 0 & R_3 \end{pmatrix}$

This is a 16 × 16 matrix and Figure 7.10 (p. 189) can be rewritten in this form as follows:

Rope of husband

	X	Q	Z	S	Y	R	T	V	Z	S	X	Q	V	T	R	Y
v	0	0	0	1	0	0	0	0	0	0	0	0	0	0	0	0
t	0	0	1	0	0	0	0	0	0	0	0	0	0	0	0	0
r	0	1	0	0	0	0	0	0	0	0	0	0	0	0	0	0
y	1	0	0	0	0	0	0	0	0	0	0	0	0	0	0	0
x	0	0	0	0	0	0	1	0	0	0	0	0	0	0	0	0
q	0	0	0	0	0	0	0	1	0	0	0	0	0	0	0	0
z	0	0	0	0	1	0	0	0	0	0	0	0	0	0	0	0
s	0	0	0	0	0	1	0	0	0	0	0	0	0	0	0	0
y	0	0	0	0	0	0	0	0	0	0	0	1	0	0	0	0
r	0	0	0	0	0	0	0	0	0	0	1	0	0	0	0	0
t	0	0	0	0	0	0	0	0	0	1	0	0	0	0	0	0
v	0	0	0	0	0	0	0	0	1	0	0	0	0	0	0	0
z	0	0	0	0	0	0	0	0	0	0	0	0	0	0	1	0
s	0	0	0	0	0	0	0	0	0	0	0	0	0	0	0	1
x	0	0	0	0	0	0	0	0	0	0	0	0	1	0	0	0
q	0	0	0	0	0	0	0	0	0	0	0	0	0	1	0	0

Rope of wife

ANALYZING SYSTEMS USING MATRIX MULTIPLICATION

The alliance matrices, which show the relation "wife-of," can be shown to be the relative product of the descent matrices, "mother-of" (M), "father-of" (F), and "daughter-of" (D).

Consider the following simple model of restricted reproduction (see Figure 4.12, p. 85):

Father	Mother	Children
1*A*	1*b*	2*A*
2*A*	2*b*	1*A*
1*B*	1*a*	2*B*
2*B*	2*a*	1*B*

Given these data it is clear that 1*A* is the father of 2*A*, 2*A* the father of 1*A*, 1*B* the father of 2*B*, and 2*B* the father of 1*B*. Letting 1*A* be group 1, 1*B* group 2, 2*A* group 3, and 2*B* group 4, these relations can be described by the matrix

$$F = \begin{pmatrix} 0 & 0 & 1 & 0 \\ 0 & 0 & 0 & 1 \\ 1 & 0 & 0 & 0 \\ 0 & 1 & 0 & 0 \end{pmatrix}$$

where rows represent fathers, and columns represent the children. The "mother-of" (M) relation can likewise be described as follows:

$$M = \begin{pmatrix} 0 & 0 & 0 & 1 \\ 0 & 0 & 1 & 0 \\ 0 & 1 & 0 & 0 \\ 1 & 0 & 0 & 0 \end{pmatrix}$$

where the rows represent mothers and the columns children.

The "daughter-of" relation is obviously the reciprocal of M plus the reciprocal of F. It is necessary to distinguish the daughter of a male from the daughter of a female. This can be represented by the matrices DB and DZ, respectively, where B stands for "brother-of" and Z "sister-of." The B and Z relations are identity matrices and they do not change the structure of matrices they multiply.

The DB relation is the reciprocal of F, and because $F = F'$, it follows that $DB = F$. Likewise, $DZ = M$. The relation "daughter-of-the-brother-of-mother-of" (DBM), that is, mother's brother's daughter, can be constructed by multiplying DB by M as follows:

$$DBM = \begin{bmatrix} 0 & 0 & 1 & 0 \\ 0 & 0 & 0 & 1 \\ 1 & 0 & 0 & 0 \\ 0 & 1 & 0 & 0 \end{bmatrix} \begin{bmatrix} 0 & 0 & 0 & 1 \\ 0 & 0 & 1 & 0 \\ 0 & 1 & 0 & 0 \\ 1 & 0 & 0 & 0 \end{bmatrix} = \begin{bmatrix} 0 & 1 & 0 & 0 \\ 1 & 0 & 0 & 0 \\ 0 & 0 & 0 & 1 \\ 0 & 0 & 1 & 0 \end{bmatrix}$$

Likewise, the father's sister's daughter (DZF) relation can be constructed by multiplying DZ by F:

$$DZF = \begin{bmatrix} 0 & 0 & 0 & 1 \\ 0 & 0 & 1 & 0 \\ 0 & 1 & 0 & 0 \\ 1 & 0 & 0 & 0 \end{bmatrix} \begin{bmatrix} 0 & 0 & 1 & 0 \\ 0 & 0 & 0 & 1 \\ 1 & 0 & 0 & 0 \\ 0 & 1 & 0 & 0 \end{bmatrix} = \begin{bmatrix} 0 & 1 & 0 & 0 \\ 1 & 0 & 0 & 0 \\ 0 & 0 & 0 & 1 \\ 0 & 0 & 1 & 0 \end{bmatrix}$$

From the reproduction scheme above, the "wife-of" (W) relation can be constructed as follows:

$$W = \begin{bmatrix} 0 & 1 & 0 & 0 \\ 1 & 0 & 0 & 0 \\ 0 & 0 & 0 & 1 \\ 0 & 0 & 1 & 0 \end{bmatrix}$$

Hence

$$W = DZF = DBM$$

In other words, in this particular case of restricted reproduction, the mother's brother's daughter and the father's sister's daughter are both classified as belonging to the marriageable category.

Consider the following simple model of generalized reproduction (see Figure 4. 17, p. 88):

Father	Mother	Child
A	b	A
B	c	B
C	a	C

Group A is the father of A, B the father of B, and C the father of C. Thus the 'father-of" matrix has the form

$$F = \begin{bmatrix} 1 & 0 & 0 \\ 0 & 1 & 0 \\ 0 & 0 & 1 \end{bmatrix}$$

By similar reasoning, the "mother-of" matrix can be constructed as follows:

$$M = \begin{bmatrix} 0 & 0 & 1 \\ 1 & 0 & 0 \\ 0 & 1 & 0 \end{bmatrix}$$

The relation DB is the reciprocal of F, thus $DB = F' = F$. The relation DZ is the reciprocal of M. Thus $DZ = M' \neq M$. Thus the father's sister's daughter relation is

$$DZF = \begin{bmatrix} 0 & 1 & 0 \\ 0 & 0 & 1 \\ 1 & 0 & 0 \end{bmatrix} \begin{bmatrix} 1 & 0 & 0 \\ 0 & 1 & 0 \\ 0 & 0 & 1 \end{bmatrix} = \begin{bmatrix} 0 & 1 & 0 \\ 0 & 0 & 1 \\ 1 & 0 & 0 \end{bmatrix}$$

and the mother's brother's daughter relation is

$$DBM = \begin{bmatrix} 1 & 0 & 0 \\ 0 & 1 & 0 \\ 0 & 0 & 1 \end{bmatrix} \begin{bmatrix} 0 & 0 & 1 \\ 1 & 0 & 0 \\ 0 & 1 & 0 \end{bmatrix} = \begin{bmatrix} 0 & 0 & 1 \\ 1 & 0 & 0 \\ 0 & 1 & 0 \end{bmatrix}$$

The "wife-of" (W) relation, which can be constructed from the table above, is

$$W = \begin{bmatrix} 0 & 0 & 1 \\ 1 & 0 & 0 \\ 0 & 1 & 0 \end{bmatrix}$$

Thus

$$W = DBM \neq DZF$$

In other words the father's sister's daughter (DZF) is in the taboo category, while the mother's brother's daughter (DBM) is in the marriageable category.

By similar reasoning the following relations can be shown to hold:

Delayed reproduction (e.g. Trobriands): $W = DZF \neq DBM$
Umeda restricted reproduction: $W = DSSZFFF$
Mundugumor restricted reproduction: $W = DSZFF$

THE MATRIX OF KINSHIP TERMS

Consider the simple restricted reproduction case. If F, M, and W are added together, a matrix (K) with fully defined off-diagonals is produced as follows:

$$K = \begin{pmatrix} 0 & W & F & M \\ W & 0 & M & F \\ F & M & 0 & W \\ M & F & W & 0 \end{pmatrix}$$

These are the precise definitions of classificatory kinship terms and it should be compared with Figure 4.16 (p. 87), the actual terms used by the Kariara. To make the two matrices strictly comparable, extra rows and columns must be added to this matrix to allow for distinctions between males and females, and to allow for the different generations. This merely allows for complications without changing the basic structure of the system.

For the generalized reproduction case,

$$K = W + DZF + F = \begin{pmatrix} F & M' & W \\ W & F & M' \\ M' & W & F \end{pmatrix}$$

where $M' = DZF$. This system splits DZF and DBM, placing the former in the taboo category for marriage purposes. This matrix should be compared with Figure 4.21 (p. 90).

Similar matrices can be construed for the other systems.

References

Akin, David, and Joel Robbins, eds. 1999. *Money and modernity: State and local currencies in Melanesia*. Pittsburgh: University of Pittsburgh Press.

Annual Reports. 1888–1970. Various annual reports on the Territory of Papua formerly British New Guinea, 1888–1970; various reports to the United Nations formerly League of Nations on the Administration of the Territory of New Guinea, 1914–1970. Commonwealth of Australia.

Appadurai, Arjun. 2013. *The future as a cultural fact: Essays on the global condition*. London: Verso.

Armstrong, Wallace E. 1924. "Rossel Island money: A unique monetary system." *Economic Journal* 34 (135): 423–29.

Austin, Leo. 1945. "Cultural changes in Kiriwina." *Oceania* 16 (1): 15–60.

Bailey, Frederick G. 1957. *Caste and the economic frontier: A village in Highland Orissa*. Manchester: Manchester University Press.

Baldwin, John W. 1959. "The medieval theories of the just price: Romanists, canonists, and theologians in the twelfth and thirteenth centuries." *Transactions of the American Philosophical Society* 49 (4): 1–92.

Baric, Lorraine. 1964. "Some aspects of credit, saving and investment in a 'non-monetary' economy (Rossel Island)." In *Capital, saving and credit in peasant societies*, edited by Raymond Firth and Basil S. Yamey. Chicago: Aldine Publishing House.

Barnes, John A. 1962. "African models in the New Guinea highlands." *Man* 62 (2): 5–9.

Barrau, Jacques. 1958. *Subsistence agriculture in Melanesia.* Bernice P. Bishop Museum Bulletin 219. Hawaii: Bishop Museum.

Becker, Gary S. 1974. "A theory of marriage." In *Economics of the family,* edited by Theodore W. Schultz. Chicago: University of Chicago Press.

Belshaw, Cyril S. 1954. *Changing Melanesia: Social economics of culture contact.* Melbourne: Oxford University Press.

———. 1957. *The great village: The economic and social welfare of Hanuabada, an urban community in Papua.* London: Routledge & Kegan Paul.

Bennett, Tony, Liz McFall, and Mike Pryke. 2008. "Editorial: Culture/economy/social." *Journal of Cultural Economy* 1 (1): 1–7.

Berde, Stuart J. 1973. "Contemporary notes on Rossel Island valuables." *Journal of Polynesian Society* 82 (2): 188–205.

Berg, Elliot. 1969. "Wage structures in less-developed countries." In *Wage policy issues in economic development,* edited by Anthony D. Smith. London: Macmillan.

Bhagwati, Jagdish N. 1971. "The generalized theory of distortions and welfare." In *Trade, balance of payments and growth: Papers in international economics in honour of Charles P. Kindleberger,* edited by Jagdish Bhagwati, Ronald Jones, Robert Mundell, and Jaroslav Vanek. Amsterdam: North-Holland.

Boas, Franz. [1897] 1966. *Kwakiutl ethnography.* Edited by Helen Codere. Chicago: University of Chicago Press.

Bohannan, Paul. 1959. "The impact of money on an African subsistence economy." *Journal of Economic History* 19 (4): 491–503.

Bohannan, Paul, and Laura Bohannan. 1968. *Tiv economy.* Evanston, IL: Northwestern University Press.

Bolton, Geoffrey C. 1967. "The Rise of Burns Philp 1873–93." In *Wealth and progress: Studies in Australian business history,* edited by Alan Birch and David S. Macmillan. Sydney: Angus and Robertson.

Bourdieu, Pierre. 1977. *Outline of a theory of practice.* Translated by Richard Nice. Cambridge: Cambridge University Press.

Brookfield, Harold C. 1973. "Full circle in Chimbu: A study of trends and cycles." In *The Pacific in transition,* edited by Harold C. Brookfield. Canberra: ANU Press.

Brookfield, Harold C., and Doreen Hart. 1971. *Melanesia: A geographical interpretation of an island world.* London: Methuen.

Brown, Alfred R. 1913. "Three tribes of Western Australia." *Journal of the Royal Anthropological Institute* 43: 143–94.

Brown, Paula. 1978. *Highland peoples of New Guinea.* Cambridge: Cambridge University Press.

Bukharin, Nikolai I. 1919. *The economic theory of the leisure class.* London: Martin Lawrence.

Callon, Michel. 1998. "Introduction: The embeddedness of economic markets in economics." In *The laws of the markets,* edited by Michel Callon. London: Blackwell.

———. 2005. "Why virtualism paves the way to political impotence: A reply to Daniel Miller's critique of the laws of the markets." *Economic Sociology* 6 (2): 3–20.

Callon, Michel, and Fabian Muniesa. 2005. "Peripheral vision: Economic markets as calculative collective devices." *Organization Studies* 26: 1229–250.

Campbell, Shirley. 1983. "Kula in Vakuta: The mechanics of keda." In *The kula: New perspectives on Massim exchange,* edited by Edmund R. Leach and Jerry W. Leach. Cambridge: Cambridge University Press.

Carrier, James G. 1995. *Gifts and commodities: Exchange and Western capitalism since 1700.* London: Routledge.

Carver, Terrell. 1975. *Karl Marx: Notes on method.* Oxford: Basil Blackwell.

Census 1971. Papua New Guinea Population Census 1971. Port Moresby: Bureau of Statistics.

Chabal, Patrick, and Jean-Pascal Daloz. 1999. *Africa works: The political instrumentalization of disorder.* Bloomington: International African Institute in association with James Currey and Indiana University Press.

Chairman's address, BPNG. 1973. [Address by Mr. J. D. O. Burns, at the Annual Shareholders' Meeting, Friday, 7th December 1973 at 10.30 a.m.]

Chowning, Ann. 1977. *An introduction to the peoples and cultures of Melanesia.* Second edition. London: Cummings.

———. 1978a. "First-child ceremonies and male prestige in changing Kove society." In *The changing Pacific,* edited by Neil Gunson. Melbourne: Oxford University Press.

———. 1978b. "Changes in West New Britain trading systems." *Mankind* 11 (3): 296–307.

Clark, John B. 1886. *The philosophy of wealth*. Boston: Ginn.

Clarke, William C., and Ian M. Hughes. 1974. "Salt-making among the Baruya people of Papua New Guinea." *Australian Natural History* 18 (1): 22–24.

Cochrane Report. 1970. Territory of Papua New Guinea. *Minimum Wage Inquiry*. Port Moresby: Government Printer.

Codere, Helen. 1950. *Fighting with property*. New York: Augustin.

Colebrooke, Henry Thomas. 1818. *Treatise on obligations and contracts*. London: For the author.

Colson, Elizabeth. 1951. "The role of cattle among the Plateau Tonga of Mazabuka District." In *Rhodes–Livingstone Journal XI*, edited by Elizabeth Colson and Max Gluckman. London: Oxford University Press.

Compendium 1973. *Department of External Territories compendium of statistics for Papua New Guinea*. Canberra, October.

Copans, Jean, and David Seddon. 1978. "Marxism and anthropology: A preliminary survey." In *Relations of production: Marxist approaches to economic anthropology*, edited by David Seddon. London: Frank Cass.

Copilowish, Irving M. 1948. "Matrix development of the calculus of relations." *Journal of Symbolic Logic* 13 (4): 193–203.

Corris, Peter. 1968. "'Blackbirding' in New Guinea waters, 1883-4: An episode in the Queensland labour trade." *Journal of Pacific History* 3: 85–105.

Dalton, George. 1969. "Theoretical issues in economic anthropology." *Current Anthropology* 10 (1): 63–102.

———. 1971. *Economic anthropology and development: Essays on tribal and peasant economies*. New York: Basic Books.

Damon, Frederick H. 1978. "Modes of production and the circulation of value on the other side of the kula ring." Unpublished Ph.D., Princeton University.

Davis, Natalie Z. 2000. *The gift in sixteenth-century France*. Oxford: Oxford University Press.

Deacon, A. Bernard. 1934. *Malekula: A vanishing people in the New Hebrides*. Edited by Camilla H. Wedgewood. London: George Routledge.

Debreu, Gerard. [1959] 1971. *Theory of value: An axiomatic analysis of economic equilibrium*. New Haven, CT: Yale University Press.

Derrida, Jacques. 1992. *Given time: I. Counterfeit money*. Translated by Peggy Kamuf. Chicago: University of Chicago Press.

Dixit, Avinash. 1973. "Models of dual economics." In *Models of economic growth*, edited by James A. Mirrlees and Nicholas Stern. London: Macmillan.

Docker, Edward W. 1970. *The Blackbirders: The recruiting of South Seas labour for Queensland, 1863–1907*. Sydney: Angus & Robertson.

Dubbeldam, Leonard F. B. 1964. "The devaluation of the Kapauku-cowrie as a factor of social disintegration." *American Anthropologist* Special Publication 66 (4), Part 2: 293–303.

Dumont, Louis. [1966] 1979. *Homo hierarchicus: The caste system and its implications*. Translated by Mark Sainsbury and Basia Gulati. Chicago: University of Chicago Press.

Einzig, Paul. 1948. *Primitive money*. London: Eyre & Spottiswoode.

Engels, Frederick. 1859. "On the materialism and dialectics of Marx." Appendix D of *Ludwig Feuerbach*. London: Martin Lawrence.

———. [1884] 1970. *The origin of the family, private property and the state*. In *Selected works of Karl Marx and Frederick Engels*. Moscow: Progress Publishers.

Epstein, T. Scarlett. 1965. "Economic change and differentiation in New Britain." *Economic Record* 41 (94): 173–91.

———. 1968. *Capitalism, primitive and modern: Some aspects of Tolai economic growth*. Canberra: ANU Press.

Feil, Daryl K. 1978. "Enga women in the *Tee* exchange." Special Issue "Trade and exchange in Oceania and Australia," edited by Jim Specht and J. Peter White. *Mankind* 11 (3): 220–30.

Fingleton, Jim. 1980. "Land, law and development: A case study of tenure conversion in Papua New Guinea." Unpublished LLM thesis, University of PNG.

Finney, Ben R. 1973. *Big-men and business*. Honolulu: University Press of Hawaii.

Fisk, Ernest K. 1962. "Planning in a primitive economy: Special problems of Papua-New Guinea." *Economic Record* 38: 462–78.

————. 1964. "Planning in a primitive economy: From pure subsistence to the production of a market surplus." *Economic Record* 40 (90): 156–74.

————. 1971. "Labour absorption capacity of subsistence agriculture." *Economic Record* 47: 368–78.

Fitzpatrick, Peter. 1980. *Law and state in Papua New Guinea*. London: Academic Press.

Fleay Report 1974. *Income wages and prices policy*. Report of Interdepartmental Committee: Port Moresby.

Forge, Anthony. 1971. "Marriage and exchange in the Sepik: Comments on Francis Korn's analysis of Iatmul society." In *Rethinking kinship and marriage*, edited by Rodney Needham. London: Tavistock.

————. 1972. "The golden fleece." *Man* (N.S.) 7 (4): 527–40.

Fortes, Meyer. 1969. *Kinship and the social order: The legacy of Lewis Henry Morgan*. London: Routledge & Kegan Paul.

Fortune, Reo. [1932] 1963. *Sorcerers of Dobu*. London: Routledge & Kegan Paul.

Fox, Robin. [1967] 1974. *Kinship and marriage*. Harmondsworth: Penguin.

Freud, Sigmund. [1913] 1919. *Totem and taboo*. Translated by Abraham A. Brill. London: Routledge.

Garnaut, Ross. 1973. "National objectives and the choice of industries." In *Alternative strategies for Papua New Guinea*, edited by Anthony Clunies-Ross and John Langmore. Melbourne: Oxford University Press.

Gell, Alfred. 1975. *Metamorphosis of the Cassowaries: Umeda society, language and ritual*. London: Athlone Press.

Godelier, Maurice. [1966] 1972. *Rationality and irrationality in economics*. London: New Left Books.

————. [1973] 1977. *Perspectives in Marxist anthropology*. Cambridge: Cambridge University Press.

Godbout, Jacques T., and Alain Caillé. 1998. *The world of the gift*. Translated by Donald Winkler. Montreal: McGill-Queen's University Press.

Godelier, Maurice, and José Garanger. 1973. "Outils de pierre, outils d'acier chez les Baruya de Nouvelle-Guinée." *L'Homme* XIII (3): 186–220.

Goody, John R., and Stanley J. Tambiah. 1973. *Bridewealth and dowry.* Cambridge: Cambridge University Press.

Gouldner, Alvin W. 1960. "The norm of reciprocity: A preliminary statement." *American Sociological Review* 25 (2): 161–78.

Graeber, David. 2001. *Towards an anthropological theory of value: The false coin of our dreams.* New York: Palgrave.

———. 2004. *Fragments of an anarchist anthropology.* Chicago: Prickly Paradigm Press.

———. 2007a. *Lost people: Magic and the legacy of slavery in Madagascar.* Bloomington: Indiana University Press.

———. 2007b. *Possibilities: Essays on hierarchy, rebellion, and desire.* Edinburgh: AK Press.

———. 2009. *Direct action: An ethnography.* Edinburgh: AK Press.

———. 2011a. *Debt: The first 5000 Years.* New York: Melville House Publishing.

———. 2011b. *Revolutions in reverse: Essays on politics, violence, art, and imagination.* London New York: Minor Compositions.

———. 2013. *The democracy project: A history, a crisis, a movement.* New York: Spiegel & Grau.

Graves, Adrian A. 1979. "Pacific Island labour in the Queensland sugar industry, 1862–1906." Unpublished Ph.D., University of Oxford.

Gregory, Christopher A. 1979. "Gifts and commodities: A critique of the theory of 'traditional' and 'modern goods' with particular reference to Papua New Guinea." Ph.D. thesis, University of Cambridge.

———. 1980. "Gifts to men and gifts to god: Gift exchange and capital accumulation in contemporary Papua." *Man* 15 (4): 626–52.

———. 1986. "A matrix approach to the calculus of kinship relations." In *Mathematical models in anthropology*, edited by Gisèle de Meur. Brussels: Free University of Brussels.

———. 1997. *Savage money: The anthropology and politics of commodity exchange.* London: Routledge.

———. 2014. "Unequal egalitarianism: Reflections on Forge's paradox." *TAPJA* 15 (3): 197–217.

Groves, Murray. 1954. "Dancing in Poreporena." *Journal of the Royal Anthropological Institute* 84: 1–16.

Gudeman, Stephen. 1978. "Anthropological economics: The question of distribution." *Annual Review of Anthropology* 7: 347–79.

Haller, Dieter, and Cris Shore, eds. 2005. *Corruption: Anthropological perspectives*. London: Pluto Press.

Harcourt, Geoffrey C. 1972. *Some Cambridge controversies in the theory of capital*. Cambridge: Cambridge University Press.

Harris, Geoff T. 1972. "Labour supply and economic development in the southern highlands of Papua New Guinea." *Oceania* 43 (2): 123–39.

Harris, John R., and Michael P. Todaro. 1970. "Migration, unemployment and development: A two-sector analysis." *American Economic Review* 60: 126–42.

Harrod, Roy F. 1961. "A review of *Production of commodities by means of commodities* by P. Sraffa." *Economic Journal* 71: 783–87.

Hart, Keith. 2012. "The informalization of the world economy." Keynote lecture for the 24th Conference of the Societa' Italiana di Economia Pubblica: "Informal economy, tax evasion and corruption," Pavia, 24–25 September 2012. http://thememorybank.co.uk/2012/10/17/the-informalization-of-the-world-economy/. Accessed 11 June 2014.

———. 2014. "Marcel Mauss's economic vision, 1920–1925: Anthropology, politics, journalism." *Journal of Classical Sociology* 14 (1): 34–44.

Healy, Allan M. 1967. *Bulolo: A history of the development of the Bulolo region, New Guinea*. Port Moresby: New Guinea Research Bulletin 15.

Hearn, William E. 1863. *Plutology, or the theory of the effort to satisfy human wants*. Melbourne: Robertson.

Heim, Maria. 2004. *Theories of the gift in South Asia: Hindu, Buddhist, and Jain reflections on dana*. London: Routledge.

Herskovits, Melville J. 1940. *The economic life of primitive peoples*. New York: Alfred A. Knopf.

Heusch, Luc de. 1958. *Essais sur le symbolisme de l'inceste royal en Afrique*. Brussels: Institut de Sociologie Solvay.

Hide, Robin L. 1971. *Land demarcation and disputes in the Chimbu District of the New Guinea highlands*. New Guinea Research Bulletin No. 40. Canberra: ANU Press.

Highlands Labour Report 1969. "The supply of agreement labour through the Highlands Labour Scheme." Unpublished research paper prepared by the Department of Labour, Port Moresby.

Hill, Polly. 1972. *Rural Hausa: A village and a setting*. Cambridge: Cambridge University Press.

————. 1977. *Population, prosperity and poverty: Rural Kano 1900 and 1970*. Cambridge: Cambridge University Press.

Himmelweit, Susan, and Simon Mohun. 1977. "Domestic labour and capital." *Cambridge Journal of Economics* 1 (1): 15–33.

Hogbin, Ian. 1967. "Land tenure in Wogeo." In *Studies in New Guinea land tenure*, edited by Ian Hogbin and Peter Lawrence. Sydney: Sydney University Press

Holloway, Barry. 1976. *Post Courier*, October 20. [A PNG daily newspaper report.]

Hopkins, Keith. 1980. "Brother–sister marriage in Roman Egypt." *Comparative Studies in Society and History* 22 (3): 303–54.

Hughes, Ian M. 1973. "Traditional trade." In *Papua New Guinea resource atlas*, edited by Edgar Ford. Sydney: Jacaranda Press.

Humphries, Jane. 1977. "Class struggle and the persistence of the working-class family." *Cambridge Journal of Economics* 1 (3): 241–59.

Hyde, Lewis. 1984. *The gift: Imagination and the erotic life of property*. New York: Vintage.

Hyland, Richard. 2009. *Gifts: A study in comparative law*. Oxford: Oxford University Press.

Isaac Report. 1970. *The structure of unskilled wages and relatives between rural and non-rural employment in Papua New Guinea*. Joseph E. Isaac for the Administrator, Territory of Papua and New Guinea.

Jevons, W. Stanley. [1871] 1970. *Theory of political economy*. Harmondsworth: Penguin.

Johnson, Harry G. 1965. "Optimal trade intervention in the presence of domestic distortions." In *Trade growth and the balance of payments: Essays in honour of Gottfried Haberler*. Chicago: Rand McNally.

Jones, Richard. [1831] 1964. *An essay on the distribution of wealth and on the source of taxation*. New York: Kelley.

————. 1859. *Literary remains, consisting of lectures and tracts on political economy*. Edited by William Whewell. London: John Murray.

Jorgenson, Dale W. 1961. "The development of a dual economy." *Economic Journal* 71 (2): 309–34.

Kahn, Miriam. 1980. "Always in hunger: Food as metaphor for social identity in Wamira, PNG." Unpublished Ph.D., Bryn Mawr College.

Kangle, R. P. 1972. *The Kautilya Arthashaastra, part II*. Bombay: University of Bombay.

Ketan, Joseph. 2004. *The name must not go down: Political competition and state–society relations in Mount Hagen, Papua New Guinea*. Suva: IPS, USP.

Keynes, John Maynard. 1921. *A treatise on probability*. London: Macmillan.

———. [1936] 1967. *The general theory of employment interest and money*. London: Macmillan, 1967.

———. 1937. "The general theory of employment ." *The Quarterly Journal of Economics* 51 (2): 209–23.

Knight, Frank H. 1921. *Risk, uncertainty, and profit*. Boston: Houghton Mifflin Co.

———. 1941. "Anthropology and economics." *Journal of Political Economy* 49 (2): 247–68.

Krader, Lawrence, ed. 1972. *The ethnological notebooks of Karl Marx*. Assen: Van Gorcum and Company.

Kuper, Hilda. 1950. "Kinship among the Swazi." In *African systems of kinship and marriage*, edited by Daryll Forde and Alfred R. Radcliffe-Brown. London: Oxford University Press.

La Fontaine, Jean S. 1973. "Descent in New Guinea: An Africanist view." In *The character of kinship*, edited by John R. Goody. Cambridge: Cambridge University Press.

Lange, Oskar. 1962. *Wholes and part*. Oxford: Pergamon Press.

Lawrence, Peter. 1967. "Land tenure among the Garia." In *Studies in New Guinea land tenure*, edited by Ian Hogbin and Peter Lawrence. Sydney: Sydney University Press.

Laycock, Donald C. and Stephen A. Wurm. 1974. "Languages." In *Papua New Guinea resource atlas*, edited by Edgar Ford. Sydney: Jacaranda Press.

Leach, Edmund R. [1954] 1977. *Political systems of highland Burma: A study of Kachin social structure*. London: Athlone Press.

———. 1961. *Pul Eliya: A village in Ceylon*. Cambridge: Cambridge University Press.

———. 1962. "Concerning Trobriand clans and the kinship category 'tabu.'" In *The development cycle in domestic groups*, edited by John R. Goody. Cambridge: Cambridge University Press.

————. 1964. "Anthropological aspects of language: Animal categories and verbal abuse." In *New directions in the study of languages*, edited by Eric H. Lenneberg. Boston: MIT Press.

————. 1970. *Lévi-Strauss*. London: Fontana.

Leach, Edmund R., and Jerry W. Leach. 1983. *The kula: New perspectives on Massim exchange*. Cambridge: Cambridge University Press.

LeRoy, John D. 1979. "The ceremonial pig kill of the South Kewa." *Oceania* 49 (3): 179–209.

Lévi-Strauss, Claude. [1949] 1969. *The elementary structures of kinship*. London: Eyre & Spottiswoode.

————. [1962] 1974. *The savage mind*. London: Weidenfeld & Nicolson.

————. [1973] 1977. *Structural anthropology*, Vol. II. London: Allen Lane.

Lewis, W. Arthur. 1954. "Economic development with unlimited supplies of labour." *Manchester School of Economic and Social Studies* 22 (2): 139–91.

Lipton, Michael. 1977. *Why poor people stay poor*. London: Temple Smith.

Lounsbury, Floyd G. 1965. "Another view of the Trobriand kinship categories." *American Anthropologist* 67 (5), Part 2: 142–86.

MacDonald, Gaynor. 2000. "Economies and personhood: Demand sharing among the Wiradjuri of New South Wales." In *The social economy of sharing: Resource allocation and modern hunter-gatherers*, edited by George W. Wenzel, Greta Hovelsrud-Broda, and Nobuhiro Kishigami. Osaka: National Museum of Ethnology.

Macintyre, Martha. 2011. "Money changes everything: Papua New Guinean women in the modern economy." In *Managing modernity in the Western Pacific*, edited by Mary Patterson and Martha Macintyre. Brisbane: University of Queensland Press.

Malinowski, Bronislaw. [1922] 1961. *Argonauts of the Western Pacific*. New York: E. P. Dutton.

————. [1925] 1974. *Magic, science, religion and other essays*. London: Souvenir Press.

————. [1929] 1968. *The sexual life of the savages*. London: Routledge & Kegan Paul.

———. [1935] 1966. *Coral gardens and their magic. Vol. I. Soil-tilling and agricultural rites in the Trobriand Islands.* London: George Allen & Unwin.

Maro Board Report 1974. Papua New Guinea rural wages determination. Port Moresby, August.

Marriot, McKim. 1976. "Hindu transactions: Diversity without dualism." In *Transaction and meaning: Directions in the anthropology of exchange and symbolic behavior*, edited by Bruce Kapferer. Philadelphia: Institute for Human Studies.

Martin, Ross M. 1969. "Tribesmen into trade unionists: The African experience and the Papua New Guinea prospect." *Journal of Industrial Relations* 11 (2): 1–47.

Martin, Keir. 2013. *The death of the big men and the rise of the big shots: custom and conflict in East New Britain.* London: Berghahn ASAO Studies in Pacific Anthropology, Vol. 2.

Marx, Karl. [1857] 1973. *Grundrisse.* Translated by Martin Nicolaus. Harmondsworth: Penguin.

———. [1859] 1970. *A contribution to the critique of political economy.* Edited with an Introduction by Maurice Dobb. Moscow: Progress Publishers.

———. [1867] 1965. *Capital. Vol. I: A critical analysis of capitalist production.* Edited by Frederick Engels. Translated by Samuel Moore and Edward Aveling. Moscow: Progress Publishers.

———. [1893] 1971. *Capital. Vol. II: A critique of political economy.* Edited by Frederick Engels. Translated by Charles H. Kerr. Moscow: Progress Publishers.

———. [1894] 1971. *Capital. Vol. III: A critique of political economy.* Edited by Frederick Engels. Translated by Charles H. Kerr. Moscow: Progress Publishers.

Marx, Karl, and Frederick Engels. [1846] 1962. "The German ideology." In *On historical materialism: A collection.* Moscow: Progress Publishers.

Mauss, Marcel. 1914. "Les origines de la notion de monnaie." In *Oeuvres 2.* Edited by Viktor Karady. Paris: Minuit.

———. [1925] 1974. *The gift: Forms and functions of exchange in archaic societies.* Translated by Ian Cunnison. London: Routledge & Kegan Paul.

Mayer, Adrian C. 1961. *Peasants in the Pacific: A study of Fiji Indian rural society*. Second edition. Berkeley: University of California Press

Mead, Margaret. 1935 [1963]. *Sex and temperament in three primitive societies*. New York: William Morrow and Co.

Meek, Ronald L. 1962. *The economics of physiocracy: Essays and translations*. London: George Allen.

———. 1967. *Economics and ideology and other essays*. London: Chapman.

———. 1976. *Social science and the ignoble savage*. Cambridge: Cambridge University Press.

Meggitt, Mervyn J. 1965. *The lineage system of the Mae-Enga of New Guinea*. London: Oliver & Boyd.

———. 1969. "Introduction." In . *Pigs, pearlshells and women: Marriage in the New Guinea highlands*, edited by Meryn J. Meggitt and Robert M. Glasse. Englewood Cliffs, NJ: Prentice-Hall.

———. 1971. "From tribesmen to peasants: The case of the Mae-Enga of New Guinea." In *Anthropology in Oceania*, edited by Lester R. Hiatt and Chandra J. Jayawardena. Sydney: Angus & Robertson.

———. 1974. "'Pigs are our hearts!' The *te* exchange cycle among the Mae-Enga of New Guinea." *Oceania* 44 (3): 165–203.

Meggitt, Mervyn J., and Robert M. Glasse, eds. 1969. *Pigs, pearlshells and women: Marriage in the New Guinea highlands*. Englewood Cliffs, NJ: Prentice-Hall.

Meillassoux, Claude. 1960. "Essai d'interpretation du phénomène économique dans les sociétés traditionelles d'auto-subsistance." *Cahiers d'Études Africaines* 4: 38–67.

———. 1964. *Anthropologie economique des Gouro de Côte-d'Ivoire*. Paris: Mouton.

———. 1972. "From reproduction to production: A Marxist approach to economic anthropology." *Economy and Society* 1 (1): 93–105.

———. 1973. "The social organisation of the peasantry: The economic basis of kinship." *Journal of Peasant Studies* 1 (1): 81–90.

———. 1975. *Femmes, greniers et capitaux*. Paris: Maspero.

Menger, Carl. [1871] 1950. *Principles of economics*. Glencoe, IL: Free Press.

Milgate, Murray. 1987. "Goods and commodities." In *The new Palgrave: A dictionary of economics*, edited by John Eatwell, Murray Milgate, and Peter Newman. London: Macmillan.

Modjeska, Nicholas. 1977. "Production among the Duna." Unpublished Ph.D., Australian National University.

Morgan, Lewis H. 1851. *League of the Iroquois*. Rochester, NY: Sage and Brother.

———. 1871. *Systems of consanguinity and affinity of the human family*. Washington: Smithsonian Institution.

———. 1877. *Ancient society*. London: Macmillan.

Moylan, Thomas. 1973. "Disequilibrium in a New Guinea local ecosystem." *Mankind* 9 (2): 61–76.

Munn, Nancy. 1977. "Spatiotemporal transformations of Gawa canoes." *Journal de la Société des Océanistes* 54–55 (33): 39–53.

Myrdal, Gunnar. 1968. *Asian drama*, Vol. I. Harmondsworth: Penguin.

Oliver, Douglas L. 1955. *A Solomon Island society*. Cambridge, MA: Harvard University Press.

Parliamentary Papers. 1867–1868, 1873, 1892. *Correspondence relative to the introduction of Polynesian labourers into Queensland*. Reports printed by order of the House of Commons. London: HMSO.

Parry, Jonathan. 1986. "The gift, the Indian gift, and the 'Indian gift'." *Man* (N.S.) 21 (3): 453–73.

———. 1994. *Death in Banaras*. Cambridge: Cambridge University Press.

Parry, Jonathan, and Maurice Bloch, eds. 1989. *Money and the morality of exchange*. Cambridge: Cambridge University Press.

Patterson, Mary, and Martha Macintyre. 2011a. "Capitalism, cosmology and globalisation in the Pacific." In *Managing modernity in the Western Pacific*, edited by Mary Patterson and Martha Macintyre. Brisbane: University of Queensland Press.

———, eds. 2011b. *Managing modernity in the Western Pacific*. Brisbane: University of Queensland Press.

Pearce, Glenn, and Patrick Maynard. 1973. "Introduction." In *Conceptual change*, edited by Glenn Pearce and Patrick Maynard. Dordrecht: D. Reidel Publishing Company.

Peterson, Nicolas. 1993. "Demand sharing: Reciprocity and the pressure for generosity among foragers." *American Anthropologist* 95 (4): 860–74.

PNGLIB9 1972. *Papua New Guinea Labour Information Bulletin No. 9*. Department of Labour and Industry. Port Moresby.

Polanyi, Karl. 1944. *The great transformation: The political and economic origins of our time.* New York: Rinehart.

———. 1957. "The economy as instituted process." In *Trade and market in the early empires*, edited by Karl Polanyi, Conrad M. Arensberg, and Harry W. Pearson. Glencoe, IL: Free Press.

Polanyi, Karl, Conrad M. Arensberg, and Harry W. Pearson, eds. 1957. *Trade and market in the early empires.* Glencoe, IL: Free Press.

Pospisil, Leopold. 1963. *Kapauku Papuan economy.* New Haven, CT: Yale University Publications in Anthropology No. 67.

Powell, Harry A. 1956. "Trobriand social structure." Unpublished Ph.D., University of London.

———. 1969a. "Genealogy, residence and kinship in Kiriwina." *Man* 4 (2): 177–202.

———. 1969b. "Territory, hierarchy and kinship in Kiriwina." *Man* 4 (4): 580–604.

Price, Charles A., and Elizabeth Baker. 1976. "Origins of Pacific Island labourers in Queensland, 1863–1904: A research note." *Journal of Pacific History* 11 (2): 106–21.

PSA . 1974. *Submission to the Urban Minimum Wages Board.* Public Service Association of Papua New Guinea.

Quesnay, Francois. [1759] 1962. "The 'tableau économique.'" In *The economics of physiocracy*, edited by Ronald L. Meek. London: George Allen.

Raheja, Gloria. 1988. *The poison in the gift: Ritual, prestation, and the dominant caste in a North India Village.* Chicago: University of Chicago Press.

Ricardo, David. [1817] 1951. *On the principles of political economy and taxation.* Vol. I of *The works and correspondence of David Ricardo.* Edited by Piero Sraffa, with the collaboration of Maurice H. Dobb. Cambridge: Cambridge University Press.

Robbins, Joel. 2009. Rethinking gifts and commodities: Reciprocity, recognition, and the morality of exchange. In *Economy and morality: Anthropological approaches*, edited by Katherine Browne and B. Lynne Milgram. Lanham, MD: AltaMira Press.

———. 2013. "Beyond the suffering subject: Toward an anthropology of the good." *Journal of the Royal Anthropological Institute* (N.S.) 19 (3): 447–62.

Rowley, Charles D. [1965] 1972. *The New Guinea villager: A retrospect from 1964.* Melbourne: Cheshire.

Sahlins, Marshall. 1972. *Stone Age economics.* Chicago: Aldine.

———. 1993. "Cery cery fuckabede." *American Ethnologist* 20 (4): 848–67.

Salisbury, Richard F. 1962. *From stone to steel: Economic consequences of a technological change in New Guinea.* Cambridge: Cambridge University Press.

———. 1970. *Vunamani: Economic transformation in a traditional society.* Melbourne: Melbourne University Press.

Samuelson, Paul A. [1947] 1971. *Foundations of economic analysis.* Cambridge, MA: Harvard University Press.

Sandel, Michael J. 2012. *What money can't buy: The moral limits of markets.* London: Penguin.

Schieffelin, Edward L. 1977. *The sorrow of the lonely and the burning of the dancers.* Brisbane: Queensland University Press.

Schneider, Harold K. 1957. "The subsistence role of cattle among the Pakot in East Africa." *American Anthropologist* 59: 278–99.

Schultz, Theodore W. 1964. *Transforming traditional agriculture.* New Haven, CT: Yale University Press.

Scott, Michael W. 2007. "Neither 'new Melanesian history' nor 'new Melanesian ethnography': Recovering emplaced matrilineages in southeast Solomon Islands." *Oceania* 77 (3): 337–54.

Shand, Richard T. 1965. "The development of trade and specialisation in a primitive economy." *Economic Record* 41 (94): 193–206.

Sharp, Lauriston. 1952. "Steel axes for Stone-Age Australians." *Human Organisation* 11 (2): 17–22.

Sierpinski, Waclaw. 1958. *Cardinal and ordinal numbers.* Warsaw: Panstwowe.

Sillitoe, Paul. 1981. "The gender of crops in the Papua New Guinea highlands." *Ethnology* 20 (1): 1–14.

Smith, Adam. [1759] 2009. *The theory of moral sentiments.* London: Penguin.

———. [1776] 1970. *An inquiry into the nature and causes of the wealth of nations.* London: Everyman's Library.

Spate, Oskar H. K. 1959. *The Fijian people: Economic problems and prospects.* Suva: Government Press.

Sraffa, Piero. 1960. *Production of commodities by means of commodities: Prelude to a critique of economic theory.* Cambridge: Cambridge University Press.

———. 1962. "Production of commodities: A comment." *Economic Journal* 72: 477–79.

Steiner, Franz. 1957. "Towards a classification of labor." *Sociologus* 7 (2): 118–29.

Stent, William R., and Roy L. Webb. 1975. "Subsistence affluence and market economy in Papua New Guinea." *Economic Record* 51: 522–38.

Stone, Laurence. 1977. *The family, sex and marriage in England, 1500–1800.* London: Weidenfeld & Nicolson.

Strathern, Andrew J. 1969. "Finance and production: Two strategies in New Guinea highlands exchange systems." *Oceania* 40 (1): 42–67.

———. 1971. *The rope of Moka: Big-men and ceremonial exchange in Mount Hagen, New Guinea.* Cambridge: Cambridge University Press.

———. 1972. *One father, one blood: Descent and group structure among the Melpa people.* Canberra: ANU Press.

———. 1973. "Kinship, descent and locality: Some New Guinea examples." In *The character of kinship*, edited by John R. Goody. Cambridge: Cambridge University Press.

———. 1975. "Veiled speech in Mount Hagen." In *Political language and oratory in traditional sorcery*, edited by Maurice Bloch. London: Academic Press.

———. 1978. "'Finance and production' revisited: In pursuit of a comparison." In *Research in economic anthropology*, Vol. I, edited by George Dalton. New York: JAI Press.

———. 1979. "Gender, ideology and money in Mount Hagen." *Man* 14 (3): 530–48.

Strathern, Andrew J., and Marilyn Strathern. 1969. "Marriage in Melpa." In *Pigs, pearlshells and women*, edited by Mervyn J. Meggitt and Robert Glasse. Englewood Cliffs, NJ: Prentice-Hall.

Strathern, Marilyn. 1972. *Women in between: Female roles in a male world, Mount Hagen, New Guinea.* London: Seminar Press.

———. 1975. *No money on our skins: Hagen migrants in Port Moresby.* Port Moresby: New Guinea Research Bulletin 61.

———. 1988. *The gender of the gift: Problems with women and problems with society in Melanesia.* Berkeley: University of California Press.

Tarski, Alfred. [1941] 1965. *Introduction to logic and to the methodology of deductive sciences*. New York: Oxford University Press.

Thomas, Nicholas. 1991. *Entangled objects: Exchange, material culture and colonialism in the Pacific*. Cambridge, MA: Harvard University Press.

———. 1993. "Beggars can be choosers." *American Ethnologist* 20 (4): 868–76.

Thompson, Edward P. 1971. "The moral economy of the English crowd in the eighteenth century." *Past and Present* 50: 76–136.

Thune, Carl E. 1983. "Kula traders and lineage members: The structure of village and kula exchange on Normanby Island." In *The kula: New perspectives on Massim exchange*, edited by Edmund R. Leach and Jerry W. Leach. Cambridge: Cambridge University Press.

Thurnwald, Richard C. 1916. "Banaro society: Social organisation and kinship system of a tribe in the interior of New Guinea." *Memoirs of the American Anthropological Association* 3 (4): 251–391.

Trade Store Survey. 1968–1969. *Survey of indigenous owned trade stores, 1968–1969*. Office of the Economic Adviser. Department of Trade and Industry. Port Moresby.

Trautmann, Thomas R. 1981. *Dravidian kinship*. Cambridge: Cambridge University Press.

Turner, Herbert A. 1965. *Wage trends, wage policies and collective bargaining: The problem for underdeveloped countries*. Cambridge: Cambridge University Press.

Tuzin, Donald F. 1976. *The Ilahita Arapesh*. Los Angeles: UCLA Press.

Wagner, Roy. 1967. *The curse of Souw: Principles of Daribi clan definition and alliance in New Guinea*. Cambridge: Cambridge University Press.

Waka Board Report. 1974. Papua New Guinea rural wages determination. Port Moresby, June.

Walras, Léon. [1874] 1954. *Elements of pure economics*. Translated by William Jaffé. London: George Unwin.

Watson, William. [1958] 1964. *Tribal cohesion in a money economy: A study of the Mambwe people of Northern Rhodesia*. Manchester: Manchester University Press.

Weber, M. [1930] 2001. *The Protestant ethic and the spirit of capitalism*. Translated by Talcott Parsons. London: Routledge.

Weeks, John F. 1971. "Wage policy and the colonial legacy: A comparative study." *Journal of Modern African Studies* 9 (3): 361–87.

Weiner, Annette B. 1976. *Women of value, men of renown.* Austin: University of Texas Press.

———. 1979. "Trobriand kinship from another view: The reproductive power and women and men." *Man* 14: 328–48.

Wicksteed, Philip H. 1910. *The common sense of political economy.* London: Macmillan.

Williams, Francis E. [1936] 1969. *Papuans of the Trans-Fly.* Oxford: Clarendon.

Williamson, Margaret H. 1979. "Who does what to the sago?" *Oceania* 49 (3): 210–20.

Wolfensohn, James D. 1996. "Annual Meetings Address, 1 October 1996." James Wolfensohn presidency 1995–2005. http://web.worldbank.org/. Accessed 14 September 2014.

Wolpe, Harold. 1972. "Capitalism and cheap labour-power in South Africa: From segregation to apartheid." *Economy and Society* 1 (4): 425–56.

World Bank. 1978. *Papua New Guinea: Its economic situation and prospects for development.* Washington: World Bank.

Young, Michael W. 1971. *Fighting with food: Leadership, values and social control in a Massim society.* Cambridge: Cambridge University Press.

Index

Dalton, George, 16, 22

Damon, Frederick H., liii, 97, 212, 216

Daribi, 82, 192

Debreu, Gerard, lx, 21

delayed gift exchange, 53, 58, 66–68, 69, 70, 71, 193, 195–196, 202–203, 211, 213-214

delayed gift reproduction, highland PNG in, 192–209 theory of, 89–95

demand sharing, xxxv–xxxvi

descriptive kinship terms, 9–11, 16

destruction strategy, 60, 61, 197, 223

differentiation, process of, 168–169

distortions, theory of, 22–24

distribution, definition of particular economies and, 32–38 twofold character of, 27

dividual, xxviii

Dobu, 41, 97, 98, 217

domination and control, relations of, 14, 46–47, 64–68, 183

Dubbeldam, Leonard F. B., 57

Dumont, Louis, 82

E

economical structure of nations, 6

economics, critique of, 107–117, 121–127, 225 defining characteristics of, lix–lxiii, 22–24 *See also* goods

elders, lix, 53, 69, 82, 106, 168, 174, 177, 184, 185, 187

elementary structures of kinship, xl, 15, 17, 28

Enga. *See* Mae-Enga

Engels, Frederick, 5, 7–9, 78

Enona clan (Kapauku), 50–51, 55–56, 100–105

Enron, xxxviii, 1

Epstein, T. Scarlett, lviii, 50, 111, 112, 128, 168, 169

ethics, xlvii

exchange. *See* circulation

exchange-order, 47, 195, 212 *See also* rank

exchange-value, 3–5

exogamy, 35, 63

F

family, Australian and PNGian compared, 78–79 delayed gift reproduction and, 89–94 generalized gift reproduction and, 87–88 Marx and Engels on, 7–8 restricted gift reproduction and, 83–87

family wage, 153–158

Feil, Daryl K., 60, 205

female/male relations, 29–39, 60, 63, 93, 157, 194–195, 204–205

fetishism of commodities, 14, 44

Fiji, xx, xxxi, xxxvi, xliii, lv, 147

finance strategy, 60, 61, 197, 203

Fingleton, Jim, liii, 174

Finney, Ben R., 174

Fisk, Ernest K., 114, 115, 122–124

Fitzpatrick, Peter, liii, 174

food, clan production of, 103–104 imports into PNG, 165–166 as nourishment, 80–81

role of neoclassical economists, 150–156
wages theory,
economics approach, 122–124
political economy approach,
125–127
Waka Board Report, 154
Walras, Léon, xlvi, lx, 19, 21
Wamira, 53, 81, 97
Watson, William, 63, 197, 227
Webb, L. Roy, 23, 112–114, 116,
122
Weiner, Annette B., 54, 82, 96, 215,
216, 228
whales' teeth, xxxi
Wicksteed, Philip H., 20

Williams, Francis E., 63
Wiru, 197, 206–208
Wogeo Island, 80
Wolfensohn, James D., xxxviii
women-gifts, 63–67, 69, 71, 93, 95,
98, 106, 177, 181–183, 188, 193,
201, 214, 215, 217, 229
Woodlark, 96, 97, 212, 216, 217
work-commodities, 62
work-gifts, 62, 63
World Bank, xxxviii, 159

Y

Yoruba, 29
Young, Michael W., xxv, 195, 197

HAU Books is committed to publishing the most distinguished texts in classic and advanced anthropological theory. The titles aim to situate ethnography as the prime heuristic of anthropology, and return it to the forefront of conceptual developments in the discipline. HAU Books is sponsored by some of the world's most distinguished anthropology departments and research institutions, and releases its titles in both print editions and open-access formats.

www.haubooks.com

Supported by

Hau-N. E. T.
Network of Ethnographic Theory

University of Aarhus – EPICENTER (DK)
University of Amsterdam (NL)
University of Bergen (NO)
Brown University (US)
California Institute of Integral Studies (US)
University of Canterbury (NZ)
University of Chicago (US)
University of Colorado Boulder Libraries (US)
CNRS – Centre d'Études Himalayennes (FR)
Cornell University (US)
University of Edinburgh (UK)
The Graduate Institute, Geneva Library (CH)
University of Helsinki (FL)
Johns Hopkins University (US)
University of Kent (UK)
Lafayette College Library (US)
Institute of Social Sciences of the University of Lisbon (PL)
University of Manchester (UK)
The University of Manchester Library (UK)
Museu Nacional – UFRJ (BR)
Norwegian Museum of Cultural History (NO)
University of Oslo (NO)
University of Oslo Library (NO)
Pontificia Universidad Católica de Chile (CL)
Princeton University (US)
University of Queensland (AU)
University of Rochester (US)
Universidad Autónoma de San Luis Potosi (MX)
University of Sydney (AU)

www.haujournal.org/haunet